amessmith. Mg

Healing the Divide

Healing the Divide

Recovering Christianity's Mystic Roots

AMOS SMITH

Foreword by
LEONARD SWEET

Afterword by
RICHARD ROHR

RESOURCE *Publications* · Eugene, Oregon

Resource Publications
An Imprint of Wipf and Stock Publishers
199 W. 8th Ave., Suite 3
Eugene, OR 97401

www.wipfandstock.com

ISBN 13: 978-1-62032-365-6

file modified 4/15/2015

Dedicated to my confidant, teacher, best friend, spouse,
and mother to our children,
Cristianne Glenn Smith

For in Christ all the fullness of the Deity lives in bodily form.

−COLOSSIANS

*It is in the paradox itself, the paradox which was
and is still a source of insecurity,
that I have come to find the greatest security.*

−THOMAS MERTON

*For Christ is our peace; who, in the flesh,
has made both groups into one
and has broken down the dividing wall . . .*

−EPHESIANS

Out of Africa came the Garden of Eden.

−MARCUS HINDS

The significance of Christ is not his maleness, but his humanity.

−JACQUELINE GRANT

Contents

PART 6: The Christian Mystics' Love of God

PART 7: Conclusion

APPENDICES

Illustrations

Foreword

"EAT THE MYSTERY"

IT'S AMAZING HOW FAR back family stories can go. When my Gramma died, my grandfather came to live with us for a few years. His name was George Lemuel Boggs, and I remember his tall (6'3"), lanky frame bending over repair projects my mother assigned him. For most of his life he worked as a sawyer in West Virginia's Allegheny Mountains. The only thing I loved to do more with Grandad than watch him work with wood or help him clean his double-barrel, twin-gage shotgun was listen to him tell mountain stories. One of his favorite lumberjack stories he claimed to have gotten from revivalist Billy Sunday (d. 1935).

It seems that a sawyer from West Virginia was going up north to help out a lumber camp in the Adirondack Mountains. His friend from their local Methodist church warned him "If those northern lumberjacks find out you're a Christian, especially a Methodist, they'll make sport of you." The sawyer went up for a couple of months. When he came back home his friend said, "Well, how did you get along with those northern lumberjacks?" The man answered, "All right. They didn't find out." Grandad would laugh at his own joke, then go silent. But you knew what he was leaving unsaid: would people have a hard time finding out who I was? Would I showcase or cover up my identity as a follower of Jesus?

My father Leonard Lucius Sweet picked up a tool about as often as my grandfather picked up a book—in other words, never. But he also liked to tell me a story that seemed to crop up in conversations about my morning paper route.

A young boy walked into a drug store and asked to use the telephone. He called information and asked for a certain number: "Hello, Dr. Anderson . . . Do you want to hire someone to cut the grass and run errands for you? Oh, you already have someone who does this? Are you completely satisfied with the person you have? . . . OK then, goodbye, Dr. Anderson."

As the lad thanked the druggist for the use of the phone, the druggist said: "Just a minute, son. If you are looking for work, I could use someone like you."

"Thank you, sir, but I have a job," the boy replied.

"But didn't I just hear you trying to get a job from Dr. Anderson?"

"No, sir," said the boy. "I'm the one who is working for Dr. Anderson. I was just checking up on myself."

Like Grandad, my father was not one to make the point explicit. But I knew the point he was making. Once in a while it might be good for me to check up on myself and see how I was doing on my paper-route. His larger point was not lost on me either: every Jesus disciple should check up on themselves to see if God is pleased with our work in Jesus' vineyard.

Amos Smith has written a book that the church would do well to use as a check-up on itself. I would phrase some things differently, frame some issues using alternative metaphors. I don't agree with everything in this book (I've never read a book in which I did, come to think of it). But this book is a needed call for originality in the church where "originality" is something cumulative, not ex nihilo; where originality is a rebooting from our origins, from the original foundings and future unfoldments of the "faith once for all delivered to the saints" (Jude 1:3).

When Christianity is recapitulated from its origins, as Amos Smith has shown, two words emerge—paradox and harmony. The Christian faith is a surround-sound spirituality. In fact, if you're hearing only one thing you're not hearing Jesus. Wholeness is not oneness. Wholeness is harmony. Wholeness is not singing with one voice. Wholeness is singing with multiple voices that are in harmony with one another. In any piece of Christian music, there is not just a melody line or one part, but many parts that commingle in melodious harmony. Even God has multiple voices: sometimes speaking to us as to Elijah–in a soft, murmuring sound; sometimes speaking to us as to Moses on Sinai–in a consuming fire.

This means that the word "mystery" cannot be banished from Christianity. This book demonstrates that the essence of biblical faith is not learning the right answers, or exploring the right questions, but living the mystery. The ancient Hebrews discovered this in their forty years of daily gathering "manna," a word which literally means "What is it?" As Ann Voskamp puts it in her devotional classic *One Thousand Gifts*: "Hungry, they choose to gather up that which is baffling. They fill on that which has no meaning. More than 14,600 days they take their daily nourishment from something they do not comprehend. They eat the mystery."[1]

Read *Healing The Divide*, and eat the mystery. It's a check-up call to your identity and mission.

—Leonard Sweet

1. Voskamp, *One Thousand Gifts*, 22.

Preface

My task has been that of the weaver and the dyer.
I take no credit at all for the cotton and the thread.

—ANTHONY DE MELLO

THE LIGHT OF THE MYSTICS

THERE ARE NUMEROUS HARROWING chapters in Christian history, including the Crusades (1100–1600), The New England Witch Hunts
(1580–1630), the subjugation of indigenous peoples in the name of mission, the religious sanction of colonialism, persistent strains of sexism
and misogyny, regressive anti-rational elements, the bombing of abortion
clinics, the pedophile priest scandal of the Catholic Church, and the per-
petuation of violence.

Through the night of these travesties, there's a light that shines so
brightly that it can counter and ultimately vanquish these shadows. That
light is the light of the Christian Mystics, who reflect Christianity's essence—the unflinching search for God through the valley of the shadow
of death (Psalm 23:4).

The light of the Christian Mystics shone most intensely and consistently for a brief period of history in the Egyptian desert. This book will
focus on the brilliance of that time and place. I will focus on the most
concentrated beam of light in Christian history, which shone from communion with the source: Jesus.

WHICH MYSTICS?

When my friend Kimberly first glanced at my book she asked the most obvious question: "To which mystics are you referring?" I often reference the term *Alexandrian Mystics*.[2] So, I need to be specific about what I mean . . .

I have charted the lineage of the Alexandrian Mystics in appendix B. Most Oriental Orthodox theologians today would agree with that list. The Alexandrian Bishops listed in appendix B carried the lineage of the Alexandrian Mystics, as contemporized in this book.[3]

During the period noted in appendix B (312–454 CE) there was profound synergy between the monks of the Egyptian desert and the Alexandrian Bishops. So *The Alexandrian Mystics* includes the monks and nuns of the Egyptian desert during this period, some of whom are better known as the Desert Fathers and Mothers.

Although people know a lot about the Desert Fathers and Mothers and there has recently been a resurgence of interest in them, few understand that there was a mystical theological core that united them, especially between 312 and 454CE. That core was the essential understanding of Jesus as Paradox—that he is "at once God and human." The Alexandrian Mystics' phrase "at once God and human" is the keystone. This mystic theology means we can never refer to Jesus' humanity aside from his Divinity. We can also never refer to Jesus' Divinity aside from his humanity. In other words, if I am a believer I can't say "Jesus is human, period." I need to qualify that statement: "the human incarnation of God." If I am a believer I also can't say "Jesus is God, period." I need to qualify that statement: "God in human form."

This profound insight illuminates the person of Jesus today, where most on the Christian left seem comfortable with Jesus' humanity only (the historical Jesus) and where most on the Christian right seem enamored with Jesus' Divinity only. Both miss the boat. According to The Alexandrian Mystics Jesus is "at once God and human"—a Paradox.

The West is familiar with the Desert Fathers and Mothers. But the West is not familiar with the theology that united them in the fourth and fifth centuries—the theology of *The Jesus Paradox*.[4]

My book is titled *Healing The Divide* because Western Christianity today is divided between those who, for all practical purposes, acknowledge

---

2. See *Alexandrian Mystics* in glossary (Appendix A).

3. See *Oriental Orthodoxy* and *Alexandrian Bishops* in glossary (Appendix A).

4. See *Jesus Paradox* in glossary (Appendix A).

Jesus' humanity only and those who acknowledge Jesus' Divinity only. The Jesus Paradox as taught by the Alexandrian Mystics has the power to heal this divide.

To give you a better feel of what I'm talking about here you can go to my website: amossmith.org, and download a PowerPoint presentation entitled *The Jesus Paradox*. People have found the PowerPoint a helpful tool to grasp the root concept of this book.

PERSPECTIVE

Tony Robinson's book, *What's Theology Got To Do With It?*, claims that Christians, especially mainline Christians like me, have lost our way because we're not sure what we believe.[5] So our task is to clarify our core convictions in light of twenty-first century challenges. Only after we have clarity about our core truths, will we have the zeal necessary to restore and rebuild our twenty-first century churches. When we believe with our heads and our hearts, the integrity of our conviction is able to move mountains.

As we seek to clarify our core convictions in light of our times Phyllis Tickle's Book, *The Great Emergence*, outlines our mission.[6] Tickle writes that every five hundred years or so the Church "feels compelled to hold a giant rummage sale."[7] At the sale we decide what things are invaluable to our faith and with which we can't part. We also decide what things we're ready to let go of in light of changing times.

In this book I identify and clarify the theological gem of The Alexandrian Mystics. For me this gem is the invaluable core of Christian tradition that we can't part with, the foundation upon which everything else depends.

I'm fascinated by the legacy of the Alexandrian Mystics passed down through the ages, revitalized with the teachings of Severus of Antioch (d. 542), and preserved in the Oriental Orthodox Church of today (not to be confused with the Eastern Orthodox Church).

Mystics are the authorities of their respective traditions. They have experiential knowledge of God that surpasses secondary ways of knowing.

5. I grew up in the Episcopal Church, then was a member of the Religious Society of Friends (FGC), then I landed in the United Church of Christ, which for me represents an integration of the two: Low Church polity like the Quakers and Christ centered like the Episcopal Church (a sweeping generalization). My history and my study are thoroughly ecumenical.

6. See *Emergent Church* in glossary (Appendix A).

7. Tickle, *The Great Emergence*, 16.

Through habitual silent prayer, the Alexandrian Christian Mystics experienced union with God. Alexandria and the surrounding desert regions of the fourth through the fifth centuries was the most fertile period of Mystic Christianity. Never before and never since was there such a concentrated number of Christian mystics collaborating with the most sophisticated theological minds of the ages. My intent is to capture the spirit of the Alexandrian Mystics and their theology for the Twenty-first Century.

This book is intended for the Christian reader in general, the Mystic Christian in particular, and for seekers interested in Mystic Christianity and its role in the Twenty-first Century.[8]

DISCLAIMERS

Most of what I've written isn't original research. It's an original distillation and contemporary synthesis.[9]

This book is sometimes edgy. The edge is intended to clarify the truth of the mystics, not to clobber people.

This book isn't a specific history. For readers interested in a more specific history, refer to the bibliography and appendices.

This book is a treatise that looks deeply into the life-giving roots of Christian tradition . . . We can't plunge into this stuff without dropping into the depths of our own souls.

The book will become more understandable and satisfying as you go along. And when you're done you'll see each section has its place and that together they form an organic whole.

REFERENCES

I encourage you to flow with the written text and not worry about the footnotes or appendices. If you have interest you can scan the very readable footnotes and appendices later. While reading, if you come across an unfamiliar or unclear word or phrase, check the glossary in appendix A.

Throughout the book I make many scripture references. Unless specified otherwise, New Testament and Psalm references are taken from

8. See *Mystic Christianity* in glossary (Appendix A).

9. I didn't consult the original languages of the ancient texts related to this work. I've relied on English translations. There are some excellent primary sources, especially of Cyril of Alexandria, which unfortunately for me, are in French.

Oxford University Press' *An Inclusive Version*[10] and Old Testament references are taken from The New International Version.

I've provided the year of death for all deceased people when first referenced, to give ready historical context.

At the end of each chapter, there are questions for reflection and discussion for study groups.

For stories I use fictitious names to protect identities.

I often use *The Philokalia*[11] as a general source for The Alexandrian Mystics (not for the finer points of their theology). I think this is admissible given that *The Philokalia* represents a consistent lineage of Eastern Mystic Christianity through the ages.

ACKNOWLEDGMENTS

I thank Robert VanDale (Professor of Ethiopian Orthodox Studies), Duane Eberhardt, Romayne Potosky, Ari Salomon, Charley Custer, Rev. Ken Barnes, Forrest Kinney, Dow Edgerton (Professor, author, and former dean of Chicago Theological Seminary), Barry Fishler, Judy Boncaro, Rev. Samuel Sawitski, and Ethiopian Orthodox monk Abba Yohannes. Without their encouragement and help in editing various early stages of the manuscript this book wouldn't have become a reality. Thanks to Cynthia Bourgeault, William Meninger, Ken Barnes, and Abba Yohannes for their endorsements. Appreciation also for Fran Stach's last round of copyediting.

What can I say about the blessing of David Sanford and Dr. Leonard Sweet? Their invaluable encouragement along the way gave me the courage for the long journey to publication. Without their help this book wouldn't have seen the light of day!

My heartfelt thanks to Richard Rohr for his eloquent afterword.

Gratitude to my primary teachers of Centering Prayer: Rev. Sandy Casey-Martus and Thomas Keating.

Gratefulness for my sister, Meredith, who is my *compadre* on a parallel spiritual path.

---

10. Gold, et al., *The New Testament and Psalms: An Inclusive Version.* I have some discomfort with the neutered language of *An Inclusive Version.* I'm waiting for a version that honors the universality of God by alternating male and female images for God. Throughout the book I avoid male pronouns for God, acknowledging that God is beyond such limitations. When "Father-Mother" is used in *An Inclusive Version,* I substitute the word "God."

11. See *Philokalia* in glossary (Appendix A).

Finally, I want to thank all the congregations I have served as pastor. Your numerous examples of integrity and service have been a lamp to my path. You have deepened and humbled my spirit.

Part 1

A Beginning

1

A Yearning Too Deep for Words

*I do not look for God because I think it is what I am supposed to do;
I do it because I need to, because of a longing that is not of my own
creation.*

–John of the Cross

M OST OF US ARE looking for a home. We're displaced people. The average American moves every five years, deals with an increasingly frantic pace of life, and has fractures, if not in the immediate family, then in the extended family. Many of us have lost our link to the past. The traditions that spoke to our ancestors no longer speak to us with the same conviction.

We find ourselves on a turbulent ocean called the Twenty-first Century, where through the internet, satellite television, air travel, and cell phones the world is at our doorstep. Vast horizons are open to us as never before. It is an incredible, fascinating time. It is also a bewildering and anxiety-ridden time.

Now, more than ever, we need a home—not just a physical home, but a spiritual one.

A recent television show depicted people trying to live like pioneers. One of the experimental pioneers said, "There are twelve-step groups, such as Alcoholics Anonymous. In these groups people start group sharing with, 'Hello my name is John and I'm an alcoholic.'" He continued, "I often feel we need support groups, not only for the chemically dependent, but for all of us living in the Twenty-first Century. In such a group I would start by saying, 'Hello my name is John and I live in the Twenty-first Century' . . ." These are overwhelming times.

When people had job security, came from stable homes, and lived in the same place their whole lives, spiritual homesickness was less acute. Now, when everything seems tenuous, we need a spiritual anchor.

Whether we act on it or simply dream of it, all of us instinctually return to our origins—to our roots. It may be to the desert to discover ourselves in its stillness (Psalm 46:10). It may be a return to Ireland to find our relatives and family name. It may be a pilgrimage to Lourdes in France, where seekers report healings and direct communication with God.

We yearn to take the journey of Abraham and Sarah—the journey through the wilderness to the Promised Land. This is particularly true in America. The Spanish conquistadors, the Puritans, the pioneers and colonizers all searched for an earthly paradise. And the migration of seekers continues—flocking to Bali or India to find their guru, to California to find the sun and its gardens of Eden, or to that church with the new young minister who promises heaven.

Most of us are searching for a Promised Land where we can lie down in green pastures, be led to still waters, and restore our souls (Psalm 23:2–3a). We yearn for the tumultuous waters to still. We long to catch our breath and connect with something far deeper than our disconnected Twenty-first Century selves. We thirst for a refuge that transcends our fragmented, internet-surfing minds. We thirst for a spiritual home that is as spacious as the starlit desert sky, yet as intimate as our spouse's body who occupies our bed.

We thirst for something at the edge of our tongues, for a spaciousness that creates space where there is no space, for light-hearted presence of mind that brings humor into the humorless situation, for something at the tips of our tongues that echoes the invisible freedom of monarch butterfly wings.

EXPOSURE TO THE WORLD'S RELIGIONS

I grew up all over the world and took in the world's religions by osmosis. Countries outside the United States where I've lived include Indonesia, Bolivia, Yemen, Uganda, and India.

Many of my peers have been exposed to the world's religions. And as a result they can no longer accept the unquestioned Christian dogmas of previous generations. Their worldview has expanded and now their faith needs broadening to stay relevant.

The task of integrating Twenty-first Century insights with Christian tradition is daunting, so many of my peers reject Christianity wholesale. Others jump ship to other spiritually rich religious traditions that speak credibly to Twenty-first Century challenges.[1] Still others retreat from organized religion in order to fashion tailor-made spiritualities borrowed from various traditions.

My approach was different. I believed Christianity had the spiritual depth to weather the Twenty-first Century storms. And I passionately sought out this depth.

The spiritual vigor I looked for wasn't taught in my childhood church. I was taught many valuable lessons of community life and humble service, but the essence of Jesus and the deep spiritual underpinnings of his teachings eluded me. I think they also eluded the minister of my youth. Yet I instinctively knew that the language to express the deepest spirituality of Christian tradition existed. So I searched.

In college and graduate school Christianity wasn't in vogue. In fact, Christianity was openly lambasted by my peers. Given the general hostility toward Christianity, especially on the West Coast, it is little wonder so many drift away.

The progressive minded Christians with whom I went to school lamented the state of American Christianity as a whole, which often champions pop-culture sentimentality and devalues reason. Yet, these progressive Christians were unable to find an alternative that gets to the heart of Twenty-first Century challenges.

My progressive Christian friends today often find themselves in mainline denominations that are losing numbers yearly. These denominations lack a unified theological stance. At worst they're wishy-washy about their faith in Christ. Or at best they appeal to the historic Jesus. Their faith also lacks the passion of their evangelical and fundamentalist sisters

---

1. Many within Christian tradition honor pluralism and interfaith dialogue and so speak credibly to Twenty-first Century challenges. The problem is this pluralism usually doesn't cohere with sound theology. In other words, the theological underpinnings of the pluralism most often seem new-agey, vague, out of step with the roots of the tradition.

and brothers. And the lack of conviction and passion is a big part of the perpetual decline of Mainline Christian Churches.[2]

The alternatives seem to be passionate yet closed-minded Christianity on the right or open-minded yet watered-down Christianity on the left. Hence the title of Jim Wallis' book, *God's Politics: Why the Right Gets It Wrong and the Left Doesn't Get It.*

NEED FOR A TWENTY-FIRST CENTURY SPIRITUAL ANCHOR

We throw our faith anchor into the Twenty-first Century Ocean and find our rope isn't long enough. The length of rope that worked for our ancestors no longer works for us. The ocean has gotten deeper. The uncharted globe has become the pluralistic global village accessible by internet, cell phone, and global positioning satellites.

The spirituality that sustained our great-grandparents doesn't seem to have enough breadth to weather the postmodern storms. When confronted with interfaith dialogue, we lack adequate answers and the holes in our faith become apparent. When all we knew was fried chicken and spuds, it satisfied. But now, across the street there's chicken curry at the Thai restaurant, Tandoori chicken at the Indian restaurant, and Kung Pao chicken at the Chinese restaurant.

The world is shrinking. And now we have access to anything, including powerfully rich spiritual traditions from the East. So, if we're going to stay with Christianity, it will have to withstand comparison shopping. Accepting Jesus as personal savior, going to church weekly, and hearing comforting words about deliverance on the last day may no longer sustain us. This may have worked for our ancestors and it may work for traditional people who have chosen not to look past their back yard. But there are many, including me, for whom the standard exclusive model of Christianity doesn't completely satisfy.

So where do we go?

The *God-shaped hole*,[3] as Augustine put it, yearns to be filled in every generation. The yearning for God may be more acute in this generation than ever before. For we live in an age of spiritual homelessness—an age of spiritual poverty. Not only do we find homeless people walking our streets.

2. See *Mainline Christianity* in glossary (Appendix A).

3. In Augustine's *Confessions* he wrote "My soul is restless, Oh Lord (God), until it rests in thee." From this sentence the phrase "God-shaped hole" was coined.

We also find the spiritually homeless—people without an anchor—people without the enduring stability and roots that come from generations-old faith communities. In America alone, there are increasing numbers of people disconnected from their spiritual source. In fact, it is estimated that thirty-five million Americans have lost their faith.[4]

Like many spiritually homeless Westerners I've had a longing too deep for words. I've been searching for a spiritual home for my head and for my heart in the Twenty-first Century. This book is about that search . . .

The Alexandrian Mystics' teaching about Jesus has the power to restore the faith of our ancestors. It has the power to answer the Twenty-first Century challenges. It can heal Christianity's present divide. It can heal our polarized tradition, careening towards fundamentalism on the one hand and rootless new age Christianity on the other.

Although virtually unknown, there was a coherent and long standing legacy of Christian mystics—a legacy passed down through generations of monks and clerics in and near the city of Alexandria, Egypt between 312–454 CE. For one hundred and fifty years there was consensus among the early Christian mystics about Jesus' essence. I've sought this teaching my whole life and it is now my spiritual home.

REFORM AND RENEWAL IN THE CHURCH

Many Christians today don't have a spiritual home. Part of the reason is the lack of a frame of reference for Mystic Christianity. So, many flock to mystics of other world religions.

I believe the teachings of the Alexandrian Mystics have the potential to cure spiritual homelessness and spawn reform and Christian renewal.

Christianity needs deep change or it will slowly diminish in influence and die out as it has in Europe. People no longer want a status quo social club. That's why fraternal orders and social club churches are going extinct. In the Twenty-first Century staid ceremonial niceties don't inspire deep commitment and transformation. People want a holistic way of seeing the world. People want a way of life characterized by the profound reverence and ecstatic celebration of the mystics.

My mission is to make the Alexandrian Mystics more accessible. For authentic and deeply rooted mysticism is the highest expression of faith and people instinctively yearn for it. The Alexandrian Mystics took God seriously—put God at the center. And we yearn to do the same. We need a

---

4. Sanford, "If God Disappeared" Lecture.

primal model for understanding Mystic Christianity. For mysticism glues together the disparate fragments of a tradition, uniting and revitalizing it.

As attested in numerous writings of The Alexandrian Mystics, union with God through prayer is the central focus.[5] Thomas Keating, a contemporary Benedictine Monk, speaks of Christian enlightenment as *Divine Union*. Our fragmented Twenty-first Century lives need the experience of unity, even if it's only for an hour in meditation or in worship. The early Christian mystics are the wellspring of this dream.

In The United States over fifty percent of marriages fail. Teen suicide, gun violence, terrorism, and environmental devastation continue to escalate. And technology continues to rocket, whirl, orbit, and overwhelm. In response to our anxious and fragmented world we seek holistic vision. Yet, unfortunately, Christianity often becomes another arena of conflict, partisan politics, and *us versus them*.

More than ever, we need Christian leadership and teaching that reflects wholeness. The Jesus Paradox of The Alexandrian Mystics has the power to heal souls yearning for a deeply rooted mystical homeland. It has the power to heal divisions in the body of Christ.

QUESTIONS FOR REFLECTION AND DISCUSSION

1) Do you think the "spiritual homelessness" Smith talks about is real? Why or why not?

2) Do you lament the state of Christianity as a whole today? Why or why not?

3) Do you think the spirituality of our great-grandparents can weather the postmodern storms? Why or why not?

4) What do you make of the "God-shaped hole" that Smith claims needs to be filled in every generation?

5) Application question: Is Christianity "in vogue" in the circles you frequent? Explain.

---

5. In my estimation the most significant of these writings is *The Philokalia.* Maximus the Confessor and Saint Peter of Damascus make the top of my list of Philokalia writers.

2

Discovering Christianity's
Mystic Roots

I still have many things to say to you, but you cannot bear them now.
When the Spirit of truth comes,
that Spirit will guide you into all the truth . . .
and will declare the things that are to come.

–The Gospel of John

Mystic roots don't meet in the middle; they hold the ends together,
which ignites the fireworks.

–Leonard Sweet

CONTINUING REVELATION & THE GOSPEL ROCK

DID THE ACTIVITY OF the Holy Spirit end with the Acts of the Apostles and the writings of Paul, Peter, James, and John? Or is there continuing revelation through the Holy Spirit?

I believe the Holy Spirit continues to work with us through history, generation after generation. Each generation of Christians adds a letter to the New Testament. Harriet Tubman added a letter entitled *My Work on the Underground Railroad*. Saint Patrick added *Bringing Christianity to Ireland*. Martin Luther King, Jr. wrote *My Work in the Civil Rights Movement*. Millard Fuller added *The Birth of Habitat for Humanity*. Nelson Mandela, Desmond Tutu, and friends wrote a letter entitled *Dismantling Apartheid in South Africa*.

In George Fox's journal, George's spouse, Margaret, attributed the following words to him: "You will say, 'Christ says this, and the apostles say this;' but what can you say?"[1] Fox's emphasis on the primacy of first-hand knowledge and personal experience stunned his hearers. In a day when clergy were all mouthing the convictions of others, Fox had the audacity to say, "I know what they all said, but what is your conviction?" If Paul and a handful of others were the only ones to write New Testament letters, Christianity would be a thing of the past. It is the generations of living witnesses that keep Christianity vital. It is up to each generation to incarnate the Word in ways appropriate for our times.

We might ask, "What in our tradition is solid and unchanging?" "What compass do we use to navigate the turbulent waters of constant change?" For me the compass is the Gospels. I compare the Gospels to Seattle real estate. Seattle real estate closest to the heart of the city is the most valuable. The further we get from the city center, the less valuable the real estate becomes. As a Christian I hold the Gospels to be the Bible's most valuable real estate.[2] If we distill the Gospels to their essence we come to Jesus.

So the key for us is to get one piece right, that is to deeply understand Jesus' essence.

---

1. Fox, *The Journal of George Fox*.

2. Carston and D'Ancona's book, *Eyewitness to Jesus*, convinced me that Matthew, Mark, and Luke were most likely written much earlier than most scholars first hypothesized. *Eyewitness to Jesus*, based on papyrus fragments of Matthew's gospel, asserts that Matthew was most likely written 60CE by an eyewitness to Jesus. This assertion is based on forensic evidence and the refined art of papyrology (the study of ancient papyrus fragments). This assertion is not founded on the current bias of the academy which is based on conjecture, theory, and interpretation. Forensic evidence, like The Magdalen Papyrus used in *Eyewitness to Jesus*, is so important to the field of biblical scholarship. Without it we have mere conjecture, with skeptics looking for earlier origination dates for scripture, and theological conservatives looking for the opposite.

TWENTY-FIRST CENTURY CHRISTIANITY'S FOUNDATION

Much theology emerging today doesn't have a foundation on which to build. It has windows, doors, ceiling tile. Meanwhile, the foundation is ignored.

Some have tried to build Christian theology on the makeshift foundation of historical criticism. Yet, as P.T. Forsyth (d. 1921) often quoted, "Historical criticism is a good servant but a dangerous master." Others have tried to build Twenty-first Century Christianity on the foundation of meticulously defined church doctrine, which seems quaint and antiquated. Some want to build today's Christianity on the back of process theology, which is only a century old. Others want to build Twenty-first Century faith on the Jesus Seminar. But this recent revisionist project lacks historic precedent and presents numerous problems. Still others want to build today's Christianity on Twenty-first Century sensibilities, like pluralism. There are many exciting prospects for Christianity's future. Yet, none of the above can serve as Christian theology's foundation. Today's social and environmental concerns also can't serve as the theological foundation to re-build Twenty-first Century Christianity.

Our essential understanding and interpretation of Jesus is the only possible foundation. "For no one can lay any foundation other than the one that has been laid; that foundation is Jesus Christ" (1 Corinthians 3:11). In order to stand squarely within the two thousand year tradition, all Christian theology must be rooted in Jesus. So in this book I turn to Jesus—Jesus according to the Alexandrian Mystics.[3]

Jesus is Christianity's obvious core. Inquiry into the essential nature of Jesus gets at Christianity's center. We're talking about foundation work here, not a little re-modeling. Inquiry into the essential nature of Jesus has implications for every corner of the vast cathedral we call Christianity. One little crack in this foundation can create a fissure decades from now. So, pay close attention!

Inquiry into the essential nature of Jesus in the context of the world's religions has primal implications for the way we think. It has profound implications for our faith and practice, for our relationships with neighbors, and for our relationships with other religious communities.

---

3. The Alexandrian Mystics of the Egyptian desert from the third to the fifth centuries, while in deep prayer, apprehended the profound inclusive nature of Jesus reflected in the Gospels far before the dawn of Twenty-first Century religious pluralism.

THEOLOGY IS NOT A GAME

The tragedy of September Eleventh convinced me of the importance of how we think about God. Theology is not a game. Theology matters. Good theology builds bridges and heals divisions in our minds and in our world. Bad theology builds walls between people and promotes violence.

Christianity's job, in the words of George Fox, is to live in the "power, life, light, seed and wisdom, by which we may take away the occasion of wars."[4]

Religions perpetuate exclusive dogmas that breed violence in the world. It is up to the guardians of Christian faith to remove seeds of violence from the Body of Christ.[5] This task requires sensitivity. To preserve orthodoxy while remaining true to the inclusive spirit of Jesus found in the Gospels is a tight-rope, yet we have trusty guides on this sojourn. Our guides are the Alexandrian Mystics.

The life changing discovery that allows me to remain Christian with integrity is a teaching of the Alexandrian Mystics on The Jesus Paradox. This teaching has the power to heal Christianity's Twenty-first Century divide. The Jesus Paradox coheres with my faith, with my Centering Prayer practice, and with my cosmopolitan Twenty-first Century mind. The Jesus Paradox is reasoned passion and passionate reason. It balances head and heart.

Healing The Divide is the first book to make Jesus' Paradoxical essence as understood by the Alexandrian Mystics accessible to the common reader. The elaborate teaching on The Jesus Paradox of the Alexandrian Mystics is not taught in the West today. It is taught piece meal by inaccessible academics.

The unique aim of my book is to make these Alexandrian Mystics' core teachings about Jesus accessible. It is also to identify these teachings as the mystic core of Christian faith.

The Alexandrian Mystics taught that Jesus' divinity with a capital D and his humanity with a lower case h are always in dynamic tension and can never be separated.[6] This mysterious Paradox is the foundation of a broad Christianity in the spirit of Thomas Merton.

---

4. Fox, *The Journal of George Fox*, October 12th, 1658. I've adapted the old English of the original quotation to contemporary English.

5. "Body of Christ" refers to the body of Christian believers united by communion (the bread and cup).

6. By capital D I mean Jesus is the Deity in the monotheistic sense of the word, not a deity in a Hindu pantheon. And by lower case h I mean Jesus is human, with all the

In recent decades, polarizing extremes have thrown Christianity into various tail spins. So, there are hundreds of thousands of Christians without a spiritual home. Mystic Christianity correctly understood can cure spiritual homelessness.

The purpose of this book is to make the crown jewel of Alexandrian theology accessible to the common reader. The tempered mysticism of the Alexandrian Mystics has the God-given potential to heal polarized Christianity and spawn renewal.

THE NEED FOR COMPREHENSIVE TEACHING ON MYSTIC CHRISTIANITY

For the early Christians, mysticism wasn't esoteric. It was their life blood. Alexandria between 250 and 450 CE had the greatest number of monastic Christian communities the world has ever known. During this period Alexandria valued monastic disciplines and cultivated mystics as no other city before or since. Alexandrians honored the experience of monks above the hierarchy of clergy. The authority of Alexandrian theology was rooted in monastic experience and silent prayer. I refer to this as Monastic Authority.[7]

Alexandrian Mystics went into profound detail about the mystical union of Jesus' full Divinity and full humanity.[8] These elegant teachings have interior depth missing from Western Christianity.[9] My hope is to communicate this depth to the Western reader.

One morning while reading up on the Alexandrian Mystics, the hair on my arms stood on end. I realized that I'd stumbled upon the gem of Mystic Christianity. I'd speculated that the Alexandrian Mystics were Christianity's greatest mystic legacy. That Saturday confirmed my hunch and changed everything.

Over the following years I dug into relevant sources and validated the hunch! As I suspected, the influence of the Alexandrian Mystics was

limitations of our humanity.

7. See *Monastic Authority* in glossary (Appendix A).

8. The most significant of these writings is *On The Unity of Christ*, by Cyril of Alexandria.

9. The wisdom of the Alexandrian Mystics is broadly reflected in the teaching of the Oriental Orthodox Church today (not to be confused with the Eastern Orthodox Church).

Collective wisdom - deeper - more multi dimensional

profound. In fact, its lineage of teachings on The Jesus Paradox heavily influenced the Desert Fathers and Mothers.

In recent years the sayings of the Desert Fathers and Mothers have enjoyed remarkable popularity. Yet, no one in the West has connected The Jesus Paradox as taught by the Alexandrian Mystics with the sayings of the Desert Fathers and Mothers. Yet, there's no question that the Alexandrian Mystics, such as Athanasius (d. 373), had a profound influence on the monasteries and hermitages of Egypt, where the Desert Fathers and Mothers lived.[10]

In the absence of knowledge about the Alexandrian Mystics and their unique lineage, there's no comprehensive teaching on Mystic Christianity. In the vacuum, there are fragments of teachings from isolated mystics. The fragmentary nature of Mystic Christianity as it has been taught in the West makes mysticism seem diffuse and unappealing.

There is an authoritative tradition of Christian Mystics who were both theologians and practitioners of silent prayer! More specifically, there was a recognized lineage of Alexandrian Mystics whose influence was felt throughout the Egyptian desert, including the Desert Fathers and Mothers.[11]

A LINEAGE OF MYSTIC TEACHINGS AND ITS RELEVANCY TODAY

Mystic traditions the world over place great emphasis on a lineage of spiritual masters. When spiritual masters through the ages wrestle with the same questions and pass down their knowledge, the collective wisdom is deeper and more multi-dimensional than isolated individual mystics can achieve.

Unknown to the West, an authoritative body of mystical teaching has been passed down through generations! This mystic core of Christian faith is important today because everywhere I go, clergy groups agree there's a divide in Western Christianity. This is especially true when it comes to debates about Jesus' person. This is precisely where the insights of the Alexandrian Mystics penetrate.

10. Brakke, *Athanasius and Asceticism.*

11. I am referring to the Alexandrian Bishops who presided in Alexandria, Egypt from 312–454 CE. See *Alexandrian Bishops* in glossary (Appendix A) and see Appendix B. Also see Sellers, *The Council of Chalcedon*, 213.

accept and appreciate creative tension

Clergy are aware of the two poles of the Jesus debate. And when I outline the original synthesis of The Alexandrian Mystics, the positive response is dramatic. No one is attempting to bridge the obvious theological divide. This book charts a new course outside the well worn conservative and liberal arguments.

For liberal Christians there is too much ambiguity and confusion about Jesus. For conservative Christians, there's too much dogmatic certainty and not enough mystery. The Alexandrian Mystics provide a fresh and compelling angle on Jesus.

WHAT IS THE ESSENCE OF THIS BOOK?

At this point you may ask, "What is this essential teaching you're getting at? Tell me!" In other words, "Where are the Cliff Notes?" This is where I respond, "Sound bite theology doesn't work for Mystic Christianity."

The most subtle teachings of a tradition can't be reduced to sound bites. They take time to understand and digest. Like a cow chewing its cud, theological insights must be chewed and re-chewed. The essence of Mystic Christianity can't be made into fast food. We say, "I want it now." The mystics tell us, "The fruit can only be picked, eaten, and digested when it's ripe."

Mysticism isn't easily expressed. It's a state of mind difficult to achieve and even trickier to put into words, which are inherently dualistic.

This book will stir up insights different from conventional Christianity. I will suggest the standard Western interpretation of Jesus is static and dualistic. Jesus as understood by early Christian mystics provides a corrective to static polarizations.

Redefining our roots as Christians today requires accepting and appreciating creative tension as opposed to getting locked in to an either/or tug-of-war mentality. The Western dualistic mindset runs deep. Redefining our Christian roots requires unlearning reams of social scripting to choose a side, to win or lose.

The genius of the Alexandrian Mystics is their ability to ferret out extremism. The Alexandrian Mystics temper absolutism on the one hand and wishy-washy noncommittal religion on the other. Absolutism is the illness of the 9/11 hijackers and of Christians who bomb abortion clinics. Wishy-washy noncommittal religion is the illness of secularism that creeps into religions and neuters them, so God is a byword. Then dogmatic atheism picks up where secularism leaves off![12] The Alexandrian Mystics avoid both extremes in favor of a higher third way.

The root conviction of the Alexandrian Mystics transforms my faith. It saves me from the precipice of absolutism on the one hand (Jesus is God period) and wishy-washy noncommittal religion (Jesus is human period) on the other. It heals divisions and divisiveness in my mind and heart.

QUESTIONS FOR REFLECTION AND DISCUSSION

1) What do you think about the ongoing revelation of the Holy Spirit through the ages? Explain.

2) Do you agree with the following statements? "Theology is not a game. Theology matters." Why or why not?

3) Do you think we need to re-evaluate and re-build Twenty-first Century Christianity in light of current challenges? Why or why not?

4) Application question: When you hear the word "mysticism" what comes to your mind?

12. Atheists such as Sam Harris, Christopher Hitchens, and Richard Dawkins have lambasted the dark side of religion and push for its non-essential role. They see religion as an inhibitor of reason and a catalyst for violence. They see "God" as a hypothesis that's failed.

3

Going Deeper Into Paradox

The great truths can only be expressed in paradox.

–THOMAS KEATING

Christianity got over the difficulty of combining furious opposites,
by keeping them both, and keeping them both furious.

–G.K. CHESTERTON

CIRCLE OR LINE?

DAYTON EDMONDS[1] IS A Native American storyteller and Christian, whose theology centers on Jesus the storyteller, the one whose parables turned everything upside-down.

A primary insight of Dayton's stories is that it really doesn't matter what story he begins with and what one he ends with because at some point they'll intersect. The same may be said of a circle. A circle has no

---

1. Dayton Edmonds is a full-blooded Native American of the Caddo Nation, who has developed a diverse ministry, lifestyle, and artistry. Dayton was a commissioned United Methodist missionary and now leads retreats and workshops. See www.daytonedmonds.net.

distinct beginning and ending point. Not so with the linear world. For our Western minds where we begin and end along a line graph is everything. And the two ends won't meet. The two points of a line are diametrically opposed and moving in two opposite directions.

There's a distinguished place for our linear Western minds and for reason in human history. Without them the sciences wouldn't have transformed the worlds of medicine, aviation, and electronics. Yet, when reason is emphasized to the exclusion of intuition and transcendence, the life of the mind is impoverished and its full genius unrealized.

As many philosophers have pointed out, when employed rigorously, reason leads to contradictory conclusions.[2] For most of us dualistic Western thinkers these contradictions are never resolved. Our Western minds are born of a historic schism between nature and civilization, mind and body, religion and science, God and humanity. We assume the polarities are diametrically opposed and can't be reconciled.

Mystics tell us there's a way beyond persistent dualisms—a way beyond the opposites. Mystics tell us dealing with polarities generates paradoxes, which offer the possibility of profound integration beyond what reason can conceive. If we consent, the incarnation can take us to the point where reason turns back on itself. It can take us to that point where the absolute difference between eternity and time, fullness (resurrection) and emptiness (the cross), God and humanity, Creator and creature, begins to break down.

PARADOXICAL SCRIPTURES

Jesus says, "Come to me, all you that are weary and are carrying heavy burdens, and I will give you rest. Take my yoke upon you, and learn from me; for I am gentle and humble in heart, and you will find rest for your souls. For my yoke is easy, and my burden is light" (Matthew 11:28–30). These verses claim the way of Jesus is easy. Then come Jesus' words, "Any one of you who looks at another lustfully has already committed adultery. . . if you say, 'You fool,' (to anyone), you will be liable to the hell of fire" (Matthew 5:28, 22). These verses maintain the way of Jesus is exceedingly difficult. So Jesus' way is paradoxical—both easy and difficult.

Jesus' sayings are paradoxical and multi-layered—"the first will be last," "turn the other cheek," "whoever is innocent should be the first to cast a stone" (Matthew 20: 16b, Matthew 5:39, John 8:7). Then we arrive at

2. Kant, *The Critique of Pure Reason.*

the essence of paradox: "Love your enemies" (Matthew 5:44). Throughout the parables the paradoxical teachings continue: Give to receive. Die to live. Lose to win. Paul mirrors Jesus' paradoxes when he exclaims, "Whenever I am weak, then I am strong" (2 Corinthians 12:10).

Many authors have pointed out the parables are paradoxical riddles. A couple of major examples suffice. . . In the parable of the prodigal son, the Jew (the chosen one) becomes the victim and the Samaritan (the despicable one) becomes the hero (Luke 15:11–32). In the parable of the lost sheep, the individual is the concern and the crowd is ignored. The person ignored by the crowd is suddenly all in all. And the all important crowd is of little consequence. Forget the opinion polls and popularity contests. The lone individual, sitting in a jail cell or on a cross, is God's ultimate concern (Matthew 18:12–14, Luke 15:3–10). This isn't the world we're accustomed to. In the paradoxical world of the parables the loafers are treated with the same largess as the diligent workers, the riff-raff get the best seats in the house and the rich are sent away empty.

Many ministers and New Testament teachers avoid Jesus' paradoxical teachings. Many prefer Paul's straightforward approach. Yet Paul wasn't God incarnate. Jesus was. And Jesus taught paradox because that's where the transformational power is. *Amen!*

OPEN ENDED ANSWERS, GIVE AND TAKE

When people asked Jesus questions, he avoided definitive answers. Instead, Jesus responded with parables because they offered open-ended answers that respect people's own processes. He never said this is the answer, period. He said "Here is a story—work with it, put yourself in it, see what happens." So, there's not one answer, but several depending on our point of view. And the story isn't complete without the listener's engagement.

Many came to Jesus expecting him to solve their problems. Instead he helped them to connect to their own faith and their own wisdom. They had a part to play. It wasn't a one-way street with Jesus taking control. The people's faith played a big part in Jesus' healings. That's why Jesus repeated "Your faith has made you well" (Matthew 9: 21–22, Mark 5: 34). Our linear minds would like to arrive at the definitive: "It was Jesus who made them well." But this isn't Jesus' point. There's a process—a dynamic in healing, which requires the consent of both healer and healed. Good storytelling requires the engagement of both storyteller and listener. It isn't a top-down linear relationship where one person dominates.

Jesus' egalitarian sensibilities run throughout the Gospels—something completely fresh and surprising in the linear hierarchical society of first-century Palestine. Jesus' example of servant leadership is extraordinary. He said, "The rulers of the Gentiles lord it over them. . . But not so with you; rather the greatest among you must become like the youngest, and the leader like one who serves" (Luke 22:25a, 26). Jesus says "Forget about hierarchies, chains of command, and pecking orders. Let's get rid of the rectangular table with the boss at the head. Let's get a circular table, where everyone's voice is heard. Everyone has a place at the table."[3]

Life is about symbiosis—give and take. I learn from you. You learn from me. Teaching is a two-way street. Both are teachers—both students. When it comes to Jesus, some don't want to admit this. Some prefer clearly defined authority—a chain of command. Everything's tidier that way. There's less room for chaos. There's also less room for mystery. The Quakers have a saying, "Don't walk in front of me. I may not follow. Don't walk behind me. I may not lead. Walk beside me and be my friend." This is the power of the incarnation. God chose to walk beside us. We have a part to play in our own transformation and healing. God incarnate grants power with, not power over. Jesus said, "I no longer call you servants, because a servant does not know his master's business. Instead, I have called you friends" (John 15:15a, NIV).

Jesus' life and teaching marks a shift from God's power over to God's power with, from inaccessibility to incarnation, from God of fear to God of love, from remote God to intimate God (Jesus used the intimate Hebrew word *Abba* (Daddy) when referring to God, shocking his listeners).

THE PARADOX OF GOD IN PROCESS WITH US

God doesn't have hands. Only we have hands. If we refuse to use our hands as conduits of the Divine will, God's hands are tied, so to speak. Not only do we rely on God, but God relies on us. Just as Jesus counted on his human disciples to spread the Gospel, God counts on us to be God's hands and feet in the world—to be the body of Christ.

Without us, God's work won't get done in the world. God doesn't twist our arms in this process, but asks for our consent. God is about responsive love, not power over. Jesus teaches by example and by compassion, not by coercion and fear. We're invited, not forced, to incarnate the

---

3. I'm using my imagination.

word of God. This is called process theology, which when brought down to earth makes a lot of sense.[4]

Process theology casts off top-down relationship to God, where our job is simply to figure out God's will and then submit. Process theology makes room for the complex and creative interplay between our will and God's will influencing each other. And in my experience, God leaves details to us. God trusts us with our calling and isn't a micromanager. A top-down micromanaging boss is much simpler to grasp, minimizing ambiguity. Process theology beholds God in process with us—even letting us take the wheel sometimes.

The paradox is that we're invited to participate in God's power. So God isn't all-powerful. Together with us God is all-powerful, but only if we consent. If we don't consent, God's hands are tied. In other words, in order for the incarnation to happen God had to say "yes" and Mary had to say "yes." If Mary had said "no" there would have been no incarnation![5] We have a major part to play and God says "bring it!"

God doesn't will any of the worlds' suffering and wants to prevent it. But God can't prevent suffering alone. God needs us. This is powerful theology, because it puts the responsibility for the state of the world back on our shoulders. It doesn't settle for cowardly nods to God's will. God's will is limited and needs us to act. If we stand by while people suffer evils we could prevent, we're faithless. If we sit around and wait for supernatural miracles, we're deluded.[6] If we roll up our sleeves and get to work, we're among the saints (James 2:17).

Throughout the Bible, God's mind is changed in response to faithful servants. In Genesis, Abraham argues with God, and at times changes God's mind (Genesis 18:16–33). Similarly, in the Gospels, a Gentile woman changes Jesus' mind (Matthew 15:21–28). In other words we share power with God. Human beings are the body of Christ!

If God's dominion comes on earth as in heaven (Matthew 6:10), it will be because Mary consented to be an instrument of God. Moses

---

4. See *Process Theology* in glossary (Appendix A).

5. God grants us free will, so God needs our consent to act in the world. God's actions are on a consensual basis, as are the actions of all lovers. God doesn't force God's will. We consent to God's will and so are given the invitation to participate in the process of creation—to become co-creators with God (Luke 1: 26–38).

6. I disagree with most process theologians on a crucial point. . . Even though supernatural interventions are rare, they do happen against all probability once in a great while, in the fullness of time.

consented. John the Baptist consented. Nelson Mandela consented. I consent. You consent.

SYNERGY BETWEEN GOD AND HUMANITY

Our destination isn't fixed, but flexible. We can change the course of history for the good. Pre-destination is just more of the same top-down relationship (God over us). Life isn't just what God makes it. It is what we make it in covenant with God. *yes*

Process theology proclaims God is intimately mingled with the ambiguities and inconsistencies of this world. God is in history, not removed. God was in the Abolitionist Movement, the Women's Suffrage Movement, the Civil Rights Movement. God isn't up there somewhere and us down here. The two intersect; there's dynamism between the two. This is the practical implication of the incarnation. God became human. God got mixed up with humanity and all its limitations and liabilities. Through Jesus, God is humbled and humanity glorified.

Wow The future isn't already fully known by God (pre-destination). We're co-creators with God of the future (free will). The future isn't only dependent on God. It's dependent on our choices.

Fundamentalists rely on God and the afterlife too much, often seeing life as a vale of tears to be endured. Secular humanists rely too heavily on humanity, denying transcendence. Both God and humanity are part of the equation. Both sustain one another.

Process theology states the life of faith isn't totally up to God/Grace. And it's not totally up to our own efforts. It is about both working cooperatively. Yes, there's in fact a paradoxical relationship between faith and works (between *Romans* and *James* in the New Testament). As Gregory of Nyssa writes, "The grace of God cannot descend upon souls which flee from their salvation, so too the power of human virtue is not of itself sufficient to raise to perfection souls which have no share of grace."[7]

INCLUDING THE MARGINALIZED IN SOCIETY AND WITHIN OURSELVES

The Gospels lead us to conclude that every person, baggage and all, has something to teach.

---

7. Lossky, *The Mystical Theology*, 197–198.

Each life has a story that needs to be told, not only for the sake of personal authenticity but for the sake of community. Each person in a faith community adds color and texture. Everyone has a place and has something important to contribute. This notion differs from the linear Western model that puts some on a perpetual pedestal and others in a perpetual gutter. And those in the gutter should be out of the way in a prison, a nursing home, or a homeless shelter. Fundamentalists, watch out! Ivy League elitists and limousine liberals, watch out!

Jesus reached out to the margins, insisting society's outcasts have a place at the table. Jesus also reaches out to the parts of ourselves we hide, repress, and deny, insisting that these parts have a place at the table. These marginalized aspects of our God-given selves are profoundly important, because they press honesty and humility. This honesty and humility is what I love about Christian author Anne Lamott. And as the Desert Fathers and Mothers have repeatedly stated, honesty and humility are the touchstones of the spiritual journey.

Repressing the marginalized in our society and repressing the marginalized aspects of our souls is just more dualistic, *us and them* bunk. God's realm moves us beyond binaries to a holistic vision, where the marginalized are no longer left to pine away outside the city gates. They're invited in, given a seat at the table, and assured of their God-given worth. When we experience new life in Christ, difficult chapters in our histories are no longer buried in our psyches, locked away in the shadows. The soft underbellies of our lives are addressed during prayer time and among people we trust, often with trembling and tears. Then shadows are accepted for what they are: our crosses. When the crosses and their emptiness are addressed, the cocoon cracks and the butterfly emerges.

Easter wasn't intended for Christ alone. It is intended for each and every member of the body of Christ and for society as a whole. And Easter can't be experienced until the cross is accepted. Easter can't be experienced until the leper within and the lepers in society are embraced. Jesus touched the leper (Mark 1:41)! Oh yes!

WORKING WITH OR WORKING AGAINST?

The West battles against the unwanted forces of nature. Unwanted creatures, like California's grizzly bears, which used to run in packs along its beaches, were annihilated. In the state of California grizzlies are no more. Rattlesnakes are killed on sight in Texas' open range. Bat colonies are

[handwritten annotations: "Chinese medicine – Paradox / Western Medicine – slave of reason"]

blasted out of caves and abandoned mine shafts in the Midwest. Yet when the rattlesnakes are gone, the mice take over. When the bats are gone, the mosquitoes get out of control. And when the grizzlies are gone the grandeur of God's creation is diminished. *[handwritten: So sad —]*

[handwritten margin note: Include] The truth is something good comes from rattlesnakes, bats, grizzlies, prostitutes, lepers, and tax collectors. Something good even comes from abhorred diseases like smallpox. For some time a number of Western scientists wanted to rid the world of smallpox—to eradicate it completely from the planet. Others prudently argued the smallpox virus should be preserved for future generations. The unique virus could prove valuable to medical research. So, the smallpox virus was saved for its innate long-term worth and possible contribution to future medicine.

Interestingly, the AIDS virus is treated completely differently by Chinese and Western medicine. Chinese medicine assumes the virus will always exist and attempts to build the human body's resistance, so the body can live with the virus. The Western approach is to eliminate the virus completely. The first approach to the virus is more holistic, the second more linear. The first has a built-in sense of paradox. The second is the slave of reason. Reason labels some things good and others bad, then plots a line from one end to the other. Progress is advancement along the line. According to this thinking, fat is bad and should be removed through liposuction. Wrinkles are bad and should be flattened with Botox; the AIDS virus is bad and should be eliminated, period.

In contrast to the dualistic Western perspective, the holistic approach concedes that good can come from the smallpox virus and from working with, rather than against, the AIDS virus.[8] Holistic methods of weight reduction and reverse aging work with the entire system, instead of isolating and eliminating the unwanteds. The holistic mind of Jesus eats at table with the disreputable scum-bags, lavishing them with God's grace. Environmentalists work with, not against, perceived pests like grizzly bears, bats, and rattlesnakes. *[handwritten: Work with, not against]*

VANQUISHING DEMONS?

Some students of religion entertain the erroneous notion that saints completely vanquish their demons, expelling them into the pit of hell. Yet, in reality, the demons never leave. The spiritual aspirant's skill in dealing with

---

8. Leong, *The Zen Teachings of Jesus.*

Cunning, baffling, powerful sits on my shoulder to help me stay awake & aware

them simply improves over time. And the demons' presence is actually a good thing, pressing humility. *Yes!*

Anger and aggression are simply vital energies that, when harnessed, move mountains. Grief, when harnessed, champions empathy and understanding. Fear, when harnessed, leads to heightened awareness. Conversely, the business man with unbounded vital energy who whips through the inbox and spanks the to-do-list usually has to give careful attention to anger management. The sensational actress, who bathes in public affection, must watch her own destructive pleasure-seeking tendencies, which spiral into binge drinking and recreational drug use. The brilliant professor who unlocks the secrets of the brain's bio-chemistry must come to grips with chronic paranoia about his research getting stolen.

Every gift has both advantages and liabilities. And liabilities can't be eliminated completely. Even Saint Paul had a "thorn in the flesh" that didn't go away (2 Corinthians 12:7). In other words, some dog breeds are prone to biting. The solution isn't to kill the dog. It's to get a leash and a muzzle.

The solution isn't to vanquish demons, but to harness and temper them. *Harness & temper demons —*

HOLDING THE TENSION BETWEEN OPPOSITES

> A culture that prefers the ease of either or thinking to the complexities of paradox has a hard time holding opposites together. We want light without darkness, the glories of spring and summer without the demands of autumn and winter.[9]
>
> –Parker Palmer

Jesus' disciple, Saint Thomas (d. 73), known as doubting Thomas, thought death and life were irreconcilable. So he wouldn't believe the resurrection without hard evidence. Thomas' disbelief is ours. How can two polar opposites meet—how can death and life be reconciled in resurrection? Thomas couldn't comprehend life and death reconciled without touching the wounds of the risen Christ (John 20:19–31).

Many of us, like Thomas, have drawn strong boundaries and disbelieve the possibility of transcending them. But this is the Easter experience. Jesus shows us that however vividly the differences between opposites strike us, they nevertheless remain completely inseparable and

9. Palmer, *Let Your Life Speak*, 100.

All opposites are essentially inseparable !

interdependent in God's realm. One opposite can't exist without the other. We're never aware of pleasure except in relation to pain. I might be feeling relaxed and comfortable now, but I'm only able to realize this because of the existence of discomfort.

We begin to understand why life is totally exasperating when viewed as a world of separate opposites. In trying to separate the opposites and clutching those we judge positive, such as pleasure without pain, life without death, good without evil, Easter without the cross, we're striving after mirages. We might as well strive for a world of days and no nights, ups and no downs.

All opposites—such as mass and energy, subject and object, life and death—are so much each other that they're perfectly inseparable. This seems unbelievable. But this is an essential point of The Alexandrian Mystics.

LIBERATION FROM OPPOSITES

The dividing lines we find in nature or that we ourselves construct don't merely distinguish different opposites; they also bind the two together in an inseparable unity. A line, in other words, isn't a boundary. A line, whether mental, natural, or logical doesn't just separate and divide, it also joins and unites. [10] We create lines in our minds to separate what can't be separated.

Thomas completely separated life and death. That's why he couldn't believe the resurrection (John 20:25). The resurrection opens a window into the profound nature of God. The resurrection gets to the heart of paradox.

Like Thomas, we don't understand that boundaries collapse in the risen Christ. "There is no longer Jew or Greek, there is no longer slave or free, there is no longer male and female" (Galatians 3:28). Christ has achieved mystical union where boundaries subside and God's realm is realized here on earth. In Christ, there is life in death and death in life. In Christ "the last will be first, and the first will be last" (Matthew 20:16). "Those who find their life will lose it, and those who lose their life for my sake will find it" (Matthew 10:39).

Christ was liberated from the tyranny of opposites. He no longer pitted life against death, but entered into an awareness that transcended

10. The idea is reiterated in Wilbur, *No Boundary*, 15–29.

them. . . into "the peace of God, which surpasses all understanding" (Philippians 4:7).

Jesus' message to Thomas and the Apostles was "Peace be with you" (John 20:26b). This *shalom* is an active peace—a peace we can participate in—that can reverberate through every part of our lives. Then everything in our life belongs, even the messes. Then everything in the Gospels belongs, including the cross. Most would like Easter without the cross. But they're inseparable.

The point isn't to divide the opposites and make positive progress, but to harmonize the opposites, both positive and negative. God transcends and encompasses conservatism and liberalism, certainty and doubt, simplicity and complexity, Divinity and humanity, crucifixion and resurrection.

UNCREATED AND CREATED

Jesus always existed. At the same time Jesus was begotten (made human). This is the perplexing and elusive mystic core of Christian faith.[11] There was contention in the early church about this point.

Some claimed to varying degrees that Jesus was Creator, period (God/eternal). Others claimed Jesus was a creature, period (human/temporal). The Alexandrian Mystics understood Jesus is both. Philo of Alexandria pressed this point when he exclaimed Jesus is both un-created and created.[12]

The incarnation seems like an absurdity, for the essential difference between God and a human being, between the Creator and the creature, seems an unbridgeable gap. Christian author Soren Kierkegaard (d. 1855) insists on the absolute difference between God and the human. So, for Kierkegaard, Jesus is the absolute Paradox, with a capital P. The impossibility of the incarnation is our salvation. It convinces us that all things are possible for God (Matthew 19:26). God can reconcile the eternal and the temporal, the absolute and the relative, the Divine and the human.

Saint Maximus (d. 662) said,

> We are astonished to see both the finite and infinite—things which exclude one another and cannot be mixed—are found to be united in him and are manifested mutually the one in the

---

11. See *Logos* in the glossary (Appendix A).
12. Urban, *A Short History of Christian Thought*, 50.

other. For the unlimited is limited in an ineffable manner, while the limited is stretched to the measure of unlimited.[13]

TRANSCENDENT AND IMMANENT

God is both being and non-being, is everywhere and nowhere, has many names and can't be named, is everything and nothing. God is mystery, surpassing the senses and all knowledge, and yet God is at the core of our being. God is unknowable, yet we meet God face to face.

Can God be evident in all things (immanence) and miraculously burst through the veil once in a while (transcendence)? Can God be in the everyday stuff of life and take human form? Can God inspire writers who shed light on eternal truths, yet are fallible and culturally conditioned (see 1 Corinthians 7:12, 2 Corinthians 11:17)? My answer is yes. Yet, most can only tolerate one interpretation or the other. Some try to limit God's transcendence, denying God ever intervenes in history. Others try to limit God's immanence, claiming God has only intervened at set times and is no longer available to us today as to the prophets of old. Yet, no matter how hard we try we can't limit the infinite. And God will ultimately bust out of any box or category. The nature of the infinite is to foil our pigeonholing schemes. God's human incarnation jettisons all limitations on our imagination. Somehow Jesus is both transcendent God and immanent human.

God is in the stuff of everyday life, as Sue Bender has enumerated in her books, *Everyday Sacred* and *Plain and Simple*. I most appreciate the Christian spiritual classic: *The Sacrament of the Present Moment*, which spells out God's immanence.[14] God is in *chronos* (*regular time* in Greek). Yet, God is also in *kairos* (*the fullness of time*—when the transcendent God bursts on the scene). Historical Christianity has lacked appreciation for God in everyday life and for the sanctity of all life (Saint Francis of Assisi, the Celts, and Christian Mystics are exceptions[15]). Yet, some Christians today are taking the everydayness of God too far, to the point of denying

---

13. Maximus, *Maximus The Confessor: Selected Writings*, Epistle of Maximus.

14. de Caussade, *The Sacrament of the Present Moment*.

15. Thoreau, Muir, Dillard, Oliver, and other nature writers have a unique affinity with these Natural Mystics and with Mystic Christianity in general. It requires great attentiveness to observe nature the way these writers do. As a result of this attentiveness there is a profound appreciation for stillness, simplicity, solitude, and silence, which are touchstones of Mystic Christianity. See *Natural Mystics* in glossary.

God's transcendence altogether.[16] Both God's transcendence and immanence are important. Our faith is poorer if we emphasize one to the detriment of the other.

This is the paradox: God is available in the present moment (immanent) and God is beyond anything we can imagine (transcendent). God's in the world and all the stuff of life. At the same time God transcends and is ultimately beyond anything we can conceive.[17]

A BELLY LAUGH

Jesus presses the tension between the sublime and the ridiculous. The incarnation, if approached correctly, will result in a belly laugh, which is perhaps the most down-to-earth expression of mystical experience. Humor helps us to find space where there is no space and to creatively embrace contradictions.

Given the overwhelming paradoxes of Jesus' very being, I'm convinced he had a profound sense of humor. There's a whisper of Jesus' humor in the Gospels. There's the neat pun on Peter's name lost in translation, "and on this rock (*petra*) I will build my church" (Matthew 16:18). There's humor lost in translation about a camel going through the eye of a needle (camel was a pun that sounded like rope) (Matthew 19:24, Mark 10:25). These aren't the rip-roarious jokes that get people crying and aching in the belly. Yet celebrating Jesus' earthy humanity and joy of living is about recovering Jesus' humor nuanced in the Gospels.

Jesus had a glass of wine with his *compadres* and threw his head back and bellowed. I know it. If the incarnation doesn't make our belly quiver, we're missing the point. I resonate with author Anne Lamott: "Laughter is carbonated holiness."[18]

---

16. Some have pitted Supernatural Theism against Panentheism. Although it's useful to distinguish between the two, I affirm a Panentheism and a Process Theology which makes room for the surprising infinite nature of God, which can burst through any and all maps we draw. An analogy. . . The earth usually behaves in predictable ways, yet every once in a while there's the erratic tidal wave, the colossal volcano eruption, the earthquake that levels the city. Some progressive Christians today seem to be pan*en*theists first and Christians second, tiptoeing around the epicenter of Christian faith—God incarnate.

17. This essentially is pan*en*theism (Everything/*pan*, in/*en*, God/*theism*), not to be confused with pantheism (everything is God).

18. Lamott, *Plan B.*

Jesus Paradox . at once God + human [handwritten]

PARADOX AS PRE-RATIONAL OR TRANS-RATIONAL

Some rationalists will think The Jesus Paradox (Jesus is "at once God and human") of The Alexandrian Mystics is like trying to push two solid objects into the same space. They'll think, "in order to make room for more of one you have to carve out some of the other." "Jesus can't be fully Divine and fully human at the same time." "That's ridiculous." "It doesn't make any sense." These thinkers have made reason a prison.

Theology at its best eventually asks the impossible. It asks us to put stock in the ridiculous and to trust absurdity. Interestingly, quantum physics does the same thing.[19] When we finally accept absurdity, the knots in our minds fall away. Quantum physics and Jesus according to the mystics both take us to the very limits of reason. This is where profound faith begins. This faith isn't simple certitude, but what I call paradoxical certitude. We have conviction. But our conviction is about a flowing river. And we never step into the same river twice. As Thomas Merton once put it, "It is in the paradox itself, the paradox which was and is still a source of insecurity, that I have come to find the greatest security."[20]

Paradox isn't irrational. It's pre-rational or trans-rational. In other words, aspects of it can be grasped by the reasoning mind. Yet ultimately reason and logic are transcended. Paradox balances the hubris that reason is the supreme and only way—that reason is the be-all and end-all of knowing.

Most people are aware of the limitations of binary thinking. In *The Zen Teachings of Jesus*, Kenneth Leong relays the story of a sophisticated computer that's asked to translate the phrase, "the spirit is willing, but the flesh is weak" (Matthew 26:41b) into Russian then back into English. The outcome was "The vodka is agreeable, but the meat is too tender." This highlights the problems with binary thinking. Traditional logic tells us "something can be either A or not A, but not both A and B at the same time." This is a reflection of our rational mind, which tries to put everything into neat boxes. The early Christian mystics go beyond this either/ or thinking. *beyond dualism* [handwritten]

For Christians, the Jesus riddle takes us beyond the persistent dualisms. He is mortal, yet immortal. He is God, yet human. He is both Creator and creature. He died. Yet he lives. In him there is defeat and victory.

19. See *Quantum Physics* in glossary (Appendix A).

20. McDonnell, *A Thomas Merton Reader*, 16.

Jesus is a symbol of self-renunciation and suffering as well as a sign of ultimate salvation and abiding joy. He is emptiness and fullness.

PROMINENCE OF INTUITION

When reason tries to formulate a consistent system of thought there's always a non-rational element that won't fit the system. This is the nature of human thought. A religious world view makes room for what doesn't fit. It allows for mystery. It makes room for a *more*.

The religious world view says there's more to life than meets the eye. There's more to life than can be explained with our five senses. Throughout the ages the intuition of our ancestors has acknowledged transcendence.[21] And paradox is the mystic's ticket to transcendence.

Paradox moves beyond the limitations of reason into the realm of intuition. It is amazing how much we rely on intuition, but how little we acknowledge it. It is often small turns of events based on intuition that most change the course of history. For instance, if a timely book decrying anti-Semitism had come out before Hitler's rise to power it may have tipped popular sentiment against him. There's no way of knowing. But, history hinges on relatively insignificant events such as the impulse to write a book.

Intuition isn't a light bulb that goes off inside our heads. It's a flickering candle that reason can easily snuff out. The Alexandrian Mystics fan the flicker into an enduring flame, then set the flame in the center of the circle.

The age of rationalism discounts intuition. It encourages us to separate everything out—to delineate our thought. The timeline is the classic example. We think historically. We're always reverting to the past or setting goals for the future. Everything we do is headed somewhere along a trajectory. We miss the ironies under our noses—that out of nothing came something and we're part of that mystery, which can be found nowhere outside of now! When we drink in the mystery long enough, we come alive, we become like children,[22] we regain our sense of humor, our pulse quickens, our eyes open.

We're hardwired for reason and intuition, for science and God. The two complement each other.

---

21. Some of these ideas are taken from Borg, *The Heart of Christianity*.
22. It's possible to become like a child without being childish.

CONCLUSION

Give to receive. Die to live. Lose to win. In this chapter I've attempted to make these paradoxical teachings of Jesus and the mystics more accessible.

In the following chapters I will take Jesus and The Alexandrian Mystics' emphasis on paradox to the next level. I will emphasize that paradox is the distilled essence of Christian tradition and that Jesus' very person is the ultimate Paradox.

QUESTIONS FOR REFLECTION AND DISCUSSION

1) What is a paradox?

2) Is paradoxical thinking useful? Why or why not?

3) Do you think of Jesus as a paradox? Why or why not?

4) If the center of our faith is a paradox, as The Alexandrian Mystics conceived, does that affect other areas of our thought and life?

5) What do you think of the phrase *paradoxical certitude*?

6) Application question: What are some contradictions or paradoxes in your life? Do these contradictions diminish or enrich your life? How?

Part 2

The Tightrope

4

Tempering the Extremes

As for us, we move along the middle of the royal road (emphasis on Jesus' Divinity versus his humanity), turning our face away from the tortuous sins on one side or the other.[1]

—Severus of Antioch

It is hard to fight an enemy who has outposts in your own head.

—Sally Kempton

Twenty-first Century Christianity is in crisis. Fundamentalists[2] (many deny this term, yet I believe it still holds) and Evangelicals on the right claim Jesus is God period, end of story. Liberal churches on the left tend to be comfortable with Jesus' humanity only, not his Divinity with a capital D.

The first approach is narrow, claiming there's only one way to God—our way. The second approach is unrecognizably Christian, discounting

---

1. "The "torturous sins," according to Severus, are emphasizing Jesus' Divinity to the exclusion of his humanity or emphasizing Jesus' humanity to the exclusion of his Divinity.

2. Many deny the term *Fundamentalist*, yet I believe it still holds.

Christianity's unique claim: God's unique human incarnation. Christianity in America and throughout the world is polarized.

The body of Christ is in a tug-of-war between fundamentalism on the one hand and rootless new age experiments on the other.

LIMITS TO OUR UNDERSTANDING

Fundamentalism mirrors an elusive phantom in the recesses of our own minds. As the world sputters and heaves and as global changes reach break neck speeds we want a security blanket—we want wholesale certainty. We want absolutes—unchangeable symbols we can return to for safety and comfort...

they divide

Such absolutes sow seeds of hatred and war.

Providentially, the Bible has built in safeguards against fundamentalism. The second commandment, loosely translated, reads "make no images of God because God is ultimately beyond human conception" (Exodus 20:4). This is the primary insight of mystics ancient and contemporary: God in the ultimate unqualified sense is beyond our limited human understanding.

To confess the limits of our understanding is the root of humility, which is lauded throughout the Hebrew Scriptures. Jesus' most profound quality was his humility—his self-limiting power—his servant leadership (Philippians 2:5–11, John 13:4–5). Pointed lines from Proverbs: "God opposes the proud, but gives grace to the humble" (James 4:6b). "A person's pride will bring humiliation, but one who is lowly in spirit will obtain honor" (Proverbs 29:23, NRSV).

When, in the spirit of the second commandment, we honor God ultimately as mystery, we shake loose from the proud absolutes, which deny huge segments of the world's population access to God.

ABSOLUTE CERTAINTY IN AN UNCERTAIN WORLD

In an uncertain world, many are on a desperate search for absolute certainty. This search compels the mind to completely identify one particular concept of God with God. When the concept is challenged, one feels that God is being challenged.[3]

3. In my experience, limousine liberals and Ivy League elitists (forgive the labeling) can cling to their absolute certainties as vehemently as fundamentalists. I'm talking about a mindset here that cloaks itself in many forms.

I can respect some semblance of the fundamentalist idea of biblical inerrancy (basic underlying congruency of scripture), except for when this idea pushes ridiculous extremes. The extreme is epitomized in an article that appeared in *Ministry Magazine* entitled *Does God Get Angry?* This article actually defends the Old Testament claim that God commanded the Israelite genocide of the Canaanites. The author's belief in "irremediable wickedness" contributed to the author's defense.[4] This extreme adherence to biblical inerrancy is scary. Genocide goes against everything Jesus taught in the Gospels. When Jesus said "love your enemies" I don't think he meant "sometimes kill them all."

Jesus is the measuring rod of faith for Christian tradition. Yet, remarkably, many fundamentalists read the scriptures flatly, as though each line carries equal weight. When I read the Bible, if an Old Testament passage is out of step with the Gospels I defer to the spirit of the Gospels. I think this is common sense. So, I'm amazed by fundamentalists who lift up Old Testament Scriptures that contradict the Gospels as *inerrant*.

Blind adherence to absolute claims led to the assassination of Israel's Prime Minister, Yitzhak Rabin, in 1995 by reactionary Jews; to the bombing of abortion clinics by fundamentalist Christians; to ongoing suicide bombings by Muslim extremists. Distressed souls use religion to strengthen arrogant absolutistic tendencies. Religion turned absolutist becomes ugly, lacking mystery, abounding in finality.

Even conventional churches soft-pedal fundamentalism today. Bill Coffin puts it this way:

> Conventional religious wisdom in Jesus' time stressed correct belief and right behavior. Conventional religious wisdom in America does the same today . . . For too many American evangelists, faith is a goody that they got and others didn't, an extraordinary degree of certainty that most can't achieve. This kind of faith is dangerous, for it can be and often is worn as a merit badge or used as a club to clobber others . . . We believe in the Word made flesh, not the Word made words.[5]

The fundamentalist letter of the Bible is secondary to the spirit of the Gospels. The spirit of the Gospels is the all inclusive love of Jesus, which jumps off the pages.

Faith cannot be about absolute certainty in the letters of the Bible and wrath against those who don't comply (Ephesians 2:15). It has to be about

---

4. Crosby, "Does God Get Angry?," 8–11.

5. Coffin, *The Heart Is A Little To The Left*, 24, 31.

overwhelming trust in God's love,[6] which as the apostle Paul confirms, is beyond the letter of law and narrow legalistic interpretations.

CHRISTIAN FUNDAMENTALISM'S GNOSTIC ROOTS

Fundamentalists and most conventional Christians are essentially Deists. They believe in an Almighty God, whose name is Jesus.

I think fundamentalism can be traced to the Gnostics. Many Gnostics believed Jesus wasn't really human—he was in fact God, period, end of story. Gnostics to varying degrees believed Jesus' flesh was a façade. Jesus didn't suffer like us or have our same liabilities because Jesus was essentially God. His humanness was a veneer—a convenient vehicle for divine intervention. His humanity was not like ours. He was only human in appearance and a few other select traits. For many Gnostics, Jesus' humanity was a mask; behind the mask was absolute Deity, unqualified, unlimited. According to Gnostics, Jesus' Divinity altogether overwhelmed his humanity.

As the world becomes more secularized, fundamentalists become more reactionary. The more biblical literalism is discredited, the more fundamentalists dig in. The more that gray areas are brought to light, the more fundamentalists retreat to absolutes.

GOING IT ALONE

The new age mindset dismisses tradition and long-standing religious organization and goes it alone. This pervasive individualist tendency of mind dismisses tradition and sends it packing. It disregards anything hinting of hierarchy, history, and order.

The adolescent impulse says "the hell with tradition and its authority structure. I'm going it alone."[7] This tendency of mind isn't something we

---

6. When it comes to promoting tolerance I appreciate the work of Interfaith Alliance and the Center for Progressive Christianity.

7. When authority structures are rigorously questioned, tyranny and patriarchy are appropriately discredited. It's when the questioning reaches a feverish pitch and leaders become targets for irrational scapegoating that society loses. A society's leaders are its most valuable assets. We need our leaders and we need to have the humility to be re-directed by appropriate authorities. This keeps the ego in check and builds an equitable society.

can pass off on the new age. It is a tendency of mind that has plagued us for centuries.

We're all tempted to pick and choose what we like in a religion and what appeals to our egos. We're enticed to disregard what we don't like, especially elements challenging our egos. We're lured to come up with a religion of our own making.

At times most of us have felt confined by communal life, traditional faith, and established religious authority. We want the resurrection without the cross; we want religion without the struggles of communal life spanning generations; we want a belief system without an authority structure.

We often feel encumbered by established religion. There are so many problems with traditional belief systems, with all their restrictions and baggage. So, we are tempted to go it alone or in loosely defined groups of our own making. The new age exemplifies our innate antiauthoritarian impulses.

It's easy to scapegoat the new age, which lets us off the hook.

The new age at its best produces *new thought*. Alcoholic Anonymous was considered *new thought* or new age in the beginning. Now it's a well established vehicle of collective transformation, which all reasonable churches consider a huge blessing. So, we exercise caution when evaluating the new age. We can't summarily reject all new age phenomena. Some of it over time will bestow profound blessings. Yet, it behooves us to resist the new age tendency of mind stalking us all, mirroring our own antiauthoritarian, individualist, and utopian impulses, which lack depth and only scratch the surface.

THE JESUS SEMINAR

For most of Christian history Jesus' Divinity overshadowed his humanity. In light of this, the search for the historical Jesus is a necessary corrective. Yet the search for the historical Jesus is not definitive because it swings the pendulum too far in the other direction, where Jesus' humanity overshadows his Divinity. An authentic balanced faith holds Jesus' mystic Divinity and his historic humanity in creative tension, never letting go of one aspect or the other.

The Jesus Seminar is a group of scholars who gather to vote on the authenticity of the Gospels based on contemporary scholarship.[8] According to the Seminar only select portions of the Gospels are authentic and more than two-thirds of the Gospels are suspect.

The Jesus Seminar has a wide and acclaimed following in numerous progressive Christian circles. Yet, it has discounted and done away with apostolic accounts of the resurrection,[9] as well as vast sections of the Gospels deemed unrepresentative of Jesus. This smacks of new age.

Granted, the Jesus Seminar's focus is the Jesus of history. Yet part of that history is Divinity, miracles, and resurrection, which are afterthoughts of the Seminar at best.[10] This is a break from Christianity, making it unrecognizable to previous generations. Historical Jesus scholar, John Dominic Crossan, who I generally respect, has the audacity to claim "Jesus' body was probably never buried but left to rot and be eaten by birds and dogs."[11] Such speculative claims make an unprecedented break from tradition, discounting centuries of witnesses.

It is one thing to claim the jury is out on the resurrection and there is no way of knowing the precise details so many centuries later. It is another thing to rule out the possibility of bodily resurrection altogether.

The Grand Canyon was not begun by a joker in Arizona dragging a broomstick on the ground behind him. It was formed by centuries of mighty geologic forces. In the same way Christianity, which now claims more than one third of the world's population, didn't start from a band of rag tag Galilean fisherman. Christianity was ignited by all powerful living

---

8. Voting on the authenticity of scripture based on contemporary scholarship is palatable when done on an individual basis that can be assimilated or refuted. But, when such an enterprise takes on such a large scale it seems arrogant. It implies that the authority of modern biblical scholarship can dismantle the centuries old Gospel witness. This is the hubris of the post-modern age, which presumes the scientific mind knows all and rules all. See Carston and D'Ancona, *Eyewitness to Jesus.*

9. Leudmann, "The Jesus Seminar Considers the Resurrection." In this public address Professor Gerd Luedmann of the University of Goettingen, Germany, argued that "Jesus' body undoubtedly decayed in the usual way." The fellows of the Jesus Seminar overwhelmingly approved this thesis.

The Gospel witness to bodily resurrection doesn't seem to phase the seminar. If Jesus had overwhelming healing powers, which explain his popularity, can we rule out the possibility of bodily resurrection? I don't think we can. The article did point out that ten percent of the Jesus Seminar fellows believed in Jesus' bodily resurrection.

10. Biblical scholar John P. Meier has gone against the grain of The Jesus Seminar by arguing that the miracle tradition was not a fabrication of the early Church, but should be traced back to the historical Jesus himself. See Meier, *A Marginal Jew.*

11. Crossan, *Who Killed Jesus?*

experiences of the resurrection, sometimes witnessed in the Gospels as bodily resurrection (Luke 24:41–43).

TEMPERING THE HUBRIS OF THE SCIENTIFIC AGE

The Jesus Seminar's dropkick to the resurrection echoes the hubris of the scientific age, which concludes that science and verifiable observations of the five senses are the only authority, period. And ancient pre-scientific witnesses can't be trusted. The Jesus Seminar would not get very far in most Catholic or East Orthodox circles. Yet, the Jesus Seminar has seen its era of prominence. And now it has fallen prey to infighting and "competing egos" as one insider put it. Even Marcus Borg, the prominent writer on the historical Jesus, now distances himself from the Seminar.

Many of the ideas of the Jesus Seminar and the research it inspired make superb contributions to the study of Jesus' life and teachings.[12] It's a blessing to bring the flood lights of modern historical and literary criticism to bear on the Gospels. Yet the hubris of the reasoning mind needs to be kept in check. To be fair to the Seminar, keeping reason in check is a tall order in today's world, where demonstrable scientific facts are ultimate authority.[13] Yet, I believe twenty-first century Christians are called to a higher standard: they are called to hold the creative tension between reason and revelation. We don't blindly accept revelation, yet we don't rule it out either.

The search for the historic Jesus has given theology of Jesus a breath of fresh air.[14] It has illuminated aspects of Jesus' humanity eluding prior generations, confirming some of Jesus' human limitations. Yet, this valuable scholarship has been coupled with rampant skepticism. A healthy dose of skepticism is a must for critical thinking and analysis. Yet Jesus Seminar enthusiasts often gravitate toward what I call skepticism run amok. For instance, Jesus' seeming misinformation about the timing of God's kingdom coming, especially in Mark, becomes "Jesus' main message was in error." And Matthew's spin on the Gospel, which is dismissive of

12. One of the good fruits of the Jesus Seminar is their serious consideration of the Gospel of Thomas. Another is a much clearer understanding of the historical background of Jesus' time—the context in which he lived.

13. Houston Smith's book, *Forgotten Truth*, is an excellent testament to religious authority in the scientific age.

14. A more technical term for "theology of Jesus" is *Christology*. See the glossary (Appendix A).

Gentiles, turns into "Jesus was exclusive of Gentiles," which goes against the bulk of the Gospels.

Many Jesus Seminar enthusiasts claim Jesus was not God on the one hand then claim Jesus tends toward megalomania on the other. So, not only was Jesus just a man according to some of these interpreters, he was a delusional man. Other Seminar enthusiasts have written that Jesus often made "egocentric" claims. From the standpoint that Jesus was only human, this is true. Yet if Jesus was God in human form, as Christianity has confessed from the beginning, the Gospel passages in question are theocentric, not egocentric.[15]

Some Jesus Seminar enthusiasts claim "anybody who can multiply loaves, walk on water, still storms, change water into wine, raise the dead, is not a credible human being. He is not one of us."[16] This is where the best intentioned scholars lose their way. It's true these miracles don't make for a credible human being. Yet, they do make for a credible incarnation, never exclusively God or exclusively human—both at the same time—a holy mystery.

To avoid the prison of traditional Christian dogma the Jesus Seminar has retreated to the historical Jesus. Yet, the Jesus of history in and of itself is a prison cell echoing the first world's obsession with technology and facts as opposed to Divinity and revelation. The tragedy of the West is Rene Descartes' (d. 1650) elevation of reason to the derision of intuition, faith, and revelation.

Many historic Jesus scholars claim Jesus was simply crucified for seditious behavior.[17] Yet Jesus entered Jerusalem, knowing the probability he would be crucified (Luke 20:9–19). And when Jesus was captured he gave no verbal defense (Luke 23:9). Attributing Jesus' arrest to his seditious behavior alone makes no sense. For Jesus was intelligent enough to evade capture by the authorities on numerous occasions (Luke 4:28–30, John 8:59). Yet, he virtually turned himself in on the fateful eve of his arrest (Mark 14:41–42).

Given Jesus knew the probable consequences, there had to be a theological reason why Jesus entered Jerusalem . . . God experiencing humanity in the full would include experiencing the full extent of human suffering and death. So I resonate with traditional interpretation: through

---

15. Sullivan, *Rescuing Jesus from the Christians*.

16. Borg, *Reading the Bible Again for the First Time*, 190–191.

17. This and the preceding ideas can be found in Sullivan, *Rescuing Jesus from the Christians*.

Jesus, God was reconciling humanity to God's self. I mean all of humanity, all that's characteristically human, including long-suffering, torture, and agonizing death. This is our redemption—out of love for us God took on our humanity and its long shadow, shattering the distance between Divinity and humanity. This is the cross' mysticism. If Jesus' death is reduced to crucifixion merely on account of seditious behavior we are left with a meager theology indeed.[18]

Some Jesus Seminar enthusiasts discount Jesus' Divinity as one more "speculation" of the early church. Yet, without Jesus' Divinity there is no viable Christianity left, only a hull.

ISN'T ONE RELIGION ENOUGH?

I appreciate writers like Brother Wayne Teasdale, Matthew Fox, and Thomas Moore. Yet, their lack of disciplined long-term commitment to a particular faith tradition and to a community of faith in time, with all its failures, is new agey and makes me uneasy.

In *The Soul's Religion* Thomas Moore writes about the ideal of down-to-earth spiritual leaders. But more often than not he gets ethereal, consistently quoting different world religions. Isn't one religion enough? What about sticking to one thing until it shines? Violin player Stephen Nachmanovitch writes: "Limits yield intensity . . . Commitment to a set of rules frees your play to attain a profundity and vigor otherwise impossible."[19] What precedent does Moore's eclectic faith set?

Brother Wayne Teasdale studied with a Hindu master for years and mixes metaphors and traditions in his writing and speech.[20] Along these lines, I find Teasdale's book, *The Mystic Heart,* too general. I would have preferred *The Christian Mystic Heart,* leaving other religions to define their own mysticism.

I remember when I visited Matthew Fox's center for Creation Spirituality in Oakland, California. One room of the center was devoted to Buddhism, one to Native American religion with a dream catcher and

---

18. The way historic Jesus enthusiasts work through some of their spurious observations about the Jesus of history is that they distinguish sharply between the preresurrection and the post-resurrection Jesus. Before the resurrection Jesus was simply human. After the resurrection he came to represent something more. Yet, didn't one follow the other? The resurrection didn't occur in a vacuum. Aren't the two inextricably connected?

19. Nachmanovitch, *Free Play*, 84.

20. Teasdale, *The Mystic Heart.*

eagle feather on the altar, another room was dedicated to Christianity, and yet another to Gandhi.

Too many sounds make the ears dull . . . Now, when it comes to world religions I am interested in prefaces and introductions. And when it comes to the religion I call my own, I save myself for her. This way my religious life is simpler and more down to earth. Yes, my Christianity is informed by East Orthodox and Oriental Orthodox tradition. But most forget Jesus is from the Middle-East! No need to look to Eastern traditions. Christianity's roots are Eastern!

Many spiritual seekers in the West have the attitude of the tourist, trying a little here, a little there, and often coming away with mere snapshots and trinkets. As soon as the ego is challenged or the path gets rough the new-ager is tempted to move on to the next tourist attraction. So, genuine spiritual teachers, who understand the fickleness of the Western mind, recommend seekers stick with one tradition, broadly defined, and select appropriate spiritual practices from within one religion.

I have great respect for teachers of comparative religion like Houston Smith. Smith doesn't mix religions together. For Smith, Buddhism stays Buddhism; Hinduism stays Hinduism; Christianity stays Christianity. And Smith remains a practicing Methodist-—the faith he was born into.

Of course comparative religion in the spirit of Houston Smith has its place. But comparative religion is the territory of the specialist. For most people, one religion broadly defined is plenty to chew on. More than this brings indigestion and heartburn.

BEYOND CUMBERSOME GENERALITIES

New age celebrates the one spirit uniting us all with vibrations echoing throughout the universe. And this cosmic celebration is punctuated with cumbersome generalities.

Recently a friend's wife came back from a meditation retreat. I asked him how it went for her. He responded, "She has fallen in love with humanity, but is having a hard time loving me." This is the new age liability. It is comfortable with generalities about energy flow and the one spirit that unites religions. Yet it's uncomfortable with the particulars such as an actual historic faith passed down through generations and an actual faith community with a street address.

Well-meaning authors like Stephen Mitchell collect generalized quotes from the world's religions, which are out of context, in anthologies such as *The Enlightened Mind* and *The Enlightened Heart*. His proses offer a universal soup outside any historic tradition. At this point I can hear people saying, "I love Mitchell—shut it!" Yet, I have to admit that after reading such books, I find myself yearning for particles of dirt, for the background and foreground, for the towel wrapped around the waist, for the foot washing and the table wine (John13:1–17). Particulars make a religious landscape come alive!

FIXATION ON ONE SIDE OR THE OTHER

Part of why new age and fundamentalist Christianity have massive appeal is they can formulate their stances so easily. New age says, "I like to try some of the various religions without thoroughly committing to any one. They all point to the same source anyway." Fundamentalism says, "Jesus is the only way to God, period." Both statements have an appealing brevity and finality in an uncertain world.

Fundamentalism fixates on one side of the equation—Jesus is God, period. New age fixates on the other side of the equation—Jesus is human, period. But, Jesus wasn't simply a wisdom teacher, nor was he God in the unlimited sense. Jesus was God self-limited by his humanity (Mark 13:32, Philippians 2:5–11). The human incarnation of God is original and unique: Jesus' Divine knowledge and power are limited by his humanity.[21]

New age thinking within Christianity doesn't take religion seriously enough and needs realignment with tradition for balance. Otherwise new age Christianity falls prey to diffuse individualistic experiments. Fundamentalism takes itself too seriously and needs some space and humor for balance. The essence of new age and fundamentalist Christianity is dogmatism about words. Both fixate on one polarity or another, losing flexibility and dynamism along the way.

So the dualistic theology[22] of the West has spawned two camps: the fundamentalist camp and the new age camp. Neither extreme attends to the untold depths of Jesus as understood by the Alexandrian Mystics.

---

21. The problem that anthropocentrism presents . . . If we make the Aristotelian claim that the human form is the highest of all life forms, then it follows that Jesus is the highest form of God's revelation. Yet it's ridiculous to make unqualified statements about the superiority of one religious form over another. Each form has its place and superiority within a given context. Weighing how one tradition is better than another is unwise. The Old Testament advises against such arrogance. See Proverbs 16:18.

22. That Jesus' person is "in two natures" (one Divine and the other human) is what the West came to accept at the Council of Chalcedon (451). This led to the dualistic

FINDING BALANCE

For balance, new age or new thought, as it was sometimes called, needs anchoring in bare-bones doctrine and in a rooted faith community. For balance fundamentalism needs a measure of uncertainty, appreciation of mystery, and humility before ultimate reality (the touchstone of the Hebrew Scriptures).

A seminary professor told me "You can be so open your brains fall out." This is the liability of the new age. Yet, its corollary is also true: "Your doctrine can be so rigid it hardens your heart." Hardening the heart is a great lament of Hebrew Scripture (Exodus 8:19, 32; Deuteronomy 15:7; 1 Samuel 6:6; Psalm 95:8). Hardening of the heart is a particular liability of fundamentalist doctrine. Both extremes require tempering.

Jesus as understood by the Alexandrian Mystics heals divisions in our minds and builds bridges. For those who err on the side of certainty (fundamentalists), a measure of uncertainty brings healing. For those who err on the side of uncertainty (new age), a measure of authentic doctrine brings healing. Erring on the side of certainty or uncertainty infects all of our minds. These imbalances also infect the church. Too much certainty sows subtle seeds of totalitarianism and violence. Too little conviction about core Christian truths like the incarnation undermines essential insights anchoring Christianity, making it a unique and viable world religion.

I understand resistance to the word *incarnation* given its exclusive historic claims to God and the dehumanization of non-believers. And I have no intention of using belief in the incarnation as a litmus test to label some *saved* and others *damned*. But, I won't tiptoe around God's human incarnation because it's where the transcendent power is.

I wholeheartedly embrace God's human incarnation without denying non-Christian's access to God.[23] This exquisite balance is the road to sanity. It's the gift of the Alexandrian Mystics.

---

understanding that Jesus has two persons (two natures). The thoroughly monastic and mystical Oriental Orthodox Church rejected this dualistic travesty. To this day the Oriental Orthodox Church asserts that after the incarnation Jesus was "one united dynamic nature": "at once God and human . . ." Ultimately, a Divine mystery—a paradox.

23. The quest for the Historical Jesus has led to a greater understanding of Jesus as a Jewish mystic, healer, wisdom teacher, social prophet, and movement initiator. Yet if we claim all of these titles for Jesus while leaving out his unique incarnate nature, we leave behind historic Christianity and the most important affirmation of Christian faith through the ages.

The Jesus Paradox as understood by the Alexandrian Mystics denies the claim of new age thinkers who assert Jesus is another wisdom teacher like Buddha, Moses, Guru Nanak, or other founders of world religions. For the unique claim of Christianity, supported by the early witnesses, is that Jesus is God's human incarnation: God in human form. No other world religion makes this claim.[24]

The Jesus Paradox also denies the claim of fundamentalists who assert, "Jesus is God, period." This thinking has infected Christianity for hundreds of years, discounting the authenticity of other world religions and claiming a monopoly on truth. For Christian fundamentalists there's only one way to God and conveniently, it happens to be "my way." The Jesus Paradox restores humility and balance.

The minds of the Alexandrian Mystics transform the Jesus tug-of-war into The Jesus Paradox. The minds of the Alexandrian Mystics transform the dualistic tension of the tug-of-war into a holistic creative tension. The Jesus Paradox applies a fresh healing balm to the body of Christ; a more balanced and nuanced theology for the Twenty-first Century. The Jesus Paradox is the mystic core of Christian faith that I've searched for all my life.

TIGHTROPE OF THE INCARNATION

Some fundamentalists will argue I'm spouting a watered down Christianity, which undermines Jesus' Divinity. But, isn't it enough to worship the human form of God? Why take it the next arrogant step and say Jesus is God, period? I embrace Jesus with both arms. Yet if Jesus is God, period, I can no longer worship him. I can no longer relate to him. If Jesus is God, period, my approach to him will always have a twinge of fear. Jesus is accessible to me because he bridges the gap between Divinity and humanity. I don't see Jesus as God in the unqualified sense. I see Jesus as "at once God *and* human." God "and" human makes all the difference. It liberates me from unyielding finality. It allows for space and humor. It saves me from a world of black and white rigidity and creates bridges in my mind.

Others have claimed Jesus is God and human. The unique claim of this book is found in the revolutionary words "at once God and human."

24. Some might argue that "God in human form" is not a unique claim of Christianity. Hinduism, for example, has Avatars, who are deities that have taken human form. Yet there's a big difference between "The Deity" in the unqualified monotheistic sense and "a deity" in the qualified Hindu sense. A "deity" is a lesser manifestation of the infinite. The monotheistic "Deity" with a capital D is the ultimate, the infinite, the great Mystery. See Colossians 2:9.

This gem of The Alexandrian Mystics shatters the prison bars of duality with paradox, breadth, and mystery. In Jesus we behold the Paradox of infinite Spirit (God) and finite form (humanity), of the Creator in dynamic union with the creature. [25]

Jesus according to the Alexandrian Mystics isn't about winning the tug-of-war. It is about accepting the creative tension in the rope, without needing to side with one extreme or the other.

MOVING BEYOND REACTIVITY

Mainline Christianity at its best frees us from the tyranny of excesses. Divisions and divisiveness plague our minds and take up permanent residence when we fall for extremes.

If we take post-Enlightenment scholarship to the point of discarding mystical awareness we're in trouble. If we allow entrenched orthodoxy to suspend our critical thinking we're in danger.

The tug-of-war between fundamentalist and new age Christianity is inherently reactive. Ironically, the two forms of Christianity are inextricably connected, feeding off each other in an endless cycle of argument that never arrives at satisfying closure, let alone harmony.

In his book, *Rescuing the Bible from Fundamentalism*, I believe Bishop Spong's intentions are good, but his writing is primarily a reaction to fundamentalists. And in railing against fundamentalist neuroses, Spong is often negative. His approach is often "against fundamentalism" rather than "for authentic and life-giving streams of Christianity."[26] Reactivity isn't the answer. The passionate, yet carefully measured response of the Alexandrian Mystics is the answer.

FROM THE TYRANNY OF EXCESSES
TOWARD THE DANCE

The unifying mysticism (dynamic unity of the incarnation) in Christian tradition is the leaven in the loaf. Yet if we lose the particulars, we have only leaven without substance/flour. Spirit (spirituality) and form (religion) are

---

25. Religious doctrine is strengthened by appropriate scientific methods of experimentation and verification, yet given the limitations of reason, especially when it comes to arrogantly codifying the infinite, there will always be limits to scientific inquiry into religion.

26. Spong, *Rescuing the Bible from Fundamentalism*.

most life-giving when they dance. The more integrated the two, the more vibrant and embodied the tradition. Traditions need spiritual electricity to energize them. They also need religious rites and forms to insulate and ground the current. Those who would discount one or the other don't understand their symmetry.

Authentic religion dances between mystery and certainty. Either, in the pure sense, won't satisfy. The Jesus Paradox intertwines certainty with mystery. Wonder of wonder! For The Alexandrian Mystics, mystery (immaterial Spirit) and certainty (material flesh) fly together like butterfly wings fresh from the cocoon.

Many are well aware of liabilities of too much certainty. Fewer are aware of problems of too much mystery. Robert G. Kemper, a mainline Protestant minister writes, "The reason for . . . calling Protestant theology agnostic is the stance we take toward mystery. We accept the basic definition of God as hidden, unknowable, wholly other. In short, God is a mystery. Always has been: always will be."[27] This statement would be fine if Kemper qualified it. But he leaves it there. So, like many mainline Protestants, he gets wishy-washy.

I affirm the mystery of God on the one hand. On the other hand I behold Jesus, who gets closer to the mystery's essence than anything I know. So I confess both my ignorance and my knowledge of God. I won't settle for mysterious agnostic soup. Nor will I settle for "God is on our side" theism, which exacerbates divisions in our world.

I behold the tension in the rope, not one side of the tug-of-war or the other. I uphold the dance, not one dance partner or the other. I behold the elegant flight of the butterfly. I don't fixate on the mechanics of one wing or the other.

CHRISTIANITY IN CRISIS

Dogma in the middle-ages up to the present gravitates toward simplistic ultimatums and hubris. The so-called dogma of The Alexandrian Mystics is of a different order. The Jesus Paradox counters static dogmatic religion by focusing on dynamic creative tension. The Alexandrian Mystics' understanding of the incarnation (The Jesus Paradox) isn't simple union, but dynamic creative union.[28]

27. Kemper, *Kind Words for Our Kind of Faith*, 42.

28. The Jesus Paradox, as taught by the Alexandrian Mystics, is not simple union (*monophysite* in Latin). It is dynamic union (*Miaphysite* in Greek). For more on the

Today's liberals often get lost in complexity and fail to define anything decisively. The Alexandrian Mystics bypass the unending thicket of complex arguments by holding fast to Jesus: God's human incarnation.

The essence of fundamentalism is the same as extreme liberalism—absolutism about words. In the hands of both, words lose flexibility and become fixed. The Christian Right asserts that "God said it. I believe it. That settles it." The Christian Left insists that "National Public Radio said it. I believe it. That settles it!"[29] Neither of these statements reflects the dynamic mystery of the incarnation—the resounding depth of The Jesus Paradox.

Political/religious convictions and agendas take a back seat to respect (Luke 6:31). Words, at their best, gracefully bear one another's burdens in mutual respect, confronting when necessary. This dynamic interchange expands horizons. Entrenched positions on the Left or Right are infuriated by this presumption! It is more satisfying to the ego to have the answers, rather than to stay open to new light, often from opponents or so-called enemies.

I appreciate the immortal words of Georges Bataille (d. 1962): "True language is poetic." Poetry doesn't make heavy-handed demands, demeaning people who miss the mark. It quietly invites transformation.

PROTECTION FROM TYRANNY AND RAMPANT INDIVIDUALISM

I've come down hard on fundamentalist and new age Christianity. Yet, I've wielded a blade of truth, which heals the wounds it inflicts. A direct word that protects our minds from toxic extremes is more loving in the long run than evasive words. A surgeon's scalpel punctures in order to heal.

Our spiritual path to the source is precious, yet precarious. So, I wouldn't leave it to un-rooted new age experiments. I also wouldn't leave it to fundamentalist religion. The Alexandrian Mystics care enough about the seeker to warn against destructive excesses. The crown jewel of the Alexandrian Mystics, The Jesus Paradox, frees us from polarizations and leads us toward dynamic union in him, with him, and through him.

The chasm between God and humanity was the greatest division imaginable to the ancient mind. By bridging the chasm Jesus becomes the great mediator, balancing unimaginable extremes. Jesus' balancing act

monophysite and *Miaphysite* see the glossary (Appendix A). Also see Appendix F.

29. Grewe, "Conversation."

has numerous implications for world affairs.[30] For, the world is teetering between tyrannies (fundamentalism) on the one hand, and unchecked individualism (new age) lacking any lasting cohesion on the other.

The threat of tyranny ran high during World War II. More recently, the threat was felt during the cold war, when the possibility of nuclear annihilation cast a shadow over my young mind. In my Virginia neighborhood in the 1980s, our neighbors had a nuclear fallout shelter in their backyard. Walking the stone steps into the underground shelter and seeing the shelves of canned food stores and survival supplies scared me to death.

Less blatant, but equally noxious, is the tyranny of runaway individualism, superficial television programming, and the *sex & money* culture, which lacks a social conscience.

The life-giving Jesus Paradox wards off tyrannies of individualism run-amok and absolutism that leads to violence. It engages new age folks and encourages them to root their spiritual practice in a historic tradition. It engages fundamentalists, affirming Jesus at the center, but encouraging a loosened grip. The adept person critiques what's wrong within a tradition while remaining in it. This dance is not revolution. It is not preservation. It is reformation.

I dream of a world free from the tyrannies of absolutism and "anything goes" individualism. I dream of a world where the balance and grace of the Alexandrian Mystics takes root and produces healing and depth.

QUESTIONS FOR REFLECTION AND DISCUSSION

1) Do you take issue with fundamentalism? If so, why? If not, why not?

2) Do you take issue with the new age? If so, why? If not, why not?

3) From what you've read so far, do you think The Jesus Paradox helps balance the extremes of Christian tradition?

4) What is your impression of the Jesus Seminar?

5) What is your take on the idea of biblical inerrancy?

6) Application question: Where do you consider yourself on the continuum from fundamentalism to new age? Why?

---

30. I will go into more detail on this later in the book.

When what is in our
heart contradicts reason,
it is a death "knell" for faith

passionate reason /
reasoned passion

Asking the Age-old Question

Jesus . . . asked his disciples . . . 'Who do you think I am?'
−THE GOSPEL OF MATTHEW

It gets darker and darker and darker, then Jesus is born.
−WENDELL BERRY

MAINLINE CHRISTIANITY IN DECLINE

MAINLINE CHURCHES ARE IN decline because they're unable to stay theologically relevant.

Vatican II (1962–65) was a tremendous leap toward relevancy. Buddhist/Christian Dialogue in America is bearing promising fruit.[1] Christian writers such as Thomas Keating, Walter Wink, Bill Coffin (d. 2006), Thomas Cahill, Eugene Peterson, Kathleen Norris, Philip Yancey, Fred Buechner, Anne Lamott, Parker Palmer, Joan Chittister, Richard Rohr,

1. In numerous instances Buddhist/Christian dialogue has helped revitalize the study and practice of deep traditions of silent prayer that exist within Christianity. The John Main (d. 1982) lectures are one example. The subject of Buddhist/Christian dialogue is vast and compelling and I might add, beyond the scope of this book. See glossary (Appendix A).

Albert Nolan, Mary Oliver, Henri Nouwen (d. 1996), Barbara Brown Taylor and a number of others carry their baton with vigor. But as a whole, Mainline Christianity is unable to remain vitally relevant. It doesn't have a broad, deeply-rooted, bare-bones theology with both a history and a future. Without a theological anchor that makes sense of our pluralistic Twenty-first Century there's a lack of conviction, a lack of passion. This lack drains the mainline.

Mainline Christianity's lack of relevancy is rooted in theology. Jesus is the head of the church, from whom the limbs take direction. If our theology of Jesus lacks conviction, the limbs will lack direction and vitality. In particular, Christian theology's inability to keep up with religious pluralism has sent the faith reeling.

Theology is not a game. It's an ultimate concern that changes how we see the world. When we take theology seriously in light of our times, we take God seriously (taking God seriously is the legacy of The Alexandrian Mystics, which we most desperately need in the West). If we cop out of doing theology in light of interfaith dialogue and other Twenty-first Century complexities, our faith in God weakens. Without a viable theological anchor, faith becomes tenuous. So it's up to us and every generation to clarify our understanding of God. Staying intellectually and emotionally relevant is the key to vigor.

Many say faith is only about believing with our hearts. And if what we believe in our hearts contradicts reason, so be it. But this is the death knell for faith. If North America keeps up this nonsense it will find itself in the same boat as Canada and Europe, where Christianity is barely holding on as a remnant.

We need a faith where head and heart meet, where reason is passionate and passion reasoned—where devotion is wedded to relevant theology.

ABSENCE OF A SATISFYING DYNAMIC
BARE-BONES THEOLOGY

Paul Tillich (d. 1965) pointed out, "The essence of theology as we know it in the West is bound to an inadequate Greek concept of 'static essence,' whereas what is needed is a set of concepts which can press 'dynamic relation.'"[2]

2. Tillich, *Systematic Theology*, Vol. 2, 138. In this quotation, instead of Tillich's words "the traditional Chalcedonian formula . . ." I interjected "the essence of theology as we know it in the West . . ." The traditional Chalcedonian formula is "the essence of

As Michael Goulder puts it, "The official stance of the majority of churches is that Jesus is in two natures, one Divine and one human. But we have no accepted account of what it means for an individual to have two natures."[3] In other words, there's a vacuum in our understanding of Jesus. Largely due to the work of Alexandrian Bishop Athanasius, the Council of Nicaea (325) reasoned Jesus is both God and human. But Nicaea and following councils didn't satisfactorily work out the relationship between Jesus' Divinity and humanity. This is the problem.

Liberal Christians retreat from theology, even the theology of Jesus, and so miss the mark. For Christianity has to be rooted in sound doctrine about Jesus. We must find words, however limited, for God's revelation in Jesus. Otherwise Jesus becomes putty for fundamentalists and new agers. We need precise words for Jesus. Otherwise, Christian theology is built on a foundation of sand.

Few can throw themselves into the dance of theology gracefully. Many end up with no theology, no starting place, and no actual window to look upon God. This is where Alan Watts' (d. 1973) book, *Beyond Theology*, takes us. Others gravitate toward systematic theology, which is rigid, exhaustive, and prison like. Few can elegantly dance between the two (no theology and exhaustive theology). Theologians are either hell-bent on mystery leaving no room for certainty of any kind, or they leave little room for mystery and nuance, which are the touchstone of the mystics.

WHO IS JESUS?

The questions we must answer to stay relevant are, "Who is Jesus today?" "Who is Jesus is light of interfaith dialogue?" These central questions require an adequate answer that makes sense through and through for our post 9/11 world. Answers I get to those most significant questions are usually dated and rigid or amorphous and confusing.

Who is Jesus in our post 9/11 world and in the larger context of the world religions? When I ask fundamentalists this question, they tell me Jesus is God period, and salvation is through him alone. Mainline clergy give wishy-washy responses lacking conviction. So, on the one hand I am

---

theology as we know it in the West" so I think Tillich would approve of this interjection (in this one instance only) for reasons of accessibility. If one mentions Chalcedon or anything smacking of that fifth century debate too soon, the reader's eyes will glaze over. I can't let that happen. I haven't even gotten started!

3. Goulder, *Incarnation and Myth*, 48.

given a fixed interpretation of Jesus condemning more than two thirds of the world's population (Jesus is God period, end of story). And on the other hand I am told Jesus is human, a wisdom teacher like other founders of world religions. And this interpretation (Jesus is a human wisdom teacher, period) is unrecognizable to our Christian forbearers.

For Jews and Muslims, Jesus was a prophet. Many Buddhists say Jesus was enlightened. Hindus call Jesus an Avatar (the human incarnation of a *deity*). I appreciated these responses, which interpret Jesus in light of different faith perspectives. Yet, I longed for a relevant and comprehensive understanding of Jesus within my own faith.

I longed for a Christian interpretation of Jesus somewhere between rigid fundamentalism and wishy-washy liberalism. Like many Christians I searched for Christianity's elusive core, that's about creative tension and mystery, not definitive resolution and either-or platitudes.

The Jesus I found in the Gospels satisfied a deep longing in my soul. But I didn't find an essential interpretation of Jesus that did him justice. I felt I was back in Jesus' day with Herod claiming Jesus is the reincarnation of John the Baptist. Others are claiming Jesus is Elijah. Still others are claiming he is like one of the prophets of old (Mark 6:14–15). In short, there's confusion.

Mainline Christians should be the guardians of a balanced path that holds the extremes in check. Yet there's a lack of a balanced path. So, mainline Christians vacillate between fundamentalism and new age.

For a long time I searched for a cure to the polarization I felt, not only in the larger church, but within my own soul. I searched in Mexico. I searched in India. I searched in Africa. I searched in Eastern Europe. I searched in the Anglican Church. I searched among Friends/Quakers[4]. I searched in the United Church of Christ. But, I couldn't come home and embrace faith in Jesus with both arms.

There was no core of Christian tradition I could stand on and call my own. I was a Christian without a theological home.

---

4. By Quakers I mean Un-programmed Quakers (F.G.C.: Friends General Conference). See Buddhist /Christian Dialogue and Prayer of the Heart in glossary (Appendix A).

GOOD FENCES MAKE GOOD NEIGHBORS

An essential quandary . . . Do we attempt to name ultimate reality?[5] If we name ultimate reality, we're susceptible to fundamentalism. If we refuse to name ultimate reality, our religion is irrelevant at worst or undisciplined at best. So where do we stand? It is a question of boundaries.

I advocate for a tightrope between absolute and relative. It's not absolutism (fundamentalism) and it's not relativism (new age). It's a boundary line creatively holding the tension between the extremes. The boundary line (doctrine) of the Alexandrian Mystics is the ticket. It's the path of sanity and balance—the way of the "Prince of Peace" (Isaiah 9:6).

At first, I wanted to avoid the turbulent waters of drawing boundaries because boundary lines are often used to exclude and bludgeon outsiders. I wanted to avoid gate-keeping that presumes to dictate who is inside and who is outside the Christian faith. Religious doctrine is so often used as a litmus test: an either/or proposition that divides people into camps. Litmus tests reduce complex issues into sound bites, pigeonholing people and flattening mystery.

In the beginning, I had a negative attitude toward all church doctrine.[6] Yet, as I got further into the early Jesus debates, I saw the importance of getting entangled. True, doctrine is often politically motivated, often insults intelligence, and often ignites violence. Yet, doctrine at its best guards against corruption and extremism. Doctrine is a protective fence around a tradition. It is the skin around the body. It is the membrane around the cell. It is the fence around the property. As the Amish say, "Good fences make good neighbors."

If religious doctrine is a fence, I recommend a chest high wire fence. With this fence around my religion I can be clear where my tradition stands, yet converse with folks from other traditions in a non-threatening way. No fence (new age) is not the answer. And a ten-foot razor wire wall (fundamentalism) is not the answer. Authentic faith is somewhere in between the extremes of rigid exhaustive doctrine and no doctrine.

---

5. Most Vajrayana and Zen Buddhist schools, for example, carefully avoid naming ultimate reality in any way.

6. During this time I read *Beyond Theology* by Alan Watts and resonated with much of it. Watts argues that we must finally go beyond theology into the ultimate mystery of the World Religions that is beyond precise language, yet accessible through experience. I agree with his thesis, except I put more confidence in language's ability to behold mystery—not dissect, prove, or corner mystery, but to stand at a respectful distance and behold!

Matters of doctrine have to be handled delicately because they often sow seeds of violence . . . If the fence around our faith is too low (no doctrine), any coyote can get into our flock. On the other hand, if our fence is too high (overly rigid and exhaustive doctrine), we'll create disparities in our souls that contribute to violence in Jesus' name. We can't communicate across a ten foot razor-wired wall.

We need a fence that establishes a clear boundary yet allows for communication.

THE MYSTERY OF GOD'S HUMAN INCARNATION

The unanimous witness of the New Testament Christians throughout the ages is that Jesus is God and human.

Jesus encompasses full Divinity beyond the limitations of conventional science or death. And Jesus encompasses full humanity,[7] living within a very particular historical context. When it comes to Jesus'

7. When we contemplate Jesus' humanity an important question comes up: was Jesus with or without sin? Many of the early authorities on the person of Jesus including Cyril of Alexandria claim that Jesus was like us (human) in every way except that he was without sin.

Let's break down sin. Sin occurs in thoughts, in words, and in deeds. I can acknowledge that Jesus didn't sin in the area of words and deeds. But, if Jesus didn't sin in the area of thoughts, then he is not really like me or with me in the full sense of my humanity, because sinful thoughts are part of my human nature. So, I believe that Jesus was tempted like us—he had sinful thoughts. This makes him fully human. I can acknowledge that Jesus didn't follow through with those thoughts into sinful words and actions. Over time Jesus probably purified his thoughts completely too. But I don't think he started that way. Otherwise, he wouldn't be fully human and develop as humans develop (Luke 2:52).

I'm getting into some hair-splitting here, by Twenty-first Century standards. Yet, I'm hammering home the point "fully human." This is a hugely important point and that's why I go into these deliberations. If Jesus didn't sin at all, even in his thoughts, then in my estimation he is not fully human.

There's another contradiction to the idea that Jesus was "without sin . . ." At the end of his life Jesus took upon himself the sins of humanity. So, he who was without sin knew sin (2 Corinthians 5:21). In other words, he was in fact human in every way, including experiencing sin and separation from God to the core of his being, even to the point of uttering the words "My God, my God, why have you forsaken me?" from the cross (Matthew 27:46). These words affirm Jesus' solidarity with all that is human, including occasional experiences of complete estrangement and utter isolation from God. This is a mystery given that Jesus was God in human form, but such is the bewildering economy of the incarnation.

humanity it's important to note the words of womanist author Jacqueline Grant: "The significance of Christ is not his maleness, but his humanity."[8]

Athanasius of Alexandria's great written works were defenses of the true Deity and true humanity of Jesus.[9] This is Christianity's starting point. The Nicene Creed (primarily the work of Athanasius) affirms Jesus was "of one being with the Father (God)" and that Jesus "was made man (human)."[10] So, for Athanasius and the Nicene bishops Jesus is fully God and fully human. The point the Nicene bishops failed to clarify is the relationship between the two.[11]

What does it mean for Jesus to be God and human? This profound question affects all Christian theology. Alexandrian Mystics knew the vital importance of this question, so they carefully answered it. Their elegant answer is the focus of the next chapter.

The Gospel of John states, "And the Word became flesh and lived among us . . . ." (John 1:14). In what sense, then, should we say the Word became flesh? The Gospel of Matthew gives us the word *Emmanuel*, meaning "God with us" (Matthew 1:23). Again, what does it mean for God to be with us? In Colossians Paul writes "In Christ all the fullness of the Deity lives in bodily form" (Colossians 2:9, NIV). Colossians says Jesus is God in human form. Again, what does it mean for the fullness of the Deity to live in bodily form?

8. Grant, *White Women's Christ and Black Women's Jesus*, 220.

9. Athanasius, *On the Incarnation*.

10. The Nicene Creed was the only creed accepted by all of Christendom. So, when it comes to historic Christian doctrine, it has the broadest authority. Protestant Creeds are based on the Nicene Creed (Protestantism may be moving further and further away from creeds, yet this one still stands). For the entire creed see Appendix C.

11. Another significant question is the relationship of the incarnation to God, the author of creation. This question was answered for the church universal in the Nicene Creed, which states Jesus was "God from God" and "true God from true God, begotten not made, of one being (of one substance) with the Father (God, The Creator)." For more of the Nicene Creed refer to Appendix C.

The Nicene bishops affirmed that Jesus was on the same level with God, the creator of all. It's interesting to note that there are a number of scriptures that indicate Jesus was subordinate to God the Creator: John 15:1, Rom. 8:31–34, 1 Corinthians 11: 3; 15: 20–28; 2 Corinthians 4:4–6. Another group of scriptures indicate that God the Creator and Jesus are on the same level: John 10:30: "(God) and I are one." Also see Matthew 11:27; 14:9–11, 20:28; Colossians 2:9; 1 John 5:20.

When it comes to his Divinity, Jesus is equal with God. When it comes to his humanity, Jesus is subordinate to God. Yet, the point of my book is that Jesus' Divinity can't be separated from his humanity. So, the incarnation is a mystery—a paradox that transcends and includes these contradictory scriptures.

Things get confusing quickly. For sometimes the human Jesus wielded the power of God, as when Jesus cursed the fig tree (Mark 11:12–14). That's probably what I would do if I wielded the power of God. On a bad day I would curse fig trees. Other times Jesus' Divinity seemed to wield his humanity, as when he calmed the storm on the Sea of Galilee (Matthew 8:23–27) and when he healed the sick. So much spiritual power poured through Jesus that if someone touched the hem of his garment they came away whole (Mark 5:25–29). Yet there's no way to spell out, "Okay, this time Jesus' humanity is at work and this other time Jesus' Divinity is at work."

In Norman Mailer's *Gospel According To The Son*, Jesus says "I had said 'it was easier for a camel to pass through the eye of a needle than for a rich man to enter the kingdom of heaven,' yet from the other side of my mouth, I had, if only for an instant, scorned the poor."[12] I'm not in agreement with Mailer's statement, but I appreciate his paradoxical treatment of Jesus.

Throughout the Gospels, there's constant creative tension between Jesus' Divinity with a capital D and his humanity with a lower case h.

TENSION BETWEEN DIVINITY AND HUMANITY

Jesus' betrayal in the garden of Gethsemane epitomizes the tension between Jesus' Divinity and humanity. In Luke's Gospel Jesus says, "Any one of you who has no sword must sell your cloak and buy one." Then the disciples exclaim, "Lord, look, here are two swords." Jesus replied, "It is enough" (Luke 22:36b–38). Then when Jesus is arrested and taken away he contradicts his prior words: "Put your sword back into its place; for all who take the sword will perish by the sword" (Matthew 26:51–52). I see this as a wrestling match between Jesus' two aspects. Just as wrestlers are often intertwined to the point we can't tell where one body ends and the other begins, so it is with Jesus. We can't tell where his Divinity ends and his humanity begins.

Anyone who reads the Gospels is struck by the contradictions. For instance the Gospel of Mark reads, "And as he was setting out on his journey, a man ran up and knelt before him, and asked him, 'Good teacher, what must I do to inherit eternal life?' Jesus responds, 'Why do you call me good? No one is good but God alone'" (Mark 10:17; Matthew 21:18–19). Jesus' prayer life also poses questions. If Jesus was God why did he

12. Mailer, *The Gospel According To The Son*, 194.

regularly pray to God? There's also Jesus' entirely human remark on the cross, "My God, my God, why have you forsaken me" (Matthew 27:46)? Then there are the scriptures where Jesus' Divinity stands out, as when he walks on water (Mark 6:48; Matthew 14:25) and says "before Abraham was, I am" (John 8:58). How do we sort this out?

ATTEMPTING TO SEPARATE JESUS' DIVINITY AND HUMANITY

Throughout church history many have separated out scripture passages pertaining to Jesus' Divinity and Jesus' humanity as follows . . .[13]

Jesus' Divinity	Jesus' humanity
1a) "In the beginning was the Word, and the Word was with God, and the Word was God" (John 1:1).	1b) "The word became flesh, and lived among us" (John 1:14).
2a) "All Things came into being through the Word, and without the Word not one thing came into being." (John 1:3).	2b) "(Jesus was) born of a woman, born under the law" (Galatians 4:4b).
3a) born of the Virgin (Luke 1:26–27)	3b) born of the flesh (Luke 2:7)
4a) declared by the voices of Angels (Luke 2:9–15)	4b) demonstrated by a lowly cradle (Luke 2:16)
5a) Jesus whom the Magi worshiped (Matthew 2:11)	5b) Jesus whom Herod tried to slay (Matthew 2:16–18)
6a) Jesus is ministered to by angels (Matthew 4:11b, Mark 1:13b)	6b) Jesus is tempted by the devil (Matthew 4: 3–11, Mark 1: 12–13, Luke 4: 3–13)
7a) to feed thousands with five loaves, to bestow living water on the Samaritan woman, to walk on the surface of the sea and to bring down the waves by rebuking the storm . . . (Luke 9:10–17; John 4: 7–42; Matthew 14: 22–33, John 6:16–21; Matthew 8: 23–27)	7b) to hunger, to thirst, to be weary and to sleep (Matthew 21:18; John 19:28; John 4:6; Matthew 8:24b)
8a) to raise Lazarus from the dead (John 11:43–44)	8b) to weep with feelings of compassion over a dead friend (John 11:35)

13. Sellers, *The Council of Chalcedon*, 244–245 (Leo's letter).

9a) to make all the elements tremble after light had been changed into darkness (after the crucifixion) (Matthew 27: 50–53, Luke 23: 44–46)	9b) to hang on the cross (Matthew 27:35, Mark 15:25, Luke 23:33)
10a) to open the gates of paradise to the faith of the robber (Luke 23: 39–43)	10b) to be pierced with nails (John 20:25)
11a) "God and I are one" (John 10:30).	11b) "God is greater than I" (John 14:28b).

Here, the two aspects of Jesus reflect two parallel spheres of being.[14] Surprisingly, the Western Church and most of the Eastern Church accepted this theology as orthodox.[15] If this thinking is taken to its logical end, Jesus' humanity died and his Divinity was resurrected.[16] Then we have a hopelessly dualistic model—two Christs. This is precisely the problem with Western theological tradition—it has separated Jesus' Divinity and humanity into two separate natures.

TAKING A STAND ON JESUS

For liberal mainline Protestant denominations there's rarely a bottom line of faith. There's waffling. We have intentionally moved away from creeds, which is a good thing. But there has to be some standard, otherwise we have no compass.

The lack of a compass is one reason why mainline Protestant denominations lose numbers yearly. For without conviction, there is little passion—sermons become dull and worship becomes a mere rallying cry to be good. Without conviction, faith is diminished. Without conviction, the celebration of transcendence wanes.

In mainline churches many ministers go through the motions. But the deep down faith reaching into the bones and into the toes is lost. Then worship attendance declines. I believe Protestants, not to mention Orthodox and Catholics, have reached a point in history where they must take a stand or become increasingly irrelevant. September Eleventh, the bombings in Madrid, London, Mumbai, the quagmire of Iraq, and struggle for

14. This was Nestorian teaching (Nestorious d. 451). See Appendix F.

15. This theology was accepted as orthodox at the Council of Chalcedon.

16. After reading Leo's letter, Severus of Antioch exclaimed "Which nature did Leo think had been nailed to the cross?"

the soul of Afghanistan are signs of more religious intolerance and terrorism to come. If we take these signs seriously they'll become an impetus to clean house and clarify our convictions. Otherwise, we shirk our responsibility at a pivotal point in the history of religions and we relinquish Jesus to fundamentalists.

As world religions collide and at times converse the question "Who is Jesus?" gets increasingly complex. Yet despite the conundrums that pluralism present, we can't retreat from the question. If mainline Christians draw back from this question and waffle, they won't be taken seriously and fundamentalists of various hues will fill the vacuum.

Many scholars of twenty-first century religion agree that "the twenty first century is the interfaith dialogue century." This is the century for Christians to clean house! We need to determine our core conviction in light of pluralism.

The heart of Christian theology, no matter the denomination, is "Who is Jesus?" Luke reads, "Once when Jesus was praying alone, with only the disciples near him, Jesus asked them, 'Who do the crowds say that I am?' They answered, 'John the Baptist; but others, Elijah; and still others, that one of the ancient prophets has arisen.' Jesus said to them, 'but who do you say that I am'" (Luke 9:18–20a). As seekers and especially as twenty-first century Christians we're each asked this question.

Where do we stand? Do we claim Jesus is God in the unqualified sense, excluding the legitimacy of other faiths? Do we claim Jesus is another wisdom teacher like many others, denying Christianity's unique historical claim: God incarnate? Some of my peers espouse these extremes because they can't find Christianity's mystic core. Others ignore the question. Still others are in limbo because they're overwhelmed by the endless questions raised by religious pluralism.

We don't have the luxury to loiter theologically. Our ancestors took their faith seriously enough to die for it. How we answer the question, "Who is Jesus," matters in our post 9/11 world. Our answer will sow seeds of peace or seeds of war.

THE ALEXANDRIAN MYSTICS
ANSWER THE AGE OLD QUESTION

The three primary branches of Christianity emphasize the authority of different vehicles. The Catholic Church emphasizes apostolic succession and the priesthood. The Eastern Church emphasizes the sacrament of Holy

Communion and counciliary governance.[17] And the Protestant church emphasizes the Bible, harkening back to Martin Luther's (d. 1546) rallying cry: "*solo scriptura.*" Yet all these authorities ultimately trace back to Jesus. So, our answer to the question "Who is Jesus" is of ultimate concern and forms the basis for all other inquiry. The answer to this question is the root from which the Christian tree withers or blossoms.

As I traveled the world and plumbed the depths of my soul I didn't solve all the riddles of faith. Thank God for that. Yet, I did stumble upon the most satisfactory answer to the age old question, "Who is Jesus?" The Alexandrian Mystics' answer to the question changed my life and restored Christian tradition for me. It restored a holistic worldview true to Christianity at its best and true to post 9/11 pluralism. The answer is true to Jesus as author of my redemption, true to the faith of my ancestors, and true to my reasoning Twenty-first Century mind.

The following chapters will give a more in-depth account of The Alexandrian Mystics' understanding of God's human incarnation. And, unpredictably, the understanding of The Alexandrian Mystics is sophisticated enough to handle post modern Twenty-first Century challenges, including religious pluralism. For good theology is broad enough to weather the storms of every age. The Alexandrian Mystics were the master theologians, whose knowledge wasn't borrowed, but came from direct experience . . . I'm talking about years of silent retreat in the desert, where seeking Jesus was the aim. If anyone comprehends the person of Jesus it is these Alexandrian Mystics whose minds were made agile and lucid through years of dedication to prayer. Their teaching sprang up in a time and place unlike any other in history, with more monks and monasteries than any other city has ever known. So the teaching of these mystics has unique authority.[18]

For the Alexandrian Mystics Jesus is the ultimate riddle, which unlocks the depths of Christian tradition. As soon as Jesus does something entirely human in the Gospels he turns and does something entirely Divine with a capital D. In the Gospels Jesus is a moving target that leaves

17. Eastern Orthodox churches decide matters of faith at councils of bishops. It's the community gathered around the communion table and the bishops gathered at councils, which have the highest authority.

18. Some will claim that third through fifth century theology can't have much to offer us in the twenty-first century. This is the hubris of the post-modern mind—that the schools of thought most relevant to us today are a century or less old. This truncated analysis of history contributes to our fragmented and discordant world. The ancients, despite their blind spots, had precious gems to teach us, which hold the key to restoring our personal and collective wholeness.

us guessing. The Alexandrian Mystics help us navigate the guessing games and bring us to Christianity's elusive mystic core.

The definitive core of the Alexandrian Mystics has unlocked the doors of my heart so I can fully and joyfully embrace Jesus.

QUESTIONS FOR REFLECTION AND DISCUSSION

1) Does religious extremism in the Twenty-first Century make the question, "who is Jesus," more urgent?

2) Is the question "who is Jesus" the most important question for Christian theology? Why or why not?

3) Do you think theology of Jesus is important and relevant? Why or why not?

4) Application question: How do you answer the question, "who is Jesus?"

6

Cyril of Alexandria Proclaims Jesus' Mystic Essence

There is one Son, and he . . . is at once God and human.

In Christ, the divine and human came together in a mysterious and incomprehensible union without confusion or change.

−CYRIL OF ALEXANDRIA

ALEXANDER THE GREAT

DURING ALEXANDER THE GREAT'S (d. 323 BCE) numerous travels he came upon the Gordian Knot in Asia. The unsolvable riddle of the knot vexed the greatest minds of the ages. The knot was surrounded with pomp, ceremony, and liturgical rites.

Given his notoriety, Alexander was invited to try his hand at untying the knot that frustrated countless other dignitaries before him. When Alexander approached the knot an elaborate ribbon cutting ceremony commenced with the same pageantry that accompanied previous attempts. After all the smells, bells, and flag waving faded Alexander stood before the knot. He paused, took a careful look, then stepped back, unsheathed his sword and clove the knot in two with one swift stroke, horrifying all in attendance.

For many students of Christianity Jesus is the vexing Gordian Knot. The Alexandrian Bishops compose the sword that cleaves the knot. The Alexandrian Bishops between 312 and 454[1] give the most satisfactory account of Jesus' essence. They give an explanation more adequate than all others, because it makes room for both reason and mystery, expanding the parameters of each. The Alexandrian Mystics' understanding of The Jesus Paradox was the root theology of the vast monastic communities in the Egyptian desert of the fourth through the fifth centuries. It was also the root theology of the Desert Fathers and Mothers.[2]

THE CITY OF ALEXANDRIA

Alexandria was founded in 331 BCE by Alexander the Great and was the port of choice for Egypt's extensive trade. The city had a number of similarities to modern cities. It was founded as a Greek-style polis with institutions of democratic self-government.[3] It was a center of trade, government and culture, so it was no stranger to diversity. In fact, its exposure to other languages, religions, and cultures rivaled all other Greek cities. Alexandria was also a headquarters of literary and textual criticism, philosophy, and mathematics. The famous library of Alexandria, founded by Ptolemy I, made the city the premier intellectual capital of the ancient world.

Given Alexandria's cosmopolitan nature, the city's theology has special relevance for our post-modern world. Out of Alexandria's open port and open majestic library came its jewel: its open-minded mystical theology.

If we follow the Alexandrian Bishops from Demetrius (189–232) to Dionysius (247–65) to Athanasius (328–73) to Theophilus (385–412) to Cyril (412–44) to Dioscorus (445–51) we find the common thread in their thinking about the incarnation.[4] This theological lineage was passed down through generations of monks and clerics.

Martin Luther tended toward Alexandrian mysticism in his writings, meaning he stressed the Divinity of Jesus with a capital D and his humanity with a lower case h. Luther affirmed the unity of Christ's dynamic

---

1. See Appendix B

2. "The Jesus Paradox" is my contemporary coining of the Greek word, *Miaphysite*. There were some monasteries that didn't line up with *Miaphysite* (The Jesus Paradox) of the Alexandrian Mystics, but they were a small minority.

3. However, this government was soon lost.

4. Sellers, *The Council of Chalcedon*, 213

nature. Yet Protestants haven't taken sustained interest in digging through the archives of church history and uncovering the essence of Jesus as taught by The Alexandrian Mystics. It was unrealistic to expect Western teachers to quarry the mystery of God made human. The primary interest of the Protestant reformers was the practical everyday affairs of burgeoning churches. Protestant leaders had limited time for silent prayer or the mystical insights and theology that followed.

The Alexandrians, on the other hand, valued monastic disciplines and cultivated mystics as no other city before or since. And the Alexandrians honored the mystical experience of monks above the hierarchy of clergy.[5] In fact a prerequisite for Alexandrian Bishops, from the Apostle Mark to the present day bishop who resides in Cairo, has been monastic experience. The authority of monastic experience in silent prayer most informed Alexandrian theology. Eastern monastic tradition, especially Oriental Orthodoxy, still honors monastic experience above all other authorities. I refer to this as Monastic Authority. The Alexandrian Mystics' emphasis on silent prayer gave their teachings interior depth missing from Western theology today.

THE JESUS PARADOX BY WAY OF ANALOGY

Alexandrian Mystics, like Cyril, used down-to-earth analogies to explain The Jesus Paradox.[6] In the following paragraphs I'll share a few analogies, inspired by the Alexandrian Mystics, Cyril in particular. Some of the analogies weren't explicitly taught by the Alexandrian Mystics, but echo their teaching.

First, the analogy of a coin . . . The Alexandrian Mystics claimed the two aspects of Christ are different sides of the same coin. In the most primal sense this means if we look at one side of the coin we always imply the other. This is the point: a Christian can't say Jesus is solely human. A Christian can't say Jesus is solely God. One side of the coin always implies the other. One side of the coin always rests on the other side.

---

5. In *Miaphysite* Ethiopia today, the monks are revered above the clergy.

6. I use analogies in order to illuminate the subtle and multi-dimensional layers of *Miaphysite*. But these analogies are all limited and ultimately don't capture the mysterious elusive essence of the incarnation. Nor do they exhaust the nuances of the incarnation. Yet, in my estimation, analogies do the best job of exploring the mystery.

The Jesus Paradox of The Alexandrian Mystics claims the two sides of the Christ coin qualify each other. The existence of one side is contingent on the other. As the Gospel of John states, "I am in God and God is in me" (John 14:10a). There's one incarnation with two sides. One side is human and the other side is God.[7] The coin forms one composite reality. Heads rests on tails, tails on heads.

Let's look at the above painting. This is the earliest representation we have of Jesus, dating back to the sixth century.[8] This is the only icon that

7. This analogy only goes so far because two sides imply two halves or a 50/50 relationship. And the incarnation is not a 50/50 reality. It's a mystical reality—a divine economy—the quintessential Paradox.

8. "This portrait of Jesus from Saint Catherine's Monastery in Sinai, is our oldest surviving icon . . . We have no earlier icons because they were all destroyed during the iconoclast controversy (from which Saint Catherine's was spared). But we know that each generation of icon painters was expected to imitate faithfully the previous generation's work and that, therefore, this icon represents a long tradition which may go back as far as the first century and even be based on eye witness accounts. Unlike the catacomb depictions of Jesus, the icon is clearly meant (like the primitive portraits of Peter and Paul) to be a portrait of a specific man. Indeed, it is obviously a genuine descendant of the encaustic funerary tradition, made with hot wax on curved wood. No print of this portrait can approach the effect of seeing it in person. The artist has used the curved surface as if it were a three-dimensional face, so that the eyes seem to look straight at you—an effect that is much reduced in a two-dimensional print" (Cahill, *Desire of the Everlasting Hills*, 162–163).

survived the fire at Saint Catherine's Monastery in Sinai, Egypt. This icon is the one artifact saved from the fire. This tells us the sixth century monks treasured this image. When we take a close look at this painting we notice Christ's two eyes are markedly different. His right eye is distinctly human with a delicate smoothness and lucidity and his right eyebrow is normal.

His left eye is rough, mysterious, and piercing and his left eyebrow is unusually raised.

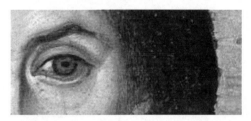

The message conveyed in this painting is Christ is one, but within one and the same skull there are two aspects. There's the human eye and the God eye. There's absolute Deity and relative humanity. There is the Creator and the creature.

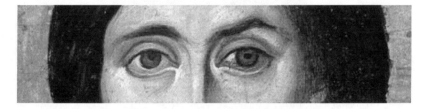

The two aspects of Christ dynamically flow in and out of one another—at the same time human and Divine.[9]

---

9. I understand that human beings have a divine nature. However a human being's divine nature is always with a lower case d. I reserve a capital D for the Divine nature of Jesus, the second person of the Trinity ("at once God and human") and for the Divine nature of the Triune God (at the same time One and Three!). Athanasius and Cyril used the same Greek word, *hypostasis*, to describe both the unity of the incarnation and the unity of the Trinity. See Sellers, *The Council of Chalcedon*, 213–214. Also see

Christ isn't a Cyclops. If Christ's right eye is removed from his face, we have a distorted and grotesque image of God. If Christ's left eye is removed, we're left with a disfigured human being. The two eyes have distinct individual differences, but they compose one and the same view. The Alexandrian Mystics' understanding of Jesus is "one united dynamic nature." The Alexandrian Mystics who painted this icon restore Christianity's holistic vision.

MORE ANALOGIES

I play hand drums. Any song on the drum is a dynamic of beats and silences. Without the silences there would be no song, just noise. Without the beats there would be no song, just silence.

The song is a dynamic union. The silence isn't mixed, compounded, or confused with the beats. There's simply a dynamic between the two that complement each other. There is only a song when there's a dynamic of beats and silences.

There is the example of my favorite cross—the Ethiopian Cross. Ethiopian crosses consist of perforated metal. These crosses articulate the two qualities of Jesus—transparent Spirit and substantial form. When we hold the cross up to a window, we can see light coming through it and we can see its substance. The Ethiopian Cross isn't solid. It's not completely see-through. It's both. The Ethiopian Cross echoes Jesus' mystical essence.[10]

Hypostasis in glossary (Appendix A).

10. Picture was taken by Amos Smith on December 2, 2010.

Another one of my favorite crosses is etched on a print Thomas Merton brought back from his Asian travels . . .[11]

Jesus is carrying the cross, yet this cross is markedly different from what we're used to. It's invisible. The cross points to how Jesus became transparent on the cross, so we can see God through him. In this painting there's the Jesus of history and the transparency of God. This transparency points beyond the limitations of words and forms—beyond the limitation of death. Through the transparent cross we see the mystical body of Christ. We also notice Jesus' head is outside the picture's frame—beyond the bounds of space and time.

FINAL ANALOGIES

One of Cyril's analogies was the relationship between soul and body in a human being.[12] Cyril asserted Christ's substantial union was like the soul-

___

11. This photo of the print was taken by Amos Smith at Monastery of the Redwoods in Whitethorn, California on March 18, 2012. Also see Merton, *The Asian Journal*, 33.

12. This analogy is not to be taken literally. What Cyril conveys with this analogy is not what his detractors claim, namely that Jesus lacked a human soul. This is definitely not Cyril's meaning, because it goes against the thrust of Cyril's whole teaching, which continually emphasized Jesus' full humanity as well as his full Divinity. In Cyril's own words, "God would hardly neglect our finer part, the soul, and have regard only for the earthly body (in the incarnation). Quite clearly in all wisdom God provided for both

body union in us. The unity affected new conditions and capacities to both elements while preserving their distinctiveness.

Cyril used two precise analogies to illustrate what The Jesus Paradox was not. He stated the union of Christ wasn't like sand and sugar (a union that did not affect or benefit either element). The union was also not like fire and wood (a union that destroys the basis of the united elements).[13] I would add the union of Christ isn't a mixture, such as a mixture of carrot and orange juice (a union that makes the two constituent parts unrecognizable from one another after they're united). Cyril points to a very precise kind of union, one where both constituents are preserved yet never independent of the other.

My final and best analogy, because it is the most dynamic, is that a crest of a wave is distinct from a trough of a wave. Yet we can't have a crest without a trough or a trough without a crest. To refer to one while excluding the other is ridiculous. Crest and trough are both part of a single dynamic called a wave.

A coin has two sides yet remains one unit. Jesus has two distinct eyes that form one view. Silences and beats form a seamless unity we call a song. The Ethiopian cross is at once transparent (Spirit) and solid (form). The crest and the trough are distinct from one another, yet are inseparable. They are one dynamic unity.

These analogies are common sense. They're the common sense of Jesus' "one united dynamic nature."[14]

the soul and the body" (Cyril, *On The Unity of Christ*, 64).

13. Cyril, *On The Unity of Christ*, 40.

14. These analogies get at Cyril's core assertion . . . Difference in the two aspects of the incarnation is allowed, but never separation or division.

There were essentially two schools of thought on the relationship of Divinity and humanity in Jesus. The first school, rooted in the theology of the Alexandrian Bishops, is *Miaphysite* (one united dynamic nature). *Miaphysite* says Jesus' aspect of being God can't be separated from his aspect of being human. *Dyophysite* theology ("two natures" in Greek), with roots in Antioch, says Jesus' aspect of being God can be separated from his aspect of being human. For more on these terms see the glossary (appendix A). Also see Appendix F.

TWO SEPARATE NATURES OR ONE UNITED DYNAMIC NATURE?

The West's "in two natures" theology of Jesus goes against common sense.[15] "In two natures" theology asserts Jesus is fully God and fully human and that these two natures can be separated. To use the above analogies, "in two natures" theology is like precisely hack sawing a coin in half so there are two thin coins with inscribed sides and blank sides. One rests these two hack-sawed coins on their blank sides next to each other and says, "See, there are two separate natures, not one." In the same way we take the one Christ and make him into two Cyclops Siamese twins, one fully human and the other fully Divine.[16] Then we say, "See, the two natures are separate."[17] Then we precisely separate out the intervals of silence from the beats in the song, claiming their division. Then we say, "See, the two natures are separate." But the unnatural separation only exists in our minds, not in reality, and comes against a wall when we get to the analogy of the crest and trough of a wave. There's no way to separate them and look at them side by side. This is the point.

Christ is fully God and fully human. We can try to separate these aspects to make it easier on our minds, but it is unnatural and counterintuitive. We have to address dynamic essence for what it is—dynamic—a moving target that can't be cornered. The myriad nuances and subtleties this dynamic creates may make us nervous because they escape precise analysis. Tough! We have to deal with the holy conundrum, without succumbing to the cheap intellectual trick of separating them for convenience. There's only one Christ who said, "God and I are one" (John 10:30a). One side of the coin always presupposes the other side. One eye works in a seamless unity with the other. The crest and trough form the same indivisible wave. Mystical union isn't a figment of the imagination or a naïve

15. The phrase "in two natures" or "two natures after the union" was always rejected by *Miaphysites*. In other words, after the incarnation one can only speak of two natures "in contemplation" (Cyril). For, after the union, the two aspects of Jesus were no longer separate in any real sense, neither could they be divided.

16. W.H.C. Frend says the opponents of the *Miaphysites* made Jesus out to be like Siamese twins with two separate life systems instead of one united dynamic nature, such as the body and rational soul of a human being, which Cyril espoused. (Frend, *The Rise of the Monophysite Movement.*)

17. Notice that this is the first time I've used the word "separate." I will use the words different and distinct when referring to the two aspects of Christ, but not "separate." The two aspects are not separate! They are indivisible! See *hypostasis* in the glossary (appendix A).

t. It is the dynamic paradoxical essence of Jesus as understood by ritual geniuses of Christian tradition.

f our approach is hopelessly dualistic we'll say, "Okay, when Jesus 'Before Abraham was I am' (John 8:58) and when he said 'I can tear down this Temple of God and rebuild it in three days,' (Matthew 26:61, Mark 14:58, John 2:19) this was Jesus' Divinity talking." "And when Jesus said, 'My God, my God, why have you forsaken me' on the cross, (Matthew 27:46, Mark 15:34) that was his humanity talking." This dualistic Western theology divides the incarnation into "two sons."[18] This theology fails us. The West has forfeited its mysticism in favor of dissecting analysis.

The Jesus Paradox is the cure, compelling a lively Christian Mysticism, which builds bridges across denominations, which drops the scalpel and beholds the mystery! I should add that the intricate theology of The Jesus Paradox is alive and well today in Oriental Orthodox tradition (not to be confused with Eastern Orthodox).

THE ALEXANDRIAN MYSTICS DEFINE JESUS

After reading the Alexandrian clerics, I discovered the Greek word that transformed my thinking and my life: *Miaphysite* (which I have coined, The Jesus Paradox). *Miaphysite* embodies the holistic healing power of The Alexandrian Mystics. Its God-given power cures Christianity's ills. This word can tear down walls and build awesome bridges.

When I came upon the word *Miaphysite* for the first time doors opened in my mind and heart, and light streamed in. The word reverberated in my soul for weeks following that first encounter. The word's encyclopedic definition wasn't revealing. But on some level, I knew the word was packed with God-given power. Its magnetic force unpacked Jesus' mystic essence. In the wake of 9/11 this powerful word's time has come.

The Alexandrian Mystics knew the word through and through. The word anchors Oriental Orthodoxy's theological core. Oriental orthodoxy is vital, yet virtually unknown to the West. The Ethiopian Orthodox Tewahedo Church takes its name from *Miaphysite*. *Tewahedo* means "one united dynamic nature" in Ge'ez, the liturgical language of Ethiopia. *Miaphysite* means precisely the same thing in Greek.

Because of the *Miaphysite* teachings of the Alexandrian Mystics I remain Christian today. *Miaphysite*, which I've coined "The Jesus Paradox," restores my faith in the living Christ. In the aftermath of 9/11, this

18. This is a Nestorian teaching (Nestorius d. 451). See Appendix F.

"one united dynamic nature"

word cradled me in the night. In the face of religious extremism this word, properly understood, is the key to balance, integrity, and poise.

THE RUNT TAKES THE THEOLOGICAL THRONE

Miaphysite or The Jesus Paradox hasn't been given the airtime it deserves or the sustained careful attention it's due. *Miaphysite* was misused, maligned, and distorted in the ancient past. The word's roots have been misrepresented due to ancient church politics and state politics[19]

The earliest split in Christendom can be traced to *Miaphysite*. Highly technical scholarship follows this word into the present.[20] Yet I have limited interest in all of this. I'm most interested in this word's primal form and its application today. I'm interested in its authentic interpretation found in Oriental Orthodox tradition.

I want to take this word out from the circle of bullies who have pummeled it for centuries, bathe it, wrap the royal robes around it and put it in its proper place, which is on a throne.

David of the tribe of Judah (d. 970 BCE) was considered the runt of his family and was the butt of his older brothers' jokes. He was off tending the sheep when Samuel came to anoint him King of Israel (1 Samuel 16:1–13). For centuries this word, *Miaphysite*, has been the runt of the Christian family. Yet, its proper place is the theological throne.

As many recent writers on the subject fail to see, *Miaphysite* isn't a byword of church history. *Miaphysite* has profound relevancy for us today, encapsulating the spirit of The Alexandrian Mystics and adding much needed depth to Christian theology.

In the twentieth century the *Miaphysite* position held by Christians in Egypt, Syria, Ethiopia, Armenia, Eritrea, and parts of India has finally been accepted by the wider Church. Both Rome and Constantinople now

---

19. See appendix G. For a thorough sketch of the politics of *Miaphysite* see Samuel, *The Council of Chalcedon Re-Examined*.

20. Even though some of the books I refer to contain the word *monophysite* (Latin) I don't use the word. I use the word *Miaphysite* (Greek). The reason for this is to emphatically and definitively distinguish between *monophysite* (one simple nature, which is a heresy of the early church) and *Miaphysite* (one united dynamic nature, which is the authentic legacy of Cyril and the Alexandrian Mystics). Many books I refer to in the notes fail to differentiate between *monophysite* (simple union) and authentic *Miaphysite* theology (dynamic union). See these terms and *The Council of Chalcedon* in the glossary (Appendix A). Also see Appendix F.

accept the alternative *Miaphysite* theology as "adequate."[21] *Miaphysite* theology, especially Cyril's, is far more than "adequate." It amounts to no less than the cure for Christianity's ills. W.H.C. Frend (d. 1958) writes "There was nothing comparable to the school of thought, which had matured slowly through two centuries of Alexandrian church history to reach its climax with the genius of Cyril."[22]

THE PRIMAL DEFINITION FREE OF MISREPRESENTATIONS

Let's look at *Miaphysite* anew. Let's look at its primal definition, free from misrepresentations. Let's look at *Miaphysite's* basic definition, first formulated by the Alexandrian Bishop Athanasius, who championed the Nicene Creed (Christianity's oldest universal creed).

The basic, universal definition for *Miaphysite* is a composite of two Greek words, *mia* and *physis, mia* meaning "one" and *physis* meaning "nature." Used as an adjective in English the term means 'of one united dynamic nature.'[23] Dynamism (differentiation) is implied in this phrase. The word *Miaphysite* asserts the two aspects of the person of Jesus (Divinity & humanity) can't be separated or divided. They are never independent of each other. They are always in dynamic interdependent relationship. As Cyril put it, Jesus is "at once God and human." [24] "At once" means both are going on at the same time: both crest and trough are part of one dynamic we call "wave." Both silence and beats are part of one dynamic we call "song." Both Divinity with a capital D and humanity with a lower case h are always present in the person of Jesus.

My technical translation of *Miaphysite* is "one united dynamic nature."

In this book I coin *Miaphysite* "The Jesus Paradox."[25]

21. Hastings, et al, *The Oxford Companion*.

22. Frend, *The Rise of the Monophysite Movement*, 88.

23. We're not talking about a reduction into one "simple nature" (*monophysite*). That's why I've used the phrase "one united dynamic nature" for *Miaphysite*. The Ge'ez (Ethiopian) word *Tewahedo* is equivalent to the Greek *Miaphysite*, which means "one united dynamic nature." "United" in Ge'ez presses dynamism.

24. Cyril, *On The Unity of Christ*, 77. When Cyril refers to man here we can safely infer human, which is the word I've substituted here.

25. This slogan, "at once God and human," quoted from Cyril is my technical Cyrilian definition of *Miaphysite* (Cyril, *On The Unity of Christ*, 77). This definition may seem a little technical. Yet, if you look into the material, you will appreciate that

THE GAME-CHANGING CLAUSE

Miaphysite means a person can't refer to Jesus as God period without qualifying that: "God in human form" (Colossians 2: 9). A believer also can't refer to Jesus as human period without qualifying that: "the human incarnation of God" (John 1:14). This lightning bolt insight repairs Christianity's ancient mystic foundation and has profound significance for the tradition as a whole.

Miaphysite reflects the most basic mystical insights of monotheism—that unity is emphasized in theology.[26] Monotheism affirms there's one source of all. Contemporary authors have called this one source "the ground of all being" (Paul Tillich) and "the tremendous mystery" (Rudolph Otto d. 1903). Monotheism addresses the very substance of reality itself at its most primal undifferentiated level, which existed before space, before time. Thomas Aquinas (d. 1274), in the spirit of monotheism, refers to ultimate reality (God) as "the first cause." Aquinas traced the law of cause and effect back to the first cause, before all effects including space and time. For Judaism and Jewish mysticism in particular the most celebrated verse in the Hebrew Bible emphasizes God's oneness: "Hear, O Israel: The Lord our God, the Lord is one. Love the Lord your God with all your heart and with all your soul and with all your strength" (Deuteronomy 6:4).[27] Jesus affirmed that this passage is the most important verse in the Hebrew Bible (Mark 12:29). So too, the Alexandrian Christian mystics assert Jesus is one: "at once God and human:" "one united dynamic nature."

Jesus embodies one interdependent dynamic that encompasses absolute Deity and relative humanity. John 14:10a puts it well: "I am in God and God is in me." In the person of Jesus God became human and a human was God.

WHY ALL THE HYPE?

Why all the hype and build up over precise translations of an ancient word? After all, faith is primarily a matter of the heart. It's not about nitpicking over words. But details are important. Truth is found or lost in the

this is a profound distillation.

26. By emphasizing unity I'm not denying the difference between Divinity and humanity. There is definitely a difference between the two. But the two are always in indivisible dynamic union.

27. Deuteronomy 6:4 is known as "The Schema."

The debate at Nicea - to include or exclude the greek letter "iota"

details. In human history, slight miscalculations have had disastrous consequences, especially when it comes to subtle sciences. Everything from launching a space shuttle to baking a cake is dependent on details. Even a simple little comma can change the entire meaning of a phrase.

If I look up *Panda* in the dictionary and the definition reads: "eats shoots and leaves," without the commas I accurately understand the Panda eats shoots and leaves from plant foliage. If I'm an alien from another planet and the definition of *Panda* reads "eats, shoots, and leaves," with the commas, I get an entirely different impression. I get the impression that pandas are clever violent mammals that enter bars, order sandwiches, eat, shoot up the place, then leave. That's the power of the comma.[28]

Some years ago a woman was visiting Paris and found a painting she wanted priced at two hundred thousand dollars. She sent a telegram to her husband on Wall Street, and asked if she could "pretty please" have the painting for her birthday. Her husband responded with the following telegram: "no, price too high." The clerk sent the telegram, except it contained one slight error. Instead of "no, price too high" the Western Union clerk wrote "no price too high." There was a complete reverse of meaning for lack of a comma!

When Emperor Constantine called three hundred seventeen bishops together to settle the question of Jesus' divinity at the Council of Nicaea in 325 CE something similar went on. Was Jesus Divine with a capital D or was he another great prophet and teacher—even a high ranking angel from God? The debate at Nicaea centered on the omission or addition of one simple letter—the Greek letter *iota*. All the bishops could return in peace and a unified empire if they would simply agree to include the letter. Who would bicker over a letter? Hadn't the churches seen enough strife and martyrdom in the prior century?

Well, there is always one trouble maker in a group. And this time it was Athanasius of Alexandria. Athanasius simply wouldn't let go of the issue. To many, he came off as an irritable stickler for detail. The Greek words being debated even sounded alike. One group, led by Athanasius, used the term *homo-ousios* to describe Jesus: "of one substance/being" with God.[29] The other group led by a bishop named Arius (d. 336) used the word *homoi-ousios* to describe Jesus: "of like substance" with God. So,

28. Truss, *Eats, Shoots, and Leaves.*

29. *Homoousios* and *Hypostasis* are both hard to translate. The precise meaning of these Greek words is especially difficult to translate into Latin. This was the crux of the dispute at The Council of Chalcedon. See *Council of Chalcedon* and *Hypostasis* in glossary (Appendix A).

"One dynamic nature" is not "two nature" [handwritten annotation]

all the difference [handwritten annotation]

why the hype? *Homoi-ousios. Homo-ousios.* "Like substance." "Same substance." Who cares?

Church members would have labeled Athanasius a rabble-rouser today. And, he didn't fare well in his own time. He was actually banished by Constantine and his successors five different times!

So did all Athanasius' gumption over this one Greek letter matter?

Athanasius didn't live to see the victory of his position. But many today accredit the preservation of the Christian faith to Athanasius. The issue was whether Jesus was the fully Divine unique incarnation of God or whether Jesus was simply another prophet. The Nicene Creed states Jesus is "God from God, Light from Light, true God from true God, begotten, not made." In other words, Jesus isn't like other prophets. He is "God become flesh."

So, Athanasius was arguing for an important iota. If the iota isn't included, Jesus is one substance with God. Then Jesus is unique. Then Jesus is God in human form; the human incarnation of God.

If the iota is included then Jesus was like Abraham or Moses or another prophet. Then God merely dwelled in Jesus. Then, like other Prophets, Jesus was filled with the Holy Spirit. Then he was a wisdom teacher who happened to found a world religion.

Athanasius and his followers, after great personal sacrifice and tenacity, prevailed at the Council of Nicaea and the iota was omitted. This omission affirms true Christian faith: something utterly unique happened with Jesus.[30] According to Nicaea, Jesus is the unique human incarnation of the Deity with a capital D. This is Christianity's unique testament among the world religions.

Miaphysite is another case of a subtle variation making a huge impact. "One united dynamic nature" is a world apart from "in two natures." The first phrase is mystical, paradoxical, holistic. The second is dualistic.

The West's "two natures" of Christ separates Jesus' Divinity and humanity, contributing to the parting of reason from nature, mind from body, Creator from creature, civilization from wilderness. The West's static dualistic understanding of Jesus contributes to an "over and against" paradigm. This mental division tears apart ecologies, economies, and communities. The holistic understanding of the mystics can heal divisions in our minds and hearts and world.

Perhaps Richard Rohr puts it best:

---

30. Thoughts in the preceding paragraphs are taken from Jewell, *Homo-ousios.*

Richard Rohr

Religion is always, in one sense or another, about making one out of two! Cheap religion is invariably about maintaining the two and keeping things separate and apart.[31]

Creed — does not clarify the relationship "between" heaven/Divine

GOD'S HUMAN INCARNATION: CHRISTIAN THEOLOGY'S STARTING POINT

The Nicene Creed is the only creed the entire Church ever agreed on.[32] The Creed makes two contrasting affirmations about Jesus. On the one hand Jesus is "God from God, Light from Light, true God from true God, begotten, not made." On the other hand, Jesus "became incarnate . . .and was made man (human)." So, the Creed clearly states that Jesus was both Divine and human. Yet, the creed never clarifies the relationships between the Divinity and humanity. Because of the lack of clarity, throughout history there have been numerous controversies around this relationship.

The #10;15;?

The Arians believed Jesus was not fully God.[33] The Gnostics believed Jesus was not fully human.[34] Some fused Jesus' Divinity and humanity together so the Divine nature dwarfed the human nature, like a light bulb swallowed by the sun.[35] Nestorius (d. 451) separated Christ's Divinity and humanity into "two sons," one Divine Son of God and a second human son of Mary. According to this theory two persons were at work in Christ, one Divine and one human. Nestorius thought Jesus' activities on earth could be separated—some falling into the Divine category (miracles, foreknowledge, resurrection . . .) and others falling into the human category (eating, suffering, death . . .).[36]

---

31. Rohr, *From Wild Man to Wise Man*, 15.

32. See the Nicene Creed in Appendix C.

33. Arians took their teachings from Arius who was rejected at the Council of Nicaea. For more on the Arian controversy see Appendix F.

34. Gnosticism is complex, but it will suffice to say here that the Gnostics didn't believe Jesus was completely material or human. Jesus' body was so spiritualized that it was no longer recognizably human. He was God. For more on Gnostics see Appendix F.

35. These views of Eutyches (d. 456) and Apollinaris of Laodicea (d. 390) are explored in Appendix F.

36. This is the Nestorian heresy of "two sons." For more on this see Appendix F.

THE ANALOGY OF LINES

We can visualize three basic schools of thought on Jesus with lines.

Miaphysite thought draws a permeable dotted line between the Divinity and humanity of Jesus. In other words the two spheres are in constant dynamic relationship with each other. We can never be certain where the Divinity ends and where the humanity begins.[37] They weave in and out of one another. Yet they are also distinct, hence the dotted line, delineating the distinction.

Divinity

· ·

humanity

Nestorian thought draws a solid line between the Divinity and humanity of Jesus, separating the two. For this model there's a Divine son of God and a human son of Mary.

Divinity

―――――――――――――――――――――――――――

humanity

Monophysite thought draws no line of distinction whatsoever between the Divinity and humanity of Jesus. And without any sense of the unique differences between them, the two are confused, mixed, and compounded into a "simple unity."[38]

Divinity

No line between the two

humanity

Jesus isn't partially God or partly human. Jesus isn't Divinity dwarfing humanity. Jesus is also not solely human—a wisdom teacher like the prophets. Jesus is utterly unique. He is Divine and human at the same time: "at once God and human."[39]

---

37. Of course the two can't be neatly divided or separated, even with a dotted line. The dotted line is an analogy that shouldn't be taken too far. Cyril was careful to point out that the "dynamic union" of the incarnation was "seamless."

38. See *monophysite* in glossary (Appendix A).

39. By "God" and "human" in this phrase, Cyril definitely meant "fully God" and "fully human." This means Jesus was "of one essence" with God as to Divinity and "of one essence" with us as to humanity. And here we don't mean humanity in a general abstract sense (i.e. humans, cats, dogs, etc.). We mean human in the real particular

THE MYSTIC KEYSTONE

The person of Jesus is the cornerstone of the Cathedral—the piece that matters most. If we get this piece of theology right, we will give future generations a vision of God incarnate that can carry them through the Twenty-first Century and beyond. If we drop this piece of theology there's no definitive compass to show the way. *Miaphysite* is the precise compass that keeps us from slipping into muddled new age thinking on the one hand or fundamentalism on the other.

Miaphysite theology/The Jesus Paradox is the cornerstone of Mystic Christianity. That's why the Syrian and Egyptian monks staked their lives on it, risking banishment and death rather than renunciation of this crucial word. It's important to note the mystics are the primary authority for any religious tradition worth its salt. If we lose the mystics' essential understanding, we lose the essence of our faith.

The Desert Fathers and Mothers experienced the dynamic unity of Jesus first-hand in prolonged periods of silent prayer. And The Jesus Paradox reflected their experience of deep desert silences. The primary insight of the monks is reflected in the words of George Fox (d. 1691): "(I had) come to know the hidden unity in the Eternal Being."[40] The Jesus Paradox also spoke to the deep silences of the fourth and fifth century Syrian and Egyptian monks as nothing else could.

The Alexandrian monks understood God in the unqualified sense that is apprehended in mystical experience beyond all utterance. Yet, when the monks returned from those mountaintop experiences, they returned to worship God's human form: Jesus. The ultimate truth for these Alexandrian Mystics was somewhere in-between the mystical silences and the name Jesus. And this balancing act was contained in the word *Miaphysite*. For the Christian, understanding Jesus' person is the culmination of the spiritual journey—the point when the mystic cries out, "I was blind, now

---

sense (i.e. the human Jim Day, the cat Morris, the dog Molly, etc.) The first (*ousia* in Greek) is an abstract and generalized union. The second (*hypostasis* in Greek) is the real particular union *Miaphysite* affirms.

In Cyril's words, "In Christ, the divine and the human came together in a mysterious and incomprehensible union without confusion or change" (Cyril, *On The Unity of Christ*, 77). "Change" is the key word. God remains fully God and humanity remains fully human. In the incarnation there is no change in the essence of Christ's Divinity or the essence of Christ' humanity. However, these two aspects do influence one another. If we think too long on this it will take us to the outer limits of reason. That's why Cyril ultimately refers to the incarnation as "mysterious" and "incomprehensible."

40. Fox, The Journal of *George Fox*, 27.

I see" (John 9:25). *Miaphysite* is how I've come to embrace Jesus without reservation. Without *Miaphysite* as my point of reference, I can't fully embrace Jesus with both my head and heart.

Understanding The Jesus Paradox can make sense of the deepest and most subtle forms of prayer. It also gives us security in the underlying fabric of reality—in what is most real. Understanding Jesus' person can also guide the practical concerns of everyday life, giving us words and forms that complete our holistic awareness. The Jesus Paradox holds the sacred silence and the sacred utterances in exquisite creative tension.

BEHOLDING THE MYSTERY

I'm not trying to solve the mystery of the incarnation. Holy mysteries are not meant to be solved.

What I am doing is sketching a way of contemplation that honors the conviction of the mystics—a conviction that always leaves room for mystery. Science and technology try to solve everything. Theology at its best doesn't seek to solve, but to behold. In beholding the mystery of the incarnation in all its depth and subtlety we deepen our intimacy with God.

In some ways naming Jesus' person is like trying to name gravity. We ascribe a name to the mysterious force, but the name doesn't explain it away. After naming it, we still don't know what gravity actually is or why it functions as it does. It's a scientific enigma. In the same way the incarnation eludes precise analysis. Yet, like gravity, we can name it: *Miaphysite.* We don't know precisely what gravity or the incarnation are. We never will. Yet there are knowable things about gravity and the incarnation. We can concede a degree of ignorance, while forging ahead to understand what we can. We can concede a degree of certitude, while always honoring an element of mystery.

Jesus is the holy conundrum of Christian faith, which is neither primitive nor nonintellectual, but primal. The incarnation gets at the root mystery of God—of formlessness and complete mystery on the one hand and form and approachability on the other. When the incarnation sifts through our minds over and over, it brings us to the limits of both reason and imagination. This is the work of God—to engage our reasoning minds while honoring mystery.

Many assert that any theologizing or speculation about Jesus is archaic and quaint. But this is the spiritual poverty of the exclusively scientific mind. It writes off centuries of serious debate over theology as something out of the dark ages. Yet, in fact, exercising the imagination and the mind in search of God is humanity's most enduring and ennobling legacy. Exercising our theological imagination can reverse the damage of unbridled reason, returning us to the awe of a child gazing in wonder at the star-lit sky. It is the loss of wonder and awe—the loss of transcendence that's most tragic in postmodern people. We need a way of beholding the transcendent higher power. *Miaphysite* is the best way I know—a way that's true to the pluralistic Twenty-first Century and true to the legacy of Alexandrian Mystics.

QUESTIONS FOR REFLECTION AND DISCUSSION

1) Which analogy about the person of Jesus, i.e. coin, wave, Ethiopian cross, stood out for you? Why? *wave - most dynamic always in motion*

2) In questions of Christian theology, to whom do you give primary authority, The Alexandrian Mystics or another authority? Why? What makes them the primary authority?

3) What do you think of *Monastic Authority*?

4) Do you think The Jesus Paradox is a useful way of understanding the relationship between Jesus Divinity and humanity? Why or why not?

5) What are some implications of this way of thinking about Jesus?

6) Does The Jesus Paradox give you a language for understanding mystical experience? Why or why not?

7) Application question: Have you had a mystical experience? If so, please describe it.

Part 3

Jesus' Exquisite Union
of Divinity & Humanity

7

Incarnation: Christianity's Soul

God was in humanity. God who was above all creation was in our
human condition; the invisible one from on high was made visible
in the flesh; God who was from the heavens and from on high was in
the likeness of earthly things; the immaterial one could be touched.

–CYRIL OF ALEXANDRIA

Be transformed by the renewing of your mind.

—ROMANS

GOD IN PROCESS WITH US

BECAUSE OF THE INCARNATION humans can experience eternity. And
as a result of the incarnation we now understand that God changes
over time.[1] Eternal and temporal no longer rule each other out. Jesus
changed the rules. Through Jesus God becomes temporal and through
Jesus humanity touches eternity.

---

1. I agree with Gregory Palamas (d. 1359), that God's essence does not change, but
God's emanations do. See Palmer, et al, *The Philokalia Vol. 4*, 377, 380, 392.

The incarnation transformed both God and humanity. With Jesus, the vindictive, jealous, and wrathful nature of God as evident in passages of the Old Testament is past. After the incarnation, God becomes first and foremost the gracious, merciful, and compassionate one. For Christians, God came of age in Jesus.

Through Jesus, God entered into humanity and consequently into change and mortality. God is eternal and unchanging, but God's emanations are subject to change.[2] God's essence is always the same, but God's energies, as manifest in the Trinity, change.[3] So the Spirit remains constant but the primal forms vary over time.

The incarnation is a process—a mysterious synergy between God's will and human will. God had to say yes and Mary had to say yes. If either had said no there would be no incarnation. Consent, not coercion, is God's way in Jesus. In the process, God is humbled and humanity is exalted.

Through the incarnation we understand not only our need for God. God also needs us! We complete each other. The incarnation took place two thousand years ago; Divine Union or the experience of being in God is possible today. It is what the monks of the early church aspired to, as testified in the most celebrated text of the Eastern Church next to the Bible, *The Philokalia.*

God says to us "Some things won't get done unless you do them. I created you. I gifted you. Creation isn't just up to me. It's up to you. Bring

---

2. Gregory Palamas developed the important notion that the essence of the Trinity can't be known. But, that the energies can. This maintains the balance between transcendent and eminent aspects of the Trinity. The two are in creative tension.

3. I am referring to the essence/energies designation of Gregory Palamas . . .

If God is changeless then *Miaphysite* is bunk, because then influence is a one way street. There can be no influence on God if God is changeless. There can only be influence on Jesus' humanity. Herein lays the importance of process theology. God changes over time (see Genesis 18:16–33). The sometimes vengeful vindictive God of the Old Testament has transformed into the compassionate one through Jesus.

Some will ask, "How can we worship a God who is not fixed?" Here we acknowledge that the source and essence of all is constant. But history is an unfolding dynamic. God changes over time. God is in process with humanity and with history as it unfolds.

Likewise God isn't omnipotent. For if God could intervene on behalf of a girl running in front of a bus, but chose not to, then God would not be all-loving. The truth is God wants to intervene on behalf of the girl running in front of the bus, but can't. God needs someone with legs and arms to intervene. God does not have legs and arms. The body of Christ has no arms and feet, but ours. In other words, God needs us as much as we need God.

Process theology is an extension of the same essential insight of *Miaphysite*, namely that of interdependence between Divinity and humanity.

See *Process Theology* in glossary

it! Incarnate it! Become a co-creator with me. Live into your God-given potential! Invent the Internet to increase human connection and networking. Create Habitat for Humanity to help stem the tide of worldwide homelessness. Be the positive role model for your adopted girls. Give them the tools to make good choices. Do the single most important thing to change the world . . . Get off your butt and roll up your sleeves."

The ultimate challenge for the Christian is to imitate Mary and incarnate the Word. Each of us in our own way is called to incarnate the Word. The winged Gabriel may be the catalyst for our calling (Luke 1:28). We may fall off a horse and be visited by a blinding light (Acts 9:3–4). Or like Symeon the New Theologian (d. 1022), we may be going about our mundane daily life, when we are suddenly overwhelmed by a brilliant light, accompanied by overwhelming love and profuse tears of joy.[4] After the duress of modern warfare in Iraq, we may wake up in a hospital bed with a whole new vision for our life. The loss of a loved one may unhinge us, then put us back together in an utterly unpredictable way. Whatever the circumstance, God is calling us. I know this in my bones. Our choices matter. Our lives matter to God. We are called. By answering the call we enter into a generations-long struggle to bring God's realm on earth as it is in heaven. Each of us has a part to play. And just as basketball teams win or lose whole tournaments based on one point, so too, a few people (even one or two) can make a huge difference in humanity's fate on this planet. Margaret Mead is always worth repeating: "Never doubt that a small group of thoughtful committed citizens can change the world; indeed, it's the only thing that ever has."

God is working through us in the world. The Holy Spirit is at work in new and fresh ways in every generation. Thank God revelation isn't fixed by the covers of the Bible. After Paul and the early church leaders wrote their letters, Albert Schweitzer (d. 1965) added another letter called *Building a Hospital in Africa*. Then Mother Teresa (d. 1997) added a letter called *My Work with India's Poor*. Then Jim Wallis added another letter called *The Sojourner Community*. Through the generations countless prophets have contributed their books. And without the subsequent books Christianity would be dead—a thing of the past, no longer of consequence, no longer pulsing, no longer shaping history. The wisdom teachers and social prophets were co-creators with God. God without Albert Schweitzer would have been without hands and feet in Gabon, Africa. God without Mother Teresa would have been without hands and feet in Calcutta, India.

4. Palmer, et al, *The Philokalia Vol. 4*, 18–19.

God the Creator is transcendent. God the creatures are eminent. If the Word is going to become flesh it has to become flesh through us, God's creatures. That's what we're created for.

The culmination of contemplating the incarnation is to incarnate the Word God has for us. If God only incarnated 2000 years ago we're in trouble. But if we become the body of Christ, we can reflect a fraction of his glory. Then there's hope, which is the only thing stronger than fear! Each of us has a part to play. Angelus Silesius (d. 1677) put it well:

Christ could be born
a thousand times in Galilee—
but all in vain
until He is born in me.

DEATH AND RESURRECTION

The dynamic unity of the incarnation is most evident in Jesus' death and resurrection. When Jesus died he didn't cease to be God. In other words God died on the cross. The immortal became mortal. At the resurrection, Jesus also didn't cease to be human. So, at Jesus' resurrection, humanity rose. Humanity rose to new potential to transcend human limitations, violence, and death. So the Divine (immortal) became human (mortal) and the human (mortal) became Divine (immortal). East Orthodox writers have pressed this point by saying, "God became human so that human beings can become divine."[5]

Jesus broke the bonds of death. Likewise, Christians prophesy there will be a day when humanity will break free from the forces that diminish, cheapen, and corrupt it. This dream inspires the labors of saints past and present, from Harriet Tubman to Martin Luther King to Mother Teresa to Millard Fuller to Nelson Mandela and countless other hidden saints. Because Jesus rose from the dead, Christians believe humanity will also rise to its full God-given potential, both individually and collectively. We may wander in the desert for decades. We may experience wave after wave of environmental disaster. But one day we'll reach the Promised Land, one person and one community at a time.

In Jesus' death, God experienced death. So, through Jesus, God moved from the infinite dimension to finite human nature. God moved

---

5. I use the word "divine" with a lower case d. Only God and Jesus are Divine (upper case).

from eternity to the limitations of time. God moved from absolute Deity to relative humanity, from invulnerability to vulnerability, from infinite to finite.

Through the cross humanity is glorified (resurrected). And God is humbled (crucified). Through the incarnation, humanity was given the possibility of overcoming its greatest liabilities—sin, corruption, and death. God also overcame God's greatest liability—distance, remoteness, and intangibility.

God's last requirement to become fully human in every way was to experience the entire range of human suffering, including torture and death. By doing this, God's solidarity with humanity through Jesus was complete.

For The Alexandrian Mystics the resurrection was the definitive evidence that God came in human form. The resurrection pioneered the way for saints and prophets through the ages, who reflected some small portion of Christ's resurrected glory. The resurrection glorified Jesus' humanity and by association, if we consent, it glorifies our humanity.

When the Alexandrian Mystics contemplate the resurrection, they don't separate the pre-Easter Jesus from the post-Easter Jesus. This is yet another ploy to separate Jesus' Divinity and humanity. Some scholars wrongly suppose Jesus was merely human before the resurrection, then after the resurrection he was glorified. So, before the resurrection: Jesus of Nazareth. After the resurrection: the Christ. The Alexandrian Mystics reject this division.

Jesus was Divine before Easter. His full glory was simply not fully recognized before then. It was latent. And Jesus was human after the resurrection, even though the humanity of the post-Easter Jesus isn't emphasized, except when Thomas touches Jesus' wounds (John 20: 25–28) and when Jesus eats fish (Luke 24: 41–43).

Jesus is at all times both God and human. This mysticism originates with the early Christian community and with scripture. It is Christianity's mystic core. Even though this Jesus Paradox is often downplayed, The Alexandrian Mystics clarify that it is the theological jewel of Christian tradition. The Nicene Creed, the most widely accepted creed of the early church, is witness to the creative tension of The Jesus Paradox: Jesus was "begotten not made" and "was made human."[6]

When Jesus died on the cross God's grace shined through his brokenness. When Jesus rose from the dead, his immortal nature glorified his

6. See The *Nicene Creed* in Appendix C.

humanity. The paradox of Jesus' death and resurrection is that the grace of God shines through brokenness. God is broken; humanity is glorified.

LIFE AS SACRAMENT

In his book, *For the Life of the World*, East Orthodox writer Alexander Schmemann reminds us that when God became human, everything human became sacred. According to Schmemann religion exists where there is separation between God and humanity. When separation is obliterated it's the end of religion.

In other words, at some point the spiritual path obliterates distinctions between religious life and secular life—between sacred and profane. When we're in Jesus, we're no longer separate from God. When we're in Jesus, we're back in the Garden of Eden, walking with God "in the cool of the day" (Genesis 3:8). There is intimacy, there is relationship. Post-modern alienation from ourselves and from others gradually heals. We're made whole. The disunited self becomes united. The fragments come together.

By taking on our humanity in its entirety, Jesus made all things human known to God's very being, including the limitations, diseases, and disorders of the body. When we're in Jesus we're no longer estranged from our own bodies. We humbly accept our bodily limitations.

We can't be bad, because God came and took on our humanity, sanctifying our flesh, our cellulite, our tears. Sleeping is sacred because God slept. Eating is sacred because God ate. Walking, playing with children, physical intimacy, laughter, sight, music, fragrance, are all sacred because they no longer belong only to human experience. Through Jesus, they belong to God.

Through Jesus, God entered into all aspects of human life. Out of love for us, God moved from inaccessibility and intangibility into all the vulnerabilities of human existence. So we're no longer alone. When we suffer, we recall Jesus suffering with us. When we're betrayed, we remember Jesus' betrayal. When we're cast from human approval and despised, we remember Jesus reviled. Jesus is in solidarity with us, especially when we suffer. And when we reach out to sufferers, we reach out to him (Matthew 25: 31–46).

Jesus is our Emmanuel: "God with us." Through Jesus, our relationship with God moves into the deepest intimacy exclaimed by the psalmist: "taste and see that God is good" (Psalm 34:8). To taste God invokes the eroticism of the Song of Songs,[7] where God is the lover we long for and pursue. It's not enough for us to smell and touch our love. We can't be satisfied until we taste our love, bringing our beloved into ourselves. This is the symbolism of communion. This is the spiritualization of life. We take God into ourselves and partake in God incarnate. Perception is transformed. The veil is lifted. Life is revealed for what it is: sacrament. There may be no observable change in outward life—in the details of what we do. But there's a complete transformation in the way we see. We come to experience ordinary life as extraordinary. Thomas Keating refers to this transformation as an opening to a fourth dimension.

We can experience the world through God's human eyes. When Jesus came into the world, God was no longer located in one particular place (the temple). When Jesus came into the world, God was available everywhere (John 4:19–21, 23). This is the re-enchantment of the world. God is in the world through Christ. When we pray "God's dominion come . . .on earth as it is in heaven (Matthew 6:10)," we pray for the re-enchantment of the world. We pray for mystical communion with him, in him, through him: "The dominion of God is not coming with things that can be observed; nor will they say, 'Look, here it is!' or 'There it is!' For, in fact, the dominion of God is among you" (Luke 17:20–21).

The point for Schmemann isn't a life to come beyond time, but an eternal sacred dimension in time—in the here and now . . .

> The modern world has relegated joy to the category of 'fun' and 'relaxation.' But there is a far deeper joy available in the present moment—"the Kingdom of God is within you" (Luke 17:21, NKJV). When this element is lost, the reason for which we were created is also lost. The presence of God's kingdom here in time is the real cause of joy for the Christian mystic and it is also the means of the transformation of the world.[8]

Each day is a small opportunity to perceive and act upon God's realm on earth as in heaven. Each hour and minute is an opportunity to make heaven reality. Here and now is our opportunity to transform the moment. If we can't transform the moment, we can't hope to transform our lives or the world. As the Shaker spiritual puts it, "Let there be peace on earth and let it begin with me." Let it begin with me in this moment.

---

7. *The Song of Songs* is a book of the Old Testament thought to be composed by King Solomon.

8. Schmemann, *For the Life of the World*, 61.

When we separate God's realm from the world, Jesus is no longer incarnate. Only when we break down the imaginary divisions do we experience life in its fullness: "I came that they may have life, and have it abundantly" (John 10:10).

When the disunited self is united, all life becomes sacred. The lines between God and our humanity fade. Then everything of the flesh and of the humus earth is affirmed. Then we echo the affirmation of Genesis 1: "God saw all that he made, and it was very good" (Genesis 1:31).

THE SACRAMENT OF THE PRESENT MOMENT

The proof of real religion is that it transforms this world. The sacramental vision of human life understands the sacred is palpable in the moment—this moment—no other. The past is gone. The future is not yet here. In essence, this moment is all we have. When this transition occurs everything changes; nothing changes.

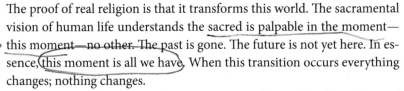

When we experience the numinous quality under the surface of things, God is incarnate once again. Then healing begins—healing from the dullness of prime-time cotton candy television and all-pervasive consumerism. We yearn for the re-enchantment of the world, which we knew as children. Union with God is re-enchantment of the here and now.

As we go through our daily routines, fly to Baltimore for the meeting, stress about the medical bills, run after our children, and try to eat more salad and less junk, we need to know there is a *More*. We need to catch glimpses of God in the moment. This is the communion we are hardwired for, the communion we long for more than any passing sensation.

The re-enchantment of the world is available. It's very familiar. It's our true home. It's what the Orthodox writers of *The Philokalia* such as Makarios call our *original purity* or *original nature*.[9] In C.S. Lewis' (d. 1963) book, *The Lion, the Witch, and the Wardrobe*, the children entered into another dimension. The children see God's realm. When we were children we saw the magic of life for what it was, a sheer gift. Only after the siege of monotonous decades, disenchantment, and secular scripting, do we lose our sight. Yet, beneath the layers of conditioning there's the buoyant wonderment of the child, who has never forgotten. That's why the Gospels say the dominion of heaven belongs to a child (Luke 18:16). The point isn't to revert to childishness, but to unlearn all the deadening adult scripting that suburbia and the market economy foist upon us. There's a

9. Palmer, et al, *The Philokalia Vol. 3*, 314, 318. Also see *Original Nature* in glossary.

mystical child in each of us, wide-eyed with rapture at the dance of life; the child who sees the fabric of light that strings everything together.

The amazing thing about transformation is it's ordinary. The human incarnation took place in an ordinary town on a speck of a planet in an average galaxy. So too, the world is transformed while reading National Geographic, shopping at the local farmer's market, or sipping a half-caff latte.

The world is thirsting for the sacrament of the present moment available in deep prayer forms and in awe-inspiring worship. Unfortunately, just when the thirst is most profound, many mainline churches can only offer a rallying cry to be good. People don't need more sentimental moral scripting. They need liturgy in the deepest sense, drenched in the transcendent. Liturgy at its best becomes like water and we the fish, embodying the mystery, incarnating Christ's body.

People thirst for God. Unfortunately, they're told Jesus is God Period—the only way. Or they're told Jesus was a historic person with a prophetic role. The first approach hits people over the head with a hammer. The other sags the body and wilts the limbs. We need God's jaw-dropping presence electrifying our nervous system, animating our every breath.

Al Whitehead writes, "Christian theology begins in wonder and when theological thought has done its best, the wonder still remains."[10] Like my Oriental Orthodox sisters and brothers, I believe the incarnation is the central mystery of the Christian faith. It's the great mystery of the world with immeasurable depths. I scratch the surface with words, but in the end I return to silent wonderment.

MYSTIC CHRISTIANITY'S FOUNTAINHEAD

My faith doesn't follow the usual framework of mainstream Western Christianity. Like The Alexandrian Mystics, my faith is centered in the incarnation. The goal of my faith isn't exclusive rights to forgiveness through Jesus. The goal of my faith is union with Christ in prayer and service to humanity in the here and now.

In Jesus, God is re-created in solidarity with our humanity. And my human nature (including my brokenness) is re-created in God. I'm a new creation in Christ! For now I realize there's a power in this world greater than death. That power is the dynamic love of Jesus, revealed to

10. Paraphrase of Whitehead about philosophy's relationship to science. See Whitehead, *Nature and Life*.

me through prayer and through service. That power can come awake in me, quicken my pulse, course through my veins. The blood flows back and forth from the center (God) to the extremities (people and other living beings).

Early Christians expected the imminent end of the world (1 & 2 Thessalonians and 1 Corinthians 15). According to Albert Schweitzer when the world didn't come to an end, the Church survived the crisis by reinterpreting the expectation. Instead of looking to Jesus' return in the world, the church began to expect Jesus' return within their souls, right here in the present moment. Maybe this was Jesus' intention all along. For the Gospel of John, eternal life is not only about life after death, it's also a quality of life here and now (John 17:3).

As the mystics remind us, the true garden of paradise is not a place but a state of consciousness . . . of union with God . . . So the incarnation wasn't just a dramatic historic event. The incarnation is a reality we experience here and now—an ever-deepening and unfolding relationship. Thomas Merton wrote, "The peak of the mystical life is the marriage of the soul with God through prayer, which gives the saints a miraculous power, a smooth and tireless energy in working for God and for people, which bears fruits in the sanctity of thousands and changes the course of history."[11]

CHRISTIANITY'S ROOT

The incarnation is Christianity's root. It's the bones upon which all the sinews and muscles are anchored. If we understand the bone structure, we have some chance of understanding the anatomy.

Who is better to guide us than the spiritual geniuses of Christian tradition—the Alexandrian Mystics? These mystics give us language to approach the dynamic essence of Jesus, the moving target, beheld by supple minds. If our minds cease their incessant striving after reward and repulsion from punishment, if our minds relax into open receptivity, the freedom of the present moment may take us by surprise. If our minds are habitually stilled and if we consent, in this moment and no other God is revealed in our flesh and we become Christ's body. We imbibe the mystery of communion.

With time, if we consent on deeper and deeper levels of our being, Jesus reveals the Word prepared for us from the beginning of time. Jesus

11. Merton, *The Seven Storey Mountain*, epilogue.

reveals our God-given name hidden beneath layers of conditioning. Beyond the habitual programs and animal instincts there is a freedom beyond imagining. This freedom is a state of mind liberated from the bondage of attachments and aversions—a state of mind the writers of *The Philokalia* refer to as *dispassion*. Just as we can't imagine the taste of a food we've never tried, so too we can't imagine this freedom until we have tasted it. And once we have tasted it, all the passing fancies of the world will seem like dross. Then we're in communion with him. Then we are graced with an abiding joy that no worldly thing can threaten. Then the soul knows profound homecoming and contentment, which desires nothing that it does not already possess. Then we are complete, whole, resplendent!

Everything from scripture to the cross to process theology to the Trinity to sacramental theology to liberation theology is informed and transformed by The Jesus Paradox. The paradox is this . . . God is in the present moment—in the nitty-gritty of human affairs. God is also transcendent mystery beyond anything we can understand. Jesus—the two syllables of the one Word—is all in all.

QUESTIONS FOR REFLECTION AND DISCUSSION

1) Do you think through the incarnation both God and humanity changed? Why or why not?

2) Christian mystics claim after God became human, human life became a sacrament? What do you think of this?

3) The Alexandrian Mystics claimed the true garden of paradise is not a place but a state of consciousness. Do you agree with this? Why or why not?

4) Application question: When do you experience your life as a sacrament? What makes life sacramental?

8

Rediscovering the Symmetry
of the Incarnation

"How is the Son (Jesus) equal to God?"
"Like sight is equal to the eyes."
—ATHANASIUS OF ALEXANDRIA

. . .the active and contemplative life begin to converge. They merge in
a sort of spiritual kinship, becoming sisters like Martha and Mary.
—THE CLOUD OF UNKNOWING

HELEN

ONE OF THE THINGS I most appreciated about traditional societies
where I lived was the respect for elders. When I volunteered with
Habitat for Humanity in Uganda, East Africa there was a Bantu term of respect used for all elders. The term was *mozay. Mozay* was a term of honor
and endearment that was used instead of someone's birth name.

The assumption in the village is that the *mozay* is someone who
can be turned to when life's challenges come. The *mozay* is someone who

has been around the block and who knows about this rough and tumble world. The *mozay* can offer perspective based on experience. The *mozay* also knows the stories of the village. He or she knows who lived where and what happened to them and can add perspective and insight. He or she knows that every choice has to be weighed carefully because each choice has consequences and ripple effects that can last generations.

One *mozay* I encountered during my years of ministry was Helen in Montana. Helen was never in a hurry. She took her time with whatever she was doing. And baking was her specialty. There was nothing like the aroma of fresh bread wafting through Helen's house. And her hot loaves were legendary. Fresh baked goods were always a perk when visiting Helen.

What I valued most was Helen's attentiveness. Even though Helen was busy with numerous activities and grandchildren, she would pause from all activity and give everyone who came to visit her full, undivided attention. Whenever I went to see her I felt like the most important person in the world. She hung on my every word and listened deeply, with understanding and compassion. Then she offered carefully chosen words that always had my best interests in mind. Helen did this with everyone who graced her home, regardless of background.

Helen was not interested in people because they were part of her affinity group, enjoyed the same hobbies, or belonged to the same political party. She had a deep caring for people, which stemmed from her belief that all people were made in God's image (Genesis 1:27). Helen knew in her soul that underneath all the layers there was "the divine indwelling (Luke 17:21b NIV). She knew this because she had dug through the layers in her own soul and come to her own truest self: free, spacious, open, and compassionate. For this reason, many came to see Helen and confided in her.

One of the things that gave Helen her depth was her devotion to prayer. Every morning for over thirty years she read from her Bible and her daily devotional booklets. She sat in stillness as the sun came up and pondered those words. Then she pondered those words all day and let them sink in. I think Helen knew how to attend to people and to listen because she attended to God and to the "still small voice" within (1 Kings 19:12). She made room to listen.

Mozays bless me with their faith that has lasted the test of time and added to the "cloud of witnesses" (Hebrews 12:1). Sometimes I look upon the pictures of some *mozays* who have touched me and made my faith what it is today. When my eyes mist I close them. Somewhere in the stillness and the luminous darkness ancestors like Helen find me and embrace me in their arms of faith.

PLUGGING IN

Anne worked for the American Friends Service Committee in Washington, DC. She tackled polarizing political issues on Capitol Hill. Her work was draining, yet she was an energetic long-term activist of 25 years—a rarity.

Anne claims her vitality and stamina on the Hill stem from her daily hour of silent Quaker-style worship. Her daily dose of silence inoculates her from burnout. Many souls who take on draining service work recharge their batteries through prayer. If we can't find constant renewal, life force dwindles.

When intimacy is established in a committed relationship time can pass with nothing being said—when there is no conversation. It's often during those times of snuggling or gazing into one another's eyes when intimacy is most felt—emotions so deep that inadequate words become awkward drivel. The same is true of relationship with God in prayer.

That intimacy inoculates us from the harsh criticism and malice of others, which we're bound to encounter in service work. That intimacy injects the love of God into our veins, so that we can't help but love ourselves, not in a self serving way, but for God's sake. We love ourselves for God's sake. Then out of that abundance we have the strength to share that love with others, no matter how it may be perceived or received.

Prayer plugs us into God's love so we can reflect it in a stable, reliable way. Constant prayer establishes God's love at the center of our lives and motivates all we do. Mystics make relationship with God their priority. They're devoted to the God of love and action. They take God seriously and have regular *heavy dates* with God.

MARY AND MARTHA

"Mary has chosen the better part, which will not be taken away from her" (Luke 10:42).

In the Mary and Martha story the point wasn't that Martha was doing the wrong thing by running around with plates in hand attending to the details of meal preparation (Luke 10:38–42). It almost doesn't matter what we're doing. It's our state of mind that counts.

If Martha had the right frame of mind there would've been no problem with her busy-body preparations. If Martha had served without anxiety it would've been beautiful. But Martha was an agitated bundle of nerves going in three directions. Evelyn Underhill, a wonderful writer on Christian Mysticism, offers:

> Many people feel unaware of any guidance,
> unable to discern or understand the signals of God;
> not because the signals are not given,
> but because the mind is too troubled,
> clouded, and hurried to receive them.

Mary knew the better part—the frame of mind at the center of our aspirations. Mary sat silently at Jesus' feet. In the end the world needs this silent attentiveness at Jesus' feet more than all our doing. We need people who have serenity, whose presence is a wellspring of calm. This peace can't be imitated. It comes from within, from a life of prayer and joy. This stillness is far more valuable than anything we could be "doing." Habitual stillness feeds our souls and nourishes our God relationship (Psalm 46:10). In a restless, harried world, habitual stillness is a beacon of light. This *blessed stillness*, as it is called by East Orthodox writers, is of more value than any external thing we can acquire.[1]

Today, chronic restlessness abounds. Excuses to stay distracted and aimlessly busy abound. Mary calls us to a still point in the midst of the storms, a solace where people can come and collect themselves . . . where people can come and feel safe . . . where people can find the spaciousness necessary to hear the Spirit . . . where there is a lightness and calm even in the most tense situation.

When I traveled in the Ukraine, I visited an Orthodox church in Kiev and asked to see the church's missions. I anticipated the priest would show me the soup kitchen downtown and homeless shelter in the church's basement. If I'd asked a minister in the U.S. to show me the church's mission, that would be the logical response. Instead, the Orthodox priest took me to the sanctuary.

This was a powerful lesson. The clear message is that from the sanctuary missions begin. From the sanctuary we move out into the world. That's the progression. It all starts with worship. We start, like Mary, by sitting at Jesus' feet. The best way to have endurance for a life of service is consistent renewal through prayer or worship. Prayer/worship and service share the

---

1. Silent Prayer is referred to as "blessed stillness" throughout *The Philokalia*. For example, see Palmer et al, *The Philokalia Vol. 2*, 317.

same symmetry as Jesus' Divinity and humanity. Authentic Christianity doesn't separate them. They're two sides of one coin. We begin in the sanctuary or the meditation hall and end up in the soup kitchen. This reminds me of a sign above a door as I exited a sanctuary: "Worship has ended. Let the service begin!"

THE GREATEST COMMANDMENT

Jesus says the greatest commandment is "Love the Sovereign your God with all your heart, and with all your soul, and with all your mind, and with all your strength. The second is this, You shall love your neighbor as yourself. There is no other commandment greater than these" (Mark 12:30).[2] The first five of the Ten Commandments pertain to our relationship with God and the second five to our relationship with people (Exodus 20: 2–17; Deuteronomy 5: 6–21). Covenant with God and covenant with humanity are the core biblical witness. The activity of the first five commandments is geared toward love of God: Mary—the other five to love of people: Martha.

Abraham Lincoln attended a Presbyterian church in Springfield and later in Washington, D.C., but never joined a church. He explained, "When any church will inscribe over its altar the Savior's condensed statement of law and Gospel: 'Thou shalt love God with all thy heart and with all thy soul and with all thy mind, and love thy neighbor as thyself.' That church I will join with all my heart."[3]

The love of God recognizes and fans the Christ light within. The love of neighbor recognizes the Christ light in all people. In the former, I treat myself with respect and care and recognize myself as a child of God. I listen deeply for the promptings of the Spirit. I cherish my soul, which is made in God's image. I lean in to hear the still small voice of my God-given conscience. In the latter, I treat others with respect and care, and recognize them as children of God, listening deeply in order to understand how best to serve. I try to non-anxiously give my undivided attention and send the clear message: you are a child of God. You matter to me!

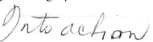

---

2. Hillel (d. 10) condensed the law into "Love God and your neighbor." So this teaching may not have originated with Jesus or with Christianity.

3. White Jr. et al, *American Christianity*, 115.

SELF EXAMINATION & SOCIAL CONSCIENCE

The Socratic imperative *know thyself* is a starting place for knowing our Maker. Inspecting an artist's craftsmanship reveals much about the artist. If we are interested in our Maker, we are interested in her/his handiwork. The psalmist exclaims,

> For it was you who formed my inward parts;
> You knit me together in my mother's womb.
> I praise you, for I am fearfully and wonderfully made . . .
> My frame was not hidden from you,
> When I was being made in secret,
> intricately woven in the depths of the earth.
> Your eyes beheld my unformed substance.
> In your book were written
> all the days that were formed for me,
> when none of them yet existed. (Psalm 139:13–16)

As we dig deeper into ourselves, we come closer to the God in whose image we're made. Contemplating our exquisite human form is the beginning of meditation.[4] Leonardo De Vinci and countless scientists have marveled at the ingenuity of the human eye and other organs, which have been billions of years in the making. The human body is the most extraordinary instrument imaginable.

From inquiry into our nature and awe for our human form comes care for ourselves, followed by care for the human family and all God's creatures. When we revere our human form we respect all the life forms leading to it, from the reptilian brain, to the mammalian brain, to the distinctively human neo-cortex. When we revere our human form we respect other human beings, who are so similar to us, for their innate worth. This is the starting place for developing a social conscience.

Self examination and social conscience are the touchstones of the spiritual life: the love of God and the love of neighbor.

Carl Jung (d. 1961) believed when the introverted elements (know thyself) and extroverted elements (social conscience) of human character

---

4. Some, who make demands on our time, would have us believe that self is a four letter word. As soon as we begin a contemplative path some may call us self-absorbed. Yet, working on the quality of our presence and deepening our communion with God in prayer is actually the greatest gift we can give others. When the quality of our presence deepens we naturally begin to bless those around us. Some will be threatened by our deepening presence of mind and will even demonize us, yet for God's sake and for the sake of the majority, we persevere on the contemplative path.

are integrated, the strongest type of personality results. People who inwardly connect to the deep promptings of their souls and outwardly connect to the world through activism and service,[5] have the greatest effects on society with marginal numbers. We need more Christians who are both mystics and activists.[6]

Thomas Keating says extroverts, contrary to popular opinion, usually make the best contemplatives. For extroverts, interior prayer is a way to recharge batteries for greater service. Those who pursue interior prayer for its own sake miss the point. Christian prayer makes little sense outside the context of service and the purpose of prayer isn't an insular self-improvement project. The purpose of prayer is a steadily increasing sensitivity to the needs of others. This sensitivity doesn't necessarily require demonstrative empathy. It is a paradigm shift—an unrelenting reverence for the innate beauty of the human soul, no matter the layers of neurosis that conceal it.

Mysticism pulls us toward service, and service toward mysticism. The more time Thomas Merton spent in his hermitage, the more driven he became to engage the world and its horrific shadow of modern warfare and the atomic bomb. Plumbing internal depths encouraged Merton to plumb external depths. Anyone who is in a service profession will tell you it's like being on the front lines of a losing battle. All soldiers in the helping professions need a refuge from the storm.

The following lines highlight the paradox between prayer and activism:

> Many have tried with more or less plausible results to link Jesus and one or more of his followers with the Essenes or the Zealots, an interesting endeavor since the one group practiced withdrawal from the world and its affairs, and the other advocated active engagement![7]

---

5. Prime examples are the historic Quaker community from George Fox on, the Church of the Savior in Washington, D.C., and Richard Rohr's Center for Contemplation and Action in Albuquerque, New Mexico. Also see Solle, *The Silent Cry: Mysticism and Resistance.*

6. A great example of the marriage of the contemplative life and the life of activism and service is found in Noe, *Finding Our Way Home.*

7. Laughlin, *Remedial Christianity,* 78.

THOSE WHO LOVE GOD LOVE THEIR SISTERS AND BROTHERS

Jesus was a fiery activist. He was executed as an enemy of the Roman state. His parables dealt with dangerous issues, which, as always, mean political and economic issues. He challenged the domination system of his time. He challenged the unjust distribution of wealth.

Bill Herzog writes,

> If Jesus had been the kind of teacher popularly portrayed in the North American church, a master of the inner life, teaching the importance of spirituality and a private relationship with God, he would have been supported by the Romans as part of their rural pacification program.[8]

This is the scandal of North American Christianity—it doesn't live up to its prophetic activist roots. Churches belong outside the status quo critiquing injustices, as Jesus did in his own time. This was the strength of the early church. It stood outside the oppressive militaristic Roman establishment and asserted God's love was the most powerful thing in the world, not military force, not Caesar.

Many social justice activists sideline their spiritual life, leaving themselves vulnerable to compassion fatigue, to bitterness, and to burn out. But spirituality and activism go hand in hand. One of the primary books in the Quaker library is *Faith & Practice*. Faith and practice weave in and out of each other. We arrive at faith through service. We arrive at effective service through faith.

We start by believing God's love is the most powerful thing in the world—so powerful nothing can overcome it, not even death. When this is no longer a fairy tale—when we solidly believe, we're transformed. Then we proclaim along with John: "We know that we have passed from death to life because we love one another" (1 John 3:14). Love of God can only be understood in the context of loving our neighbors.

As First John reminds us, loving people brings us closer to God and loving God brings us into loving relationships with one another: "Those who say, 'I love God,' and hate their sisters or brothers, are liars; for those who do not love a brother or sister whom they have seen, cannot love God whom they have not seen" (1 John 4:20).

"God is love" is Christianity's primary insight (1 John 4:8). Yet our faith can't end there. Yes, God loves us—always has, always will. Yet, there

---

8. Herzog, *Parables as Subversive Speech*, 27.

remains the infinitely challenging job of living from there—of making the longest journey we'll ever make—from our head to our heart and hands. "Faith without works is dead . . . you will know them (the faithful) by their fruits" (James 2:26, Matthew 7:20). We start with faith in God's love (head), then we reach out to people with compassion (heart), then we follow through with measurable results (hands).

The sketch below may be primitive, but it gets at the mysticism behind Jesus' greatest commandment.

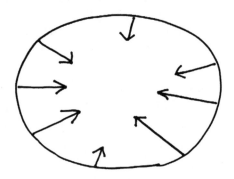

In this circle the center represents God and the arrows represent individuals. As we get closer to the center (God) we automatically get closer to other arrows (people). As we get closer to the other arrows (people in our lives) we automatically get closer to the center (God): two sides of the same coin.

This sketch doesn't do justice to the profound paradox. Yet, I'm compelled to stumble around in the darkness of silence and probe the mystery . . . As I touch the depths within I'm more able to touch and know you, not to mention the depths of our common humanity. In other words, if you know yourself, then you know me very well.

A disunited self wreaks havoc on the world. A united self creates unity and harmony in family, in community, and in the world. *Know thyself* and *love thy neighbor*. Both are infinitely simply and infinitely difficult. They are the head and the heart of the spiritual path, the Divinity and the humanity. As we get to know ourselves we see the traces of our Maker. As we open our hearts to our loved ones we find ourselves.

George Fox wrote,

The Lord taught me to be faithful in all things, and to act faithfully two ways, viz., inwardly to God and outwardly to man (people).[9]

BEING & DOING

At a Centering Prayer retreat some people lamented their full schedules and calendars. A retreatant mentioned she had heard a talk by Taoist Master Ni Hua Ching . . . After his talk in Santa Barbara on acupuncture and Chinese herbs, there was a brief question and answer period. A man asked, "What is some general spiritual advice you can give us Americans?" Master Ching took a long pause . . . Then he said two words: "Do less."

Master Ching's statement reflects the spiritual poverty of the West. Most of us are running all the time. Most households have two wage earners; there are kids to tend to, and relentless technology. Of course, it's possible to maintain presence and composure in the midst of multitudinous activities. But this is the graduate course in practicing the presence of God.

I've spent a lot of time in stillness and silence because that's what's lacking. Thomas Beckett may have expressed the essential ingredient missing from anxious and acquisitive Western culture: "nowhere to go, nothing to do." We long for this freedom—freedom of a child at play (Mark 9:36–37).

When I'm in balance I find my personal center of gravity. Each person has a balance between introversion and extroversion, between reading and reflecting and getting things done, which is right for them. My time at work and my time giggling, running, and playing with my toddler when I get home, balance each other. My feverish morning push through the inbox and my twenty minutes of centering prayer before lunch balance each other.

When my center of gravity is off, even just five minutes of deep breathing and presence of mind can bring me back to the center.

The popular Nike ad epitomizes the West's imbalance: "just do it." Nike Corporation, you're only working one angle! You can't smell the flowers on a galloping horse. What about "just be?" What about these celebrated words of Ralph Waldo Emerson (d. 1882): "Who you are speaks so loudly, I can hardly hear what you're saying."

9. Fox, *The Journal of George Fox*, 1.

In *The Way of All the Earth* John S. Dunne tells an old German story: God sends God's right hand into the world to take human form: Jesus. The right hand holds all the truth. But God isn't satisfied. So God continues to send the left hand into the world. That hand is empty. It's the hand open to wandering, searching . . . the desert. We can't receive the gifts of the right hand without the left. "A full left hand has no room to receive anything. It's cluttered. It's distracted. It's saturated. As the left hand empties it becomes more clear, focused, and open."[10]

The two hands of the Father in Rembrandt's (d. 1669) *Prodigal Son* portray God's dynamic nature. One hand is receptive and one is active, contrasting two aspects of God. The receptive hand is empty, gentle and womb-like. The active hand is rough, stout and chisel-like. The receptive hand is the wisdom of God. The strong activist hand is God's solidarity with the vulnerable.

The most exquisite lives find symmetry between gentle receptive listening and courageous forthright action. May we lay aside the frenzied caffeinated hand more often and attend to the receptive unoccupied hand.

10. Edwards, *Living Simply Through the Day*, 7.

THE KINGDOM WITHIN & THE KINGDOM COME

John's Gospel presents the dominion of God as a reality we can enter here and now. God's realm is also the coming reign of justice and peace—a realm yet to come.

Jesus' life speaks to the personal "kingdom within" (Luke 17:21, NKJV) and the collective "kingdom come" (Matthew 6:10, NIV). The kingdom within is the transformed presence of our minds and hearts here and now. The kingdom come is the transformation of the world through compassionate service and solidarity with the vulnerable, which is to come.

The Hebrew prophets understand something is deeply wrong with the world (God's dominion is yet to come). The mystics understand there is something deeply right with the world (God's dominion is already here). Both are true. But rarely do we encounter this balance. Usually, one is emphasized to the exclusion of the other. We need both; we need the ecstatic mystic reveling in the present moment and we need the lamenting prophet decrying the horrific injustices in our cities.

The prophets demonstrate the occupational hazards that come with working toward the justice of God's "kingdom come." By modern standards, Isaiah was manic, Jeremiah depressive, and Ezekiel psychotic. If we take a prolonged gaze into the heart of our collective demons (corporate demons of violence, cruelty, and domination) we risk permanent damage to our hearts and psyches. Likewise, Christian mystics warn against the excesses of silent prayer for its own sake. Thomas Keating and others advocate silent prayer not as an end in itself, but as a means of becoming a more patient, reliable, and effective servant.

Activists enter the fray of the world's injustices and risk the scarring likely to come from those encounters. Contemplatives seek the still small voice within for respite from the storms and for reconnection with the joyous freedom at our source. The two together move mountains.

Union with God is in the present tense—"Before Abraham and Sarah were, I am" (John 8:58). Solidarity with oppressed people is in the future tense. We look to something God is going to do. God will bring us through the wilderness and into the Promised Land. It may not happen in our generation or in our lifetime. Like Moses we may not live to see the promised day of freedom and justice (Deuteronomy 34:1–8). But one day we will shatter oppression in its numerous guises, which currently abound . . . sex trafficking, preemptive military strikes, insane nuclear arsenals poised to kill millions, the ongoing decimation of the Amazon rainforest, unsustainable dependency on oil, unsustainable human population growth, the United States' proliferation of warplanes and weapons in developing countries . . .

Contemporary disciples work toward God's realm both in the present tense (changing the reference point for our lives through prayer) and in the future tense (changing the world). The love of God is cultivated in the monastery or in some form of sustained spiritual practice and the love of neighbor is cultivated in our city streets. Jesus demonstrates the symmetry between the two with his forty days in the wilderness and his frequent retreats and prayer vigils lasting "all night" (Matthew 4:1–11, Luke 4:1–13; 6:12). Yet Jesus is fully engaged in the world, regularly tolerating the crowds pressing in on him (Luke 5:1; 8:45).

Jesus was contemplative and activist, mystic and prophet, Spirit and form, God and human, absolute and relative, Creator and creature, existing for eternity and existing in time.

LOVE'S TWOFOLD DYNAMIC

Some will want a singular name for the dynamic between Jesus' Divinity and humanity. And I'll respond: love (1 John 4:8; 1 Corinthians 13). Yet, I avoid talking about love, because it's a nebulous and misused term. Love is too easy on the mind as a catch-all word for the Christian Spiritual Journey. So I use it sparingly. When probing the ultimate mystery of Jesus, dropping the L word is misleading, because love is a moving target, not a stagnant term with stayed letters. If love is a moving target, it is most telling to name the specific targets themselves: God and neighbor. What's even more telling than naming the potentially polarizing targets is naming the singular dynamic that unites them: The Jesus Paradox!

Christian author and activist, Jim Wallis, tells the following story . . . Jim was in a soup line in Washington D.C. when a sixty year old black woman was asked to give the prayer. She prayed: "Jesus we know you are in this line today. When we meet you help us to treat you right." This is the essence of Christian faith. Through Jesus, God belongs to us and shares our humanity. God is in fact one of us. This is the practical conclusion of Matthew 25: 31–46: Jesus says, "When I was hungry, you fed me. When I was in prison you visited me . . ." "When Lord?" they asked. Jesus responds, "Whatever you did to the least of these sisters and brothers, you did to me."

"I'm not my brother's keeper" is the lie infecting our streets and our neighborhoods (Genesis 4:9). This lie alienates us from God and one another. Responsibility to one another and to our neighbors begins with identification with our sisters and brothers. God belongs to us and we belong to each other. This is the Gospel's distilled essence. This is the meaning of the incarnation. This is the stunning truth that re-enchants the world.

CONTEMPLATION AND ACTION

Christian prayer's distinguishing characteristic is its focus on service. Enlightenment isn't the central point. The point is intimacy with God, which spawns more effective servanthood.

Saint Thomas, a disciple of Jesus and an apostle of the early church, taught there are three vocations: There's the active life, there's the contemplative life, and there's the mixture of both. He believed the best path is the mixture. The life solely focused on prayer, such as the stereotypic monastic life, is limited. The active life, solely focused on service, is also limited. The combination is dynamic and earth moving.

Activism used to be divorced from faith. Now we're seeing more and more kinship between them. This is good! We need a spiritual refuge we can return to again and again and we need a cause. May more activists find their spiritual refuge in Jesus' dynamic essence and in prayer and may more Christians turn activist!

People interested in interior silence used to be separated from active ministries and family life. Now this is changing. Thomas Keating writes, "The persons I know who are most advanced in prayer are married or engaged in active ministries, running around all day to fulfill their duties."[11]

Silent prayer isn't necessarily about external structures like monasteries, but about the actual cultivation of interior silence accessible to all. A person can have the robe of the monk and not the heart of the monk. Likewise a person can have the heart of a monk (a committed spiritual practice) and dress in street clothes. Outward appearances are secondary to the motivations of our hearts. Saint Maximus enumerates:

> He who has renounced such things as marriage, possessions and other worldly pursuits is outwardly a monk, but may not yet be a monk inwardly. Only he who has renounced the impassioned conceptual images of these things has made a monk of the inner

11. Keating, *Open Heart*, 33.

self, the intellect. It is easy to be a monk in one's outer self if one wants to be; but no small struggle is required to be a monk in one's inner self.[12]

May more and more people reconcile world-denying asceticism[13] on the one hand with God-denying humanism on the other. May more Christians emulate Jesus by loving *The Creator and* taking care of *the creatures*, by communing with God and serving our neighbors.

Without activism, contemplation is in constant danger of becoming what Thomas Merton called "consecrated narcissism." Without contemplation, activism is in invariable danger of turning into a humanistic enterprise stripped of its vital connection to God as source of inspiration and refuge from the storm.

QUESTIONS FOR REFLECTION AND DISCUSSION

1) Smith asserts Western culture's incessant activity is unbalanced. Do you agree with this? Why or why not?

2) Do you think balance between contemplation of God and service to humanity is Christianity's essence? Why or why not?

3) Do you agree "God belongs to us and we belong to each other?" What do you make of this phrase?

4) Application question: What can you do to achieve a more balanced life of contemplation and action?

---

12. Palmer, et al, *The Philokalia Vol. 2*, 106.

13. Tempered asceticism is actually liberating. See *Asceticism* in glossary.

Part 4

Clarity & Conviction about Jesus in a Pluralistic World

9

Christian Theology's Essence for the Twenty-first Century & Beyond

Jesus graced everything under heaven with the economy of the incarnation.

–CYRIL OF ALEXANDRIA

Never place a period where God has placed a comma. God is still speaking.

–GRACIE ALLEN

LOSS OF FAITH

PEOPLE WANT TO BELIEVE—THEY want to hold on. But they begin to lose the struggle and faith silently slips away. When faith no longer hits home people begin going through the motions.

Then deadening inertia plops down on the couch and absorbs the values of television and the sex and money culture. Then discernment gets compromised. Then life takes on a dull meaningless quality void of transcendence, void of religion. Then people are vulnerable to simplistic toxic varieties of religion. Then people are more vulnerable to fixations and disintegration. Then there is a hollow sinking feeling that needs to be filled with pornography, alcohol, and video game addiction. Then people forget what's most important: our primary relationship with God and one another.

If we can't connect to God as revealed to us and to our people (Jesus), then alienation takes on new power, disconnecting us from our soul's depths and from our ancestors. If we cut ourselves off from the deep abiding memory of God preserved in our tradition, we soon become strangers in an alien land, forgetting where we came from and where we're going.

The loss of religion in our culture is staggering. At public ceremonies prayers are often given and they are sincere, yet they often amount to tokens—drops in the bucket of secularism. And many in our culture, void of deep authentic faith, seek inverted forms of worship, losing themselves in addictions, Monday night football, and gambling. People are instinctively religious. And it shows in their devotion to television, sports, money, work, and sex. These are all indirect approaches to spirituality—fixations to fill the *God-shaped hole*. Saint Seraphim (d. 1853) stated, "In the times in which we live, we have reached such a degree of lukewarmness, almost everywhere, in the holy faith in Jesus Christ, such an insensibility towards communion with God, that really we can say, we have departed almost entirely from the true Christian life."[1]

Even though I disagree with my fundamentalist sisters and brothers on many substantial points of faith, I concur with them on this: Western Civilization's abandonment of historic faith is deeply unsettling. It is a travesty. For, as Russian author Fyodor Dostoevsky (d. 1881), observed in *The Brothers Karamazov*, "When people no longer believe in God, any and all horrors become possible."[2]

In his book, *Behold I Do a New Thing*, Christian author Kirk Hadaway says the Church is primarily about personal transformation.[3] Yet Hadaway doesn't directly address the basis of personal transformation . . . The basis of transformation is belief in God, better yet, immersion in God. Fundamentalists know this instinctively but their faith is narrow and limiting. Secularists don't know it and so lose themselves in surrogate faiths like sports, chemical addictions, and other fetishes. All the while there's a nagging emptiness.

1. Motovilov, *St. Seraphim of Sarov's Conversation*.
2. Dostoevsky, *The Brothers Karamazov*, The Legend of the Grand Inquisitor.
3. Hadaway, *Behold I Do a New Thing*.

My hope is that more open-minded and educated people will arrive at a life-giving, open-minded faith for our times based on personal experience and mystical theology. The taste of freedom that comes from mystical experience brings fulfillment like nothing else. It brings healing, deep meaning, and purpose.

SECULARIZATION OF CLERGY

Today there's a terrible secularization of seminaries and of clergy. This isn't limited to Protestant clergy. When I talked to a Catholic priest friend, he confided in me that the whole environment at clergy retreats he attends is often irreverent and secular. The lack of deeply rooted faith makes many ministers anxious, aloof, or neurotic.

Clergy are becoming increasingly secular. And Academics ignore theology. Yet clergy are the glue of Christian tradition and theology is humanity's most ennobling and enduring legacy.

The lack of Christian mystics and profound broad-minded Christian theologians in the world is a sign of cultural deterioration. This deterioration is also evident in the industrialized world's diminished population of artists, poets, dreamers, and idealists. At many top American colleges today we find abundant funding for the Sciences, with fully stocked laboratories and a capable team of teaching assistants. The Arts and Humanities, on the other hand, are usually grossly underfunded and understaffed. The Arts and Humanities' primary reason for being isn't science and profit, so they're undervalued. In a society that values technological progress and the almighty dollar, other values take a back seat.

Western society favors the left brain of the engineer over the right brain of the mystic. It values the left brain of the church administrator over the right brain of the visionary leader. But, without the genius of mystical theology and the connective tissue of the mystics there's no container for all the pieces. There's no hope of transcendent peace, lasting unity, passionate dynamism.

THE BYZANTINE ERA

Theology and monasticism were pillars of the Byzantine era (330–1453). In the Byzantine era even local craftsman debated theological truths. Theology was of general interest, not just the domain of monks and clerics.

The Byzantine era was marked by thriving monastic communities everywhere. During the Byzantine the Egyptian city of Alexandria had three hundred monastic communities in its general vicinity. Some of these were house monasteries housing only three or four brothers. Others covered vast tracts of land, with a commercial arm requiring the labors of hundreds of brothers. Monastic women were common, such as Melania (d. 439), abbess at the Mount of Olives in Jerusalem, who guided young Evagrius (d. 399) into monastic life. Evagrius later became one of the most influential Greek mystic writers.[4]

My hope is that in the Twenty-first Century a practical monasticism will again penetrate the West from every angle: Catholic, Protestant, Orthodox, clergy, and lay. By practical monasticism, I mean the heart and soul of it, which is a daily personal practice of silent prayer coupled with regular retreats. People often think mystical experience is the abode of specialists and ascetics. Not so.

If centering prayer is practiced for two twenty-minute sessions a day and if a practitioner takes a weeklong centering prayer retreat yearly, Thomas Keating and numerous others guarantee results. The transforming grace of centering prayer has nothing to do with effort and is a grace. Yet, discipline is necessary. We have to show up and sit on our cushion or chair for the prescribed time. That part is up to us. One time Keating said, "You can't expect to have a chance of winning the lottery unless you buy lottery tickets." Likewise, God's transforming grace won't work its way through us unless we practice. Yes, a discipline of silent prayer requires stamina, but so does any worthwhile endeavor. There's no substitute for regular practice. What I'm describing is variously named neo-monasticism, new monasticism, or lay monasticism. It's a surprising development among tens of thousands of people across the United States and Europe, who are serious practitioners of silent prayer, but who are not members of a monastery or cloister.

In the Byzantine there were many monks and nuns who practiced silent prayer. After they became established in their practices, people sought them out for spiritual advice and to experience their magnetic and sometimes healing presence. I pray for more contemporary Christian mystics who will lead normal lives, yet provide the spiritual leaven for their communities.

---

4. The Byzantine period, as we know it, began to crumble after the Council of Chalcedon. The Council of Chalcedon began the unraveling.

I also hope more Christians will take theology seriously and give it the respect it is due. For two millennia people understood that theology is the essence of philosophy both East and West. Theology is compelling and inspiring, even to post-moderns, if its foundation is solid and authentic. It's time for Christian theology to echo rich mystical overtones of old. It's time for Christian theology to move from pre-enlightenment moorings into the Twenty-first Century.

It's time for Christian theology to return to its essence—Jesus . . . The Jesus we take seriously, but not more seriously than he took himself; the Jesus whose Divinity springs forth in every word and action, but who always remains human.

A FAITHFUL REMNANT

Paul Tillich, a towering twentieth century theologian, wrote "We should not imagine that we have nothing to learn from them (The Eastern Church). It may happen that with centuries of more intimate contact, the dimension of depth may again enter Western thinking."[5]

I'll spend my life fanning the flames of The Jesus Paradox and silent prayer, for they've been my truest introduction to Jesus' essence. Yet, I'm not naïve about The Jesus Paradox. I know the extremes are initially more attractive than balance. People are heavily scripted in the either/or tug-of-war mentality. So to ask Christians to let go of their end of the tug-of-war may ask too much. "Contemplate the creative tension in the rope itself? Are you kidding? I'm comfortable holding on to my side of the argument." To admit the merits of the other side chafes the ego and challenges our need to be right. So, for a time The Jesus Paradox will probably hang on with the Oriental Orthodox Church and with a remnant of Christian mystics East and West. Yet the Bible is filled with stories of how God can use a faithful remnant to transform history. The Hebrew prophets never had a majority, and yet they had important things to say. Their powerful witness was about faithfulness and relevancy, not numbers. Moral authority isn't a function of size. Isaiah prophesies . . . "Though a tenth remains in the land (of the righteous), it will be laid waste. But as the terebinth and oak leave stumps when they are cut down, so the holy seed will be the stump in the land" (Isaiah 6:13).

The prophets place overwhelming importance on the faithful remnant. This remnant is the few who make ancient scriptures relevant and

5. Tillich, *A History of Christian Thought*, 97.

:cessible to each generation; the few who don't settle for dusty hardback academic treatises, the few who don't settle for cotton candy televangelists. We need faith that's ancient and contemporary—faith that beams from the fiery eyes of mystics—faith that's anchored in Jesus' primal essence.

I pray for a faithful remnant of Christians in the West who learn from their Oriental Orthodox sisters and brothers and who return to the center, avoiding the errors of fundamentalism and new age. I pray that the deepest spiritual roots of Christian tradition (The Jesus Paradox) fan out, supporting an ever widening grove of mystics, who transform Christianity because of their conviction and breadth. This Christianity is in stark contrast to the *convicted, yet narrow* and the *broad, yet wishy-washy* brands of Christianity. For Christian renewal, we need both conviction and breadth.

If a more balanced Christianity takes hold in the West, it will spawn more bridge building between denominations and greater unity among Christians of different stripes. It will also generate more secure and honest interfaith dialogue, making Christianity more relevant.

LINEAGE

In the tradition and writings of the Eastern Church we're always reminded of the importance of lineage.[6] Both the theological wisdom and the mystic spirit of the Eastern monks were passed down generation to generation.[7]

Christian tradition needs a lineage of spiritual teachers, whose wisdom is passed down through generations. We need realized practitioners who embody the Gospel and who have experienced heaven on earth. We need clergy who have been on silent retreat, who have a spiritual practice, and who have a mystical tradition to anchor their spirituality. We need teachers, who themselves had reliable teachers—a lineage of spiritual masters.

When it comes to the lineage of Christian mystics through the ages I think of an axe passed down generation after generation. The axe handle is Centering Prayer as taught by Thomas Keating, Basil Pennington, Cynthia Bourgeault, and others, which makes the oldest and deepest prayer forms

---

6. Patristic writings are those passed down through generations, which reflect the best theological minds of the ages. The emblem of this legacy in the Eastern Orthodox and Oriental Orthodox Churches is *The Philokalia*.

7. Christian tradition experienced a flowering of monasticism between the third and the fifth centuries in the deserts of Egypt. The genius of this period was encapsulated in the lineage of Alexandrian Bishops between the fourth and the fifth centuries. For more on this lineage see appendix B.

of Christian tradition contemporary. The axe head is The Jesus Paradox, which is the theological legacy of the Alexandrian Mystics and the Oriental Orthodox Church. Perhaps this book is the small wedge holding the two together in Twenty-first Century minds as the two were held together in the minds of The Alexandrian Mystics.

The Christian Native American storyteller Dayton Edmonds tells the story of an axe passed down to him from his great-great-great uncle. He received the axe as a gift on his birthday. It came to him as a family heirloom, with much fanfare. He was overjoyed. It meant the world to him to have an axe passed down through so many generations.

After the excitement waned, Dayton took his mother aside and began to inquire about the axe. "Is this really my great-great-great uncle's axe?" "Yes it is," his mother replied. "This is the actual handle and head that my great-great-great uncle wielded generations ago" Dayton excitedly inquired? "Oh no," said his mother. "The handle has been replaced several times and I think the head was replaced once too, but it's the same axe!"

This is the essence of tradition. It's not something we can pinpoint and calcify. That's its power. The spirit of The Alexandrian Mystics remains alive through the ages and goes where it will even after it's been seemingly lost. It has a life of its own that lives in the memory of our people—of our Christian grandmothers and grandfathers. Those meant to find it will. Their seeking hearts won't let them down. They will seek and find (Matthew 7:7).

If we seek the mystical essence of Jesus, Jesus will in turn seek us out through a word, through a practice, through a teacher, through a book. Even though seeking requires effort on our part, we remind ourselves it's God who brings all forms of authentic teaching to us. And our authentic teachers are our greatest treasure.

MAKING ANCIENT WISDOM CONTEMPORARY

The mystical theology of Nicaea (The Nicene Creed) and of the Trinity (God is one and three at the same time), as taught by Athanasius, is well known. But the mystical legacy of the Alexandrian Mystics, as taught by Athanasius, Cyril, and subsequent Alexandrian Bishops and monks (The Jesus Paradox), is relatively unknown. The Jesus Paradox brings Christian mystical theology full circle, tempering dualistic extremes and ushering in holistic understanding and dynamism.[8]

8. In this book I have no intention of dishing out the master theology that must

The point of The Jesus Paradox is to "Exalt the One over the dyad—the single over the dual—and to free its nobility from all commerce with dualism . . .to bring into unity what was divided and to reconcile all things."[9] These words of eleventh century monk, Nikitas Stithatos (d. 1090), resonate powerfully today. With all the scientific and technological advancements of our post modern world, there seems to be more fragmentation of the soul than ever. The early monks may have had blind spots by twenty-first century standards, yet they name our blind spot more precisely than any. The Jesus Paradox and the unitive state of mind that produced its mystical theology can heal the fractured twenty-first century soul.

I've attempted to make the theology of Jesus as understood by The Alexandrian Mystics as contemporary as possible. This work isn't the meat. It's the salt in the meat. It isn't the loaf. It is the leaven in the loaf. It isn't the floodlight. It's the candle. It's not the teaching of mainstream Christianity. It's the teaching of the lineage of The Alexandrian Mystics in contemporary language.

QUESTIONS FOR REFLECTION AND DISCUSSION

1) Do you affirm that when people no longer believe in God any and all horrors become possible? Why or why not?

2) Do you think lineage is important? Why or why not?

3) Do you think theology and conviction are related? If so, how?

4) What do you make of Smith's vision of a faithful remnant of Christian mystics who trace their tattered lineage back to The Alexandrian Mystics?

5) Application Question: Do you have clarity and conviction about your faith that brings passion to your life?

---

be accepted in toto. Theology's depth is beyond the human mind's scope and cannot, I believe, be grasped in toto. This book is also not about solving Christianity's problems by simply plugging in the correct formula. *Miaphysite* gets at something much deeper. And that's the exquisite symmetry of God's human incarnation—of finding that primal balance, which frees us from the choke hold of dualistic thought, tempers extremes, and invites the peace that passes understanding.

9. Palmer, et al, *The Philokalia Vol. 4*, 143–144.

10

Fragmentation to Wholeness

Religion is always, in one sense or another,
about making one out of two!
Cheap religion is invariably about maintaining the two
and keeping things separate and apart.

–RICHARD ROHR

The Christian of the future will be a mystic or will not exist at all.

–KARL RAHNER

INDIVIDUALISM RUN AMOK

AUGUSTINE WAS THE FIRST human being to say "I" in his *Confessions*, which was the first autobiography of the ancient world. Before then, the individual was eclipsed by group-think of the herd. After Augustine Western Civilization moved quickly to Descartes, who took the individual as the starting place for all knowledge.

Now the pendulum has swung from the tyranny of group-think to the tyranny of individualism. Rampant individualism threatens the underlying fabric of relationships and communities across the industrialized world. When individualism is our starting point we become married singles, not married couples. When individualism is our starting point we become individuals in community, not the beloved community that Jesus envisioned.

Individualism run amok, also known as independence, isn't the answer. Clinging and clutching to another, also known as co-dependence, isn't the answer. Intimacy and responsibility, also known as inter-dependence, is the answer.

This book is a prayer for unity, for inter-dependence, for cosmic glue to hold the beloved tradition together through the ages, even through the breakneck technological progress of the last century, even through the post modern bevy of divorces from history, from religion, and from spouses.

With Augustine, humanity took a quantum leap forward to *self-consciousness*. Now we desperately need *community-consciousness* to be recast and to flourish once again—not community organized around the profit motive, hobbies, or special interest groups. Rather, community that has the breadth which only longstanding faith traditions can provide . . . Community that's an umbrella for family, for spiritual practice, for caring, for social justice . . . Community that provides continuity through generations, where our loved ones are baptized, married, and buried . . .[1] Community where there's both profound intimacy and good boundaries. Imagine that! Where there is a refreshing absence of litmus tests for membership or an inner circle which decides who's in and who's out. Where all are welcomed, no matter who they are and no matter where they are on life's journey. This is the beloved community Jesus inaugurated in the Gospels that yearns to become incarnate in your church and mine.

Many in my generation write off the faith of previous generations as "quaint" and "old hat." This cuts us off from previous generations and increases our isolation and anxiety. Deeply connecting with our faith connects us with our extended families of origin. It connects us to the history

---

1. An aside about communal life . . . When I was traveling in India I met a woman from Canada who was conducting research on the longest lived communities on the planet. She had visited Find Horn in Scotland, some Quaker communities, The Iona Community off the coast of Scotland, and some collective farms and co-operatives around the world. She found that the most long-standing communities throughout the world all have spiritual traditions built into their community life. These communities understand that without spiritual practice we can't unravel our personal baggage and without spiritual practice we can't cultivate the personal serenity and breadth needed to deal with the baggage of those around us. The Twenty-first Century global village requires deep collective commitment to spiritual practice to insure cohesion in the face of daunting social and cultural upheaval.

of civilization and its architects. When there's connection with the past and hope for the future . . . This is the essence of the Bible—continuity between past and future. When Christians ask, "How will God be revealed in the future?" the answer is another question, "How was God revealed in the past?" The way God was revealed in the past points to how God will be revealed in the future. God was revealed in the unity of Christ. Through his ministry the disunited self, the disunited relationship, the disunited community, were united. Through faith in him and communion with him, we can become united . . . Even the most disparate realities such as crucifixion and resurrection can be integrated! A devoted heart is a great start on the path. A holistic mind transformed by The Jesus Paradox pioneers a path up the mountain of The Alexandrian Mystics.

As Western societies become increasingly individualized and the bonds of group life, including the family, steadily weaken, healing will come through restoration of the most exalted form of group life: the faith community.[2] Committing to the faith passed to us and making it our own in the present will bring healing to our extended family of faith, which stretches back generations. Christian faith is anchored in God's revelation to our ancestors: God became human. The Alexandrian Mystics give us a satisfying account of what this means. They give us clarity about Jesus that weathers the postmodern storms.

May Jesus' primal mystic root move us from dualistic fragmentation to dynamic wholeness. May it move us from tug-of-war binaries to dynamic unity, where there's cooperation instead of competition, where there's creative tension between opposites as opposed to gridlock. May The Alexandrian Mystics move us toward a life-giving open-minded faith for our times based on personal experience and rooted in mystical theology.

RECLAIMING JESUS

Collective spiritual truths handed down through the ages are the basis of wisdom. Without them we're lost. Of course Christianity isn't the only player on the field. But it's the central player for one third of the world's population. And it has an extraordinary place within the larger vision of God.

---

2. In medieval Europe the church wasn't just the symbolic center of community life. It was the actual center. In many towns throughout Europe, the Cathedral was intentionally built in the very center of the town.

The Jesus Paradox is The Alexandrian Mystics' theological beacon. The point isn't to get fixated on the beacon, but to glance at it periodically, which orients us and protects our vessel from destruction. The beacon or lighthouse doesn't pretend to create the light, only to channel it usefully to save lives from the perils of the open sea—from the coral reef on the one side and the sand bar on the other.

Our current definition, interpretation, and understanding of Jesus is unbalanced, apparent in the fragmentation of the global church with its various camps. To remedy this situation I pray that mainline churches keep their sights on Jesus according to The Alexandrian Mystics.

If Christians enter this century equipped with a clearly defined theology, there is hope. If not, Christianity will continue to fall into excesses and fragmentation. Yes, relationship with Jesus is about devotion from the heart. It's also about responsible thinking that accounts for the rest of the world. Devotion to Jesus is about both intimacy and responsibility. Intimacy without responsibility is dangerous. And responsible theology without heartfelt devotion is hollow.

Jesus' life was an exquisite balancing act. He seems to have had a fast, furious, and bumpy ride on this earth. Yet he had as smooth a ride as possible given he was executing the most daring balancing act the world has seen. On the surface Christianity doesn't seem to be about balance. I disagree. We balance the Divinity with the humanity, the love of God with the love of neighbor, responsibility with intimacy. We balance the infinite with the finite, eternity with time, revelation with reason, subjectivity and objectivity.

RECLAIMING THE CENTER

> There are many levels of the quality of being a Christian—from Jesus the Christ to Torquemada the inquisitor . . .a similar qualitative range exists in every religious tradition. Our aim is to move closer and closer toward the mark: Jesus.[3] –Ravi Ravindra

May the holistic vision of The Alexandrian Mystics further the unfinished work of the Holy Spirit! May more and more people return to the spiritual depths at the center: Jesus.

Jesus is the point of entry into Christian faith and the point of return. Jesus isn't the sum total of the faith, but the anchor, the foundation we return to again and again. We can explore the mysteries of the universe

3. Ravindra, *The Gospel of John*, 7.

Early church relationship to the pe.
of Jesus and
mystical communion with Jesus. Fragmentation *to Whole.*

because we are anchored in God's human incarnation. This gives us the security and stability to take risks and explore. When Jesus is the anchor we have the courage to survey the ocean. While exploring we encourage the homeless and wayward to experience meaning and purpose in his all-pervasive love. And when we meet people grounded in other faiths, we respect and learn from them. Yet we expend most of our energy in our own garden, cultivating the seeds our Christian mystic ancestors tilled generations ago.

The Jesus Paradox is a powerful antidote to the addictive process. It's an especially potent counter to spiritual materialism: the desire to accumulate as many spiritual experiences as possible from as many traditions as possible. The Jesus Paradox teaches Christian holistic consciousness, bypassing the need to acquire esoteric teachings about non-dual awareness in Bali, Indonesia or Sri Lanka. Christian tradition has its own wisdom tradition dating back to the second century! The Jesus Paradox is also a powerful antidote to absolutism, insisting truth is a moving target, not an inflexible list of fundamentals. The Jesus Paradox has a way of stretching our comfort zones and generating insecurity. Yet, ironically, I now find my greatest security in the creative tension of that Paradox.

For the early church faith was about relationship to a person: Jesus. It was about mystical communion with him. The law is for children. When we mature, Christ's inclusive love as demonstrated in the Gospels, takes precedence over the law. Instead of writing a fifteen point checklist for us, Paul writes, "God has sent the Spirit of Christ into our hearts" (Galatians 4:6).

Communion with Christ requires our whole selves: body, heart, mind, and spirit (our physical, emotional/social, intellectual, and spiritual lives). Our love for Jesus can't succumb to mere sentimentality, to swaying back and forth like a love struck teenager. Our love for Jesus can't be reduced to a "Jesus is my boyfriend" approach to praise music. Open-hearted tasteful praise music within a larger context of a responsible and life-giving theology of Jesus is beautiful. But, if Jesus becomes about my insular teen heartthrob relationship and doesn't try to make sense of him within the larger context of our pluralistic world, we're lost.

We need passion for Jesus that is reasoned (rooted in life-giving theology). We also need reason that is passionate (quickened by the fire of The Alexandrian Mystics). May concerned Christians catch the fire at the center!

..ING THE DIVIDE BETWEEN HEAD AND HEART

..tent struggle, from which no humans are immune, is the struggle
.. .. .ce head and heart. This is a tenuous balance and we usually err
on one side or the other. Here are some of the persistent tensions between
head and heart

Head	Heart
1a) Thinking	1b) Feeling
2a) Theology	2b) Experience
3a) Professional	3b) Personal
4a) Self	4b) Relationship
5a) Stand apart	5b) Stand in solidarity with
6a) Analyze w/ objective distance	6b) Listen deeply w/ compassion
7a) *I* Statements	7b) *We* statements
8a) Individualistic	8b) Communal
9a) Independent	9b) Dependent
10a) "Know thyself"	10b) Social conscience
11a) Self-defined	11b) Defined by family, community, tribe
12a) Renounce everything (monk)	12b) Love everyone (minister)
13a) *Dyophysite* (dualistic theology)[4]	13b) *Monophysite* (theology of simple unity)[5]

Jesus' Third Way was not violence and not passivity, but non-violent-
ly standing up for what is right.[6] Jesus spent many hours with the crowds
pressing in on him, then went to solitary out-of-the-way places to pray.
Instead of standing apart like the Essene hermits of his time he entered the
fray of people and their tangled motivations and projections. Instead of
standing in solidarity with people without the appropriate distance to be
prophetic, Jesus often stood apart, sought God in prayer, and went on personal retreats. Instead of settling for the diminishing prospects of standing
apart or standing in solidarity, Jesus entered the synergistic dance of self in
relationship, where self-development and community development mutually enhance each other in surprising ways.

Binaries, like those charted above, become most generative when
held in creative tension. Instead of a hard heart or a bleeding heart, we

4. See *Dyophysite* in the glossary.
5. See *Monophysite* in the glossary.
6. See *Jesus' Third Way* in the glossary.

discover a soft heart. Instead of childlike dependence or aloof independence, we arrive at mature inter-dependence. Instead of everyone toeing the same line for the sake of unity, we accept diversity within unity. The German Lutheran theologian of the early seventeenth century, Rupertus Meldenius (d.1651), once wrote in a tract: "In essentials unity, in non-essentials diversity, in all things charity." Yes!

Instead of heartless capitalism or unrealistic communism, we arrive at Franklin Roosevelt's New Deal (1933–36) and Lyndon Johnson's Great Society (1961–63). Instead of settling for tyranny in its various collusive and manipulative guises, we become cooperative leaders with integrity. Instead of Martyrs we become servants. Servant leaders know when it's necessary to sacrifice, but not to the point of self-abasement. Servant leaders also know how to take a stand for what is right, even when it means standing apart from the crowd and risking ostracism.[7] Instead of militant autocracy or cumbersome consensus, we arrive at participatory democracy.

Creative tension, imagination, and integration lead us from diminishment, lopsidedness, and fragmentation to wholeness. At the heart of this creative tension is The Jesus Paradox. Instead of simple unity (*monophysite*) or duality (*dyophysite*) we arrive at the dynamic unity of The Jesus Paradox, infinitely imaginative and infinitely creative![8]

May disunited selves find wholeness! May a divided body of Christ find healing and greater unity!

QUESTIONS FOR REFLECTION AND DISCUSSION

1) Do you think Individualism has run amok in our society? Why or why not?

2) Do you think Jesus according to The Alexandrian Mystics can help move us individually and as a society from dualistic fragmentation to dynamic wholeness? Why or why not?

3) Does The Jesus Paradox according to The Alexandrian Mystics make sense to you? Is it relevant to you? Why or why not?

4) Application question: Is there a divide between your head and your heart? Please explain. If so, how can you heal the divide?

---

7. Greenleaf, *Servant Leadership.*

8. See *Monophysite* and *Dyophysite* in glossary.

Part 5

The Christian Mystics' Love of the Human Being

11

The Least of These

*As you did it to one of the least of these brothers and sisters of mine
. . . you did it to me.*

−JESUS

*To get into heaven you need to have a letter of recommendation from
the poor.*

−ANNE LAMOTT

EXPOSURE TO THE LEAST OF THESE

AFTER GRADUATION FROM HIGH school I worked for Habitat for
Humanity in Uganda, East Africa. I'll never forget Semunyo, an elderly gentleman with an oozing foot infection. His leg had begun to swell
and gangrene was days away. My friend Matovu took me to see Semunyo.
When I first saw him, it was obvious to me that he needed penicillin. The
sorry fact was Semunyo didn't have enough money to pay for penicillin
shots at the local clinic. So Matovu and I put Semunyo in a wheelbarrow
and rolled him to the clinic. I paid five dollars for penicillin, which saved
Semunyo's life.

Many Americans have lost touch with the Semunyos of the world. Semunyo is the tip of the iceberg. In fact Semunyo is a tame example of third world realities.

If a jumbo jet went down in North America it would be headline news. If two jumbo jets went down on the same day in North America it would be huge news, congressional committees of inquiry would form, a media shakedown would commence, and reparations would be made.

Every day the equivalent of two jumbo jets goes down in Africa. In other words, over four thousand Africans die from AIDS daily.[1] This is a travesty. We add to the inhumanity of the situation by turning away. Where are the headlines in the daily blogs and daily papers? Where are the congressional committees meeting around the clock to solve the crisis? These human beings are flesh and blood. They're Christ's body.

Cambodia is another sobering story. According to the Cambodian Mine Action and Victim Assistance Authority there are an estimated four to six million live land mines in Cambodia today—a country with a population of eight million.

Every day families tilling the land have the persistent horrific fear they'll hear an explosion. Then their daughter, mother, or husband will come back soaked in blood, missing a foot, a leg, an arm.

Yes, there are organizations like Church World Service addressing the problem. Yet, here again, in general we don't hear about it. It doesn't make the news.

OUT OF TOUCH

A memory from a 1994 trip to Dharamsala, India stands out for me . . . One morning at a local restaurant I sat on a bench by a robed Tibetan monk. As I sat taking in the morning rays, he reluctantly showed me his simple bowl and chop sticks, which were all he owned to eat with. Then in broken English he tried to ask me about knives, forks, spoons, plates, cups, etc. He was perplexed by all the unnecessary complication of these extra implements.

A friend of mine, Dorothy, came to Los Angeles from Uganda on a UCLA economics scholarship. She relayed her first experience in a U.S. grocery store. Upon seeing the long aisles, each containing thousands of choices, Dorothy froze. She was overwhelmed and unable to continue shopping. In Ugandan village grocery stores there are two kinds of flour,

1. Boyce, Blog.

one kind of salt, five kinds of nails, and two kinds of sugar, all in burlap sacks lining the walls. In the U.S. the average grocery store displays at least twenty-five kinds of toothpaste alone.

Matovu is a good friend of mine who lives in Uganda, East Africa. He has a two-room mud-brick house with a thatched roof and dirt floor. Everything he owns fits into one trunk, which he stores beneath his bed. Incidentally, he is hands down the most joyful soul I've ever known.

To have numerous dishes and utensils, many of which are never used, to make dozens of choices in every store aisle, and to own so much stuff it fills two storage units is the American way. My parents have a two car garage full of boxes, half of which haven't seen the light for fifteen years. One day I asked my parents what would happen to all the stuff. My dad replied dryly, "You'll figure it out when the time comes."

Americans make numerous bewildering choices every day, from our toothpaste, to our wireless service, to our shoes. The poor don't have this luxury. They simply want to survive. While many North Americans are worrying about which fork to use at the French restaurant, many families in Uganda are worrying about where they'll get their one daily meal.

The reason I'm going into this: if we take Jesus' humanity seriously we'll take the welfare of our fellow humans seriously. If God became human out of love for us, the least we can do is wake up from our Western world's collective amnesia about the poor.

The prophet Jeremiah exclaims: "Did not your father eat and drink and do justice and righteousness? Then it was well with him. He judged the cause of the needy; then it was well. Is not this to know me says the Lord" (Jeremiah 22: 15–16, ESV)? What would Jeremiah say about our current state of affairs, where we spend much of our time deciding what brand of cheese or cereal we will buy, while roughly a million and a half Africans die every year from AIDS?

The Bible reminds us that kindness counts above all else. This is the mark of our humanity—kindness to the poor, to the sick, to the homeless, to the AIDS victim, to the dying. Kindness is the core prophetic witness. Kindness redeems our humanity.

JESUS' SOLIDARITY WITH THE LEAST OF THESE

Jesus' solidarity with "the least of these" plants him among the prophets (Matthew 25:40). Jeremiah and Isaiah said the measure of a society is how it treats its least powerful. How would America measure up?

How do we treat those without adequate health care? How do we treat the elderly who can't afford their medicine? How do we treat our poor neighboring countries? What are our priorities? Are they as George Herbert Walker Bush put it, to be a "kinder and gentler nation?" Do we send neighboring countries the food and medicine they need or do we send them fighter planes and guns? Our obligation to the poor and powerless has deep biblical roots, echoing through the generations of prophets leading up to Jesus.

In the fullness of time, God entered the messiness of history. God entered into solidarity with the human family to show us the way. Jesus walked the dusty streets of Palestine in sandaled feet. Jesus entered into solidarity with the poor and suffering. Authentic Christianity continues to enter into the fray of poverty and affliction. This is Christianity's legacy— to show God's love through service to "the least of these."

African American theologian James Cone often reiterates, "Jesus Christ is a symbol of opposition to oppression."[2] Jesus' primary mission, exemplified in Luke's Gospel, is liberating the oppressed. One easy way to distinguish the true Christian prophets from the false is to listen closely to their messages. If God speaks on behalf of the wealthy, the powerful, and the privileged, then the prophet's authenticity is questionable. If God speaks on behalf of the poor, the powerless, and the oppressed, the prophet's authenticity is verified.[3] Jesus embodied the prophetic tradition of solidarity with the oppressed.

Jesus' first words in Luke's Gospel are words from the prophet Isaiah (d. Seventh Century BCE): "The Spirit of God is upon me, who has anointed me to bring good news to those who are poor, who has sent me to proclaim release to those who are captive and recovery of sight to those who are blind, to let those who are oppressed go free, to proclaim the year of God's favor" (Luke 4:18–19, Isaiah 61:1). Jesus claimed Isaiah's words were fulfilled in him. These first words of his public life set the tone for his entire ministry. From Mother Teresa's Sisters of Charity to Millard Fuller's Habitat for Humanity, reaching out to the poor is still the fast ticket to the heart of the Gospel.

When Jesus was baptized by John in the Jordan, he stood in line with the peasants, the disfigured, the lame, the destitute. John said to Jesus, "Aren't you the messiah? You don't need to stand with the riffraff and it isn't right for me to baptize you. I'm not worthy to stoop down and untie

2. Cone, *God of the Oppressed.*

3. Bill Coffin often cited this acid test of prophecy.

your sandals."[4] Jesus said in effect, "don't mess with me now, I know what I'm doing, like Gandhi I ride the third class train, I wear simple clothes, and prefer simple fare to the elaborate meal. I was born in a stable with barn animals. My parents were peasants like your parents. Blessed are the poor . . . The greatest among you is the servant of all." John, humbled by those words, baptized God's human incarnation.[5]

Some think God stands aloof, God is distant; God doesn't get involved in the nitty-gritty details of the human condition. Yet Jesus chipped his tooth on a stone in the bread, he drank a little too much at the wedding in Cana, he was the life of the party. Jesus never stopped Peter from telling colorful jokes. Don't forget the time Jesus laughed so hard he fell off his chair![6] Jesus' beard was long. He had rough edges.

Jesus was human. He was earthy. As Cyril of Alexandria put it, "God suckled, God wept, God died." To send the point home we could continue: God urinated, sweated, got wax build up in his ears. God's breath smelled after eating garlic.

Jesus, the colorful rebel, often enjoyed himself and reclined at table with the wayward backsliders. He befriended the greasy-fingered homeless man living in his pickup. He took the cause of the blond BMW-driving cocaine addict.

Jesus would've been startled by many evangelicals, whose every word is polished, whose every hair is in place, who are perfumed, plucked, shaved, and pressed. Jesus was more comfortable warming his hands at a campfire with drifters outside Nazareth than hobnobbing with upstanding church folk in a spotless fellowship hall.

Jesus dispensed with the grooming and fine tuned morals and went straight for the mark—solidarity with those who suffer. He didn't distinguish himself above others, with fine linens or the best seat in the house (Philippians 2:7). He was often found in the kitchen carrying on with the hired hands, who were the subjects of his parables. He was humble—a word that comes from the root *humus*—"of the earth."

Love of neighbor marked Jesus' whole ministry. His ministry wasn't about staying up on the mountaintop above the cries of the dispossessed. Jesus was always in trouble for reaching out to the most despicable, dirty, and degenerate. The fact "he touched the leper" was electrifying (Matthew 8:1–4). Those who heard those four words were sent reeling. In Jesus' day,

---

4. My dynamic translation of Mark 1:7.
5. My dynamic translation of Matthew 5:3, 23:10.
6. I'm using my imagination here.

lepers came around people pelted them with stones. No one looked —per, much less considered touching one.

Jesus stuck his neck out for prostitutes, tax collectors (extortionists), addicts, relentless gossips, and the terminally-ill. In today's context, Jesus would have stuck his neck out on behalf of gays, gang members, and Muslims (not necessarily in that order). We can also deduce that he would go out on a limb and risk his good name on behalf of death row convicts, pimps, and pushers. The revolutionary nature of Jesus' witness is lost on most Christians today. Its scandal is misunderstood and misrepresented.

Jesus stuck his neck out repeatedly for outcasts and derelicts! This outrage led the sanctimonious priests to conspire against him. Jesus ate with sinners and balked at the purity codes of religious purists. This got his neck pressed against a wood beam by a Roman Soldier at Golgotha (Luke 23:33).

GOD'S PREFERENTIAL OPTION FOR THE POOR

The usual translation of Matthew 5:3 is "Blessed are the poor in spirit." When I traveled in Mexico I saw a Cathedral wall that donned the following words: "*Dichosos espiritu de los pobres.*" These words were a revelation—they revolutionized my understanding of Matthew 5:3. They translate: "blessed is the spirit of the poor."[7]

This Spanish translation of Matthew 5:3 speaks to my experience. When I spent a year working with the poor in rural Uganda, I was transformed. I came away from experiences working alongside the poor with gratitude for the abundance I was given. I found myself envying the joy and contentment reflected in lives that were spiritually rich in inverse proportion to their material wealth. It's as though material prosperity blinds us to the simple pleasures of life and to the blessing of close-knit community. My experience is that the poor have often found the key to abundant life. This abundant life has little to do with the West's fixation on material

---

7. God's preferential option for the poor and oppressed is the basis of Liberation Theology. Bartolome de Las Casas (d. 1566), the Dominican priest who passionately championed Indian Rights, was a forerunner of Liberation Theology. Some won't read liberation theologians like Gustavo Gutierrez because of some academic agenda, such as liberation theology's lack of full adherence to the non-violent Jesus or because of Liberation Theology's Marxist overtones and critique of capitalism. But, the fact remains—Liberation Theologians address the West's blindness to the poor better than other theologians. See *Liberation Theology* in glossary.

gain and appearances. Rather, abundant life is a vital beating heart thriving on simple pleasures and enduring relationships.

I'm not romanticizing poverty and the terrible suffering it harvests. I'm pointing out that I've experienced more joy among the materially poor than I have among the materially rich. My experience with the poor echoes countless Peace Corps volunteers, who've been transformed by the spirit of the poor. "Blessed is the spirit of the poor"—indeed!

Why is it that the materially poor seem more likely to be content than the rich? Perhaps it is because "those who know when enough is enough, will always have enough."[8]

VILLAGE LIFE AND ACCOUNTABILITY

My time in a Ugandan village opened my eyes. My friend Matovu regularly invited elders of the village over to his house to share the family meal. There wasn't enough food to go around. But there was always room for the village elder, Bumpenje, who was revered and welcomed with open arms. The family cherished his wisdom, which came from decades of village experience.

I remember Matovu's stories about people who fell ill in the village and didn't have the money for medical attention. Each time villagers offered what they could to get their neighbor medical help. The villagers of Wobulenzi, Uganda aren't self-reliant or financially independent. They're financially inter-dependent.

When I hear old timers in America talk about Great Depression days (1929–1934) there's a glimmer in their eyes. Charles Dickens's epic phrase from *A Tale of Two Cities,* "It was the best of times, it was the worst of times," rings true for Depression veterans. Depression Era Americans relied on each other financially. There's something about relying on one another financially that makes us spiritually rich. A communal insurance policy as opposed to a corporate one brings out the best in people. When we realize our interconnection and interdependence in practical ways we're less prone to treat each other as means to some professional end. In a community where we know one another and are known there's no anonymity. Living in community makes us accountable.

In many ways, my experience in rural Montana mirrored my experience in a Ugandan village. Rural Montanans take it upon themselves to look out for each other. I know a Montanan woman named Susan who

8. Tzu, *Tao Te Ching*, Chapt. 46.

got fed up with the number of drunk driving accidents in her community. One Saturday she decided to do something about it. She slammed down the local paper with the dismal drunk driving statistics, marched to the bar a block from her home and cornered the bartender. She said, "For the love of God, when you see someone has had too much to drink, take away their keys and send them to my basement. The door is unlocked. They can sleep there." That was twenty-five years ago. Now, on weekends, when there's ample bar traffic, there is a sign on Susan's unlocked basement door: *Leave Your Shoes Outside*. On any given weekend night there's a handful of inebriated people passed out on her basement carpet or on the couch covered with a blanket. Because of Susan and the cooperation of the local bar, intoxicated people aren't stepping into their pickups and putting everyone at risk. They have a refuge.

Those who stand among the widows, orphaned, poor, elderly, and sloshed, stand with Jesus. Those who don't aren't of his kind. They don't bear his mark. In Jesus' day, the Pharisees worried about fine-tuned personal morality and the best seats in the house. Jesus rejected appearances and legalism about letters of the Hebrew Scriptures while neglecting compassion for the "least of these." Like the Hebrew prophets before him, Jesus admonished leaders for neglecting poverty stricken widows, orphans, and homeless. Jesus told his followers, "Just as you did it to one of the least of these who are members of my family, you did it to me" (Matthew 25:40).

Our ability to walk with sufferers makes us human. This ability made the Hebrew prophets and Jesus the light of the world. To give voice to those who have no voice, to speak on behalf of those who can't speak, to defend the vulnerable . . . These are the actions of God incarnate. All human beings are vulnerable, regardless of stature. The wealthy are vulnerable to chronic anxiety and a loss of meaning. They need the Gospel to counter the ephemeral values of money, appearances, chemical pleasures, and amusement park sex.

The role of the prophet isn't to predict the future but to change it. The prophet has a vision of a shared humanity, a realm where people look after each another. This prophetic vision begins in our own backyards. Dorothy Day (d. 1980) started in her backyard, providing shelter for New York's homeless. The Catholic Worker Movement was an organic extension to that primary impulse to look out for "the least of these."[9]

Charitable acts cut to the heart of social problems. They are rare because isolated acts in solidarity with the poor seem utterly insignificant. At

9. See *Catholic Worker Movement* in glossary.

one point Gandhi said: "Serving the poor can feel like trying to empty the ocean with a bucket. Nonetheless it's crucial that we continue."

The compulsion to reach out to the poor in their various forms is humanity's hope. Like Jesus, Dorothy Day, Albert Schweitzer, and the like, we begin by ministering to people, children, animals, and ecosystems in our own backyard.

TAKING ON THE GOVERNMENT

Solidarity with the poor requires taking on the government. Christian minister and author, Bill Coffin, writes:

> In the 1990s, both the Million Man March and the Promise-Keepers let the political order off the hook. Theirs was a purely spiritual message that just happened to parallel the antigovernment message of the Republicans. By contrast, Martin Luther King Jr. led the 1963 March on Washington and later the Poor People's March to confront the government, to put the government on notice . . . in a free society 'some are guilty but all are responsible' . . . In short, it is not enough to be a Good Samaritan, not when, from Philadelphia to East Oakland, whole communities lie bleeding in the ditch. What the poor need today is not piecemeal charity but wholesale justice.[10]

Coffin claims when we lessen our anger at injustice we lessen our love for the people. Jesus loved the exploited of his day and lashed out at their comfortable oblivious exploiters. Anger at injustice is a hallmark of the prophets. We have the responsibility to speak the truth. If we don't witness to the crudeness and brutality of our society, which disregards the homeless, poor, hungry, and dispossessed, who will?

For Martin Luther King, Christ's innocent suffering is the key to understanding the Crucifixion's saving power. It's also the key to conquering social evils. Unmerited suffering, like the Crucifixion, brings "to light the things now hidden in darkness and will disclose the purpose of the heart" (1 Corinthians 4:5). King believed willingness to suffer in order to expose injustice is the deepest form of love.

In the Old Testament, zeal for justice translates into land ownership being distributed evenly every fifty years, forbidding interest, and periodically canceling debts. Prophets like Nehemiah found debt and debt-slavery rampant in Judah, threatening the foundations of an equitable society.

10. Coffin, *The Heart Is A Little to the Left*, 17, 19, 21.

Jesus built on the Jewish prophetic vision of a just God. God's realm is to be sought here and now in social conditions.

The Hebrew Sabbath was a temporary reprieve from inequality, a day of rest for all: humans, animals, slaves and owners, children and adults. It was a day of symbolic egalitarianism, which is God's realm on earth as it is in heaven.

According to a UNICEF report published in the New York Times, a billion children in the world suffer extreme deprivation because of war, disease, and poverty.[11] Which politicians stand for the interests of the poor today,[12] for the interests of children, education, appropriate tax bracketing, and human rights? Those politicians have my support. Politicians who stand primarily for the interests of big corporations, weapons contractors, and the one percent of millionaires and billionaires don't need my support.

THE U.S. NATIONAL BUDGET

A glaring injustice of our times is how the United States spends its national budget. The Pentagon "defense" budget for 2010 was four hundred sixty three billion dollars compared to roughly fifty billion spent on children's health, thirty eight billion spent on kindergarten through twelfth grade education, thirteen billion spent on humanitarian foreign aid, six billion on job training, two billion on renewable energy research, and eight billion on the Environmental Protection Agency. And little has changed between 2010 and today.

The United States could meet basic human needs at home and abroad by reducing obsolete Cold War weaponry by ten percent and investing the savings. For the 2010 budget that would have broken down as follows:

1) Provide healthcare for uninsured US kids: $8 billion/year

2) Rebuild America's schools over 10 years: $14 billion/year

3) Gain energy independence w/ clean tech.: $13 billion/year

4) Double US aid to poor countries: $13 billion/year

5) Reduce debts of impoverished nations: $10 billion/year

11. UNICEF Report, New York Times, A1.

12. The ONE campaign (ONE.org) effectively addresses extreme poverty and global disease.

After 9/11, U.S. spending on anti-terrorism appropriately rose. But the Pentagon budget still includes nuclear and other weapons used during Cold War escalation. Former admirals, generals, and Pentagon officials agree the U.S. can safely reduce the yearly Pentagon budget by ten percent (fifty eight billion dollars). Along these lines it's significant to note the United States and its allies spend roughly seven hundred twenty four billion a year on defense compared to Russia (seventy billion), China (fifty billion), Iran and North Korea (eight billion).[13]

In light of glaring social ills, the yearly Pentagon budget is grotesque. Jesus said "To whom much is given, much is required" (Luke 12:48). The United States is the richest country in the world and we have a responsibility to lead by example and by compassion, beginning with responsibility to the world's poor.

> Wash yourselves, make yourselves clean; remove the evil of your doings from before my eyes; cease to do evil, learn to do good; seek justice, rescue the oppressed, defend the orphan, plead for the widow (Isaiah 1:16–17).

WORLD MISSIONS

When it comes to world missions, churches falter. Statistics of the National Council of Churches show individual church members give less than three dollars a year to help provide doctors, nurses, schools, and other assistance to people served by missions abroad. Church World Service has had a hard time raising as much as five million dollars to finance overseas relief work.

Christian charity can't serve as a Band Aid for our conscience—highly visible but ineffective. If Christianity is to experience revival, spirituality needs to be wedded to activism. We need more activists like the Quakers with their phenomenal history of working toward the abolition of slavery, women's suffrage, prison reform, and human rights. We need activism that tends to the widows and orphans of our time . . . those dying of AIDS in Africa.

I'm enamored with Bono of the rock band U2. Bono's historic initiatives save thousands of lives and generate billions of dollars to fight AIDS in Africa. Every day four thousand Africans die of AIDS. The organization Bono sponsors, DATA (Debt, AIDS, Trade, and Africa) pushes African disparities and injustices into public awareness. Bono's fundraising tactics

13. The above numbers were provided by TrueMajority.org

have teeth . . . Once senators were hedging on the amount of money they'd give for African relief. Bono then told the senators he'd display the names of all who didn't support the relief bill on huge banners at rock concerts: "These senators didn't support the fight against AIDS in Africa . . ."[14] We need more of this guerilla philanthropy. This is the church of the future, reclaiming the margins like the prophets of old.

Bono's prophetic message is "Christianity without Social Justice is empty."[15] Churches that honor Jesus' prophetic witness minister to the AIDS patient at the end of life, the smiling woman with Down's syndrome learning how to buy her own groceries, and the homeless man pocketing blueberry muffins in the church fellowship hall.

When we serve actual people, with an actual history, which includes their political and economic life, our faith takes root in actual soil, instead of remaining in the clouds. We can't just speak to people's souls. We must speak to their immediate situation. The only way we can understand people's problems is to contextualize—to look at the social, economic, and political background of their problems.[16]

Dom Helder Camara, former Archbishop of Recife, Brazil, remarked, "I give people bread and they call me a saint. I ask why they don't have any bread and they call me a revolutionary." As in Jesus' time, solidarity with the poor is always dangerous. It asks the charged political and economic questions and threatens the lopsided status quo.

SOCIAL JUSTICE ON A HUMAN SCALE

I am overwhelmed by the scale of suffering in the world, especially after torrents of environmental disasters: earthquakes, hurricanes, floods, tsunamis, oil spills, nuclear disasters, global warming. Yet few of us are called to save the world on such a magnificent scale. Most of us are called to reach out to the handful in our midst. Sometimes this is as simple as visiting sick people in our community. Rabbi Harold Kushner comments:

> At some of the darkest moments of my life, some people I thought of as friends deserted me—some because they cared about me and it hurt them to see me in pain; others because I reminded them of their own vulnerability; and that was more than they could handle. But real friends overcame their discomfort, and

14. See DATA.org

15. Editorial, "Bono's Thin Ecclesiology."

16. This is a primary insight of Liberation Theology.

came to sit with me. If they had no words to make me feel better, they sat in silence (much better than saying, 'You'll get over it,' or 'It's not so bad; others have it worse') and I loved them for it.[17]

How will the Gospel's command to love one another transform our broken world? It may seem simplistic, but I believe the transformation of our world will take place as a result of numerous acts of kindness. These acts of kindness affirm our deep interconnectedness and water the seeds of compassion and joy. Mother Teresa said, "In this life, we're not called to do great things, only small things with great love."[18]

Love transmitted from person to person in acts of service has the power to transform our families, our communities, and our world. Love transformed Jesus' disciples and planted seeds that blossomed into a movement greater than anyone could have imagined.

A Montanan minister of German descent told this story: World War II was over and he was alone in a bombed out building in Germany, tortured by extreme hunger. He was thirteen. An American soldier drove up and offered him a ride. The boy was fearful and suspicious but had run out of options, so he went along in the GI's jeep. Along the way to a nearby shelter, the American soldier was gracious toward his young German passenger, could see he was hungry, and offered him a bagged lunch with an apple and sandwich. This experience transformed the boy. He had been indoctrinated to believe Americans were brutish, degenerate, and inhospitable. When he experienced the opposite it challenged years of Nazi propaganda. The young officer had no idea that his simple act of charity was having a huge impact. The G.I. had just done what had come naturally and attended to the situation at hand with his God-given humanity.

As a result of the experience that German boy learned English and became a Christian minister in rural Montana. One kind American transformed the boy's worldview and future.

CHRISTIAN SERVICE NOT GRAND OR GLORIOUS

In light of profound challenges facing the world, we may become discouraged about our relatively insignificant attempts at social justice and activism. But Christian service doesn't have to be dramatic or glorious.

17. Kushner, *When Bad Things Happen*.
18. PBS, "Mother Teresa."

Christian service doesn't require giving up a job and going into the mission field in Guatemala or Mongolia. It doesn't require putting everything on hold and volunteering service in a foreign country. There are many inspiring examples of radical calls to service. Yet Christian service is often expressed in the smallest ways.

Disciples of Christ preacher and writer, Fred Craddock, said we sometimes assume responding to the call to serve is like taking a thousand dollar bill and laying it on the table: "Here I am, God. I'm giving it all." In reality, though, God sends us to the bank and has us cash in those thousand dollars for quarters. We go through life spending twenty-five cents here and fifty cents there: listening to the neighbor kid's troubles instead of saying "get lost;" giving a cup of water to a shaky old woman in a nursing home; caring for children in a homeless shelter while their parents are looking for jobs, staying married and keeping the family together despite awesome challenges, seeing past peoples' projections and finger pointing to their underlying humanity. Service isn't grand or glorious. More often, service is a timely compassionate text message, a small gesture, or a random act of kindness.

Jesus proclaimed the realm of God was near, and he invited his followers to work for the fulfillment of God's reign in tangible ways. But when we consider all this entails—feeding the poor, clothing the naked, sheltering the homeless, comforting the sick, receiving the stranger, working for peace, appealing for justice—our natural reaction is to shrink from the enormity of the task. The charge is momentous. Our own efforts can seem puny by comparison. Where do we begin? Why even try?

There is this line in the ancient book of wisdom, *The Tao Te Ching:* "The journey of a thousand miles begins with a single step."[19] This reminds us not to focus on the immense journey ahead, but to take it one step at a time. Often the humble act of alighting one foot in front of the other is all that's required.

Sometimes when we think of Mother Teresa, we think of the amazing missionary to the world's poor. But Teresa didn't intend to build a huge missionary society. She began where she lived, daily going out by herself to wash and bandage the wounds of destitute Calcutta street urchins. After Teresa bathed them with her hands she dressed their lesions and fed them. That's all she did for more than a year. Later people joined her efforts and together created a missionary society.

19. Tzu, *Tao Te Ching*, Chapt. 64.

Jesus declared the realm of God doesn't start on a grand scale. It starts out small. It all begins with something no larger than a mustard seed. The tiniest of all seeds grows into a tree large enough for birds to nest (Matthew 13:31–32; Mark 4:30–32; Luke 13:18–19).

Desmond Tutu, the black Episcopalian Archbishop of South Africa who won the 1984 Nobel Peace Prize for his ongoing nonviolent struggle against Apartheid, was asked to recall his formative experiences. Tutu replied, "One incident comes to mind immediately. When I was a young child I saw a white man tip his hat to a black woman. Please understand that such a gesture is completely unheard of in my country. The white man was an Episcopalian bishop and the black woman was my mother."[20] This small act of kindness planted the seed in young Tutu's mind to become an Episcopalian minister and eventually to become a bishop.

In his memoirs the great Anglo-Irish poet and playwright Oscar Wilde (d. 1900) told of being brought from prison, where he was held after being found "guilty of homosexuality." He wrote . . .

> When I was brought down from my prison between two policemen, a man I know waited in a long dreary corridor so that, before the whole crowd, whom an action so sweet hushed into silence, he might gravely raise his hat to me, as, handcuffed and with bowed head, I passed him by . . . I do not know to the present moment whether he was aware that I was even conscious of his action. I store it in the treasure house of my heart. I keep it there as a secret debt that I am glad to think I can never possibly repay . . . when wisdom has been profitless to me and philosophy barren, and the proverbs and phrases of those who have sought to give me consolation as dust and ashes in my mouth, the memory of that little lovely silent act of love has unleashed for me all the wells of pity, and brought me out of the bitterness of lonely exile into harmony with the wounded, broken, and great heart of the world . . .[21]

These two stories remind us God's realm can start with something as small as a mustard seed. Even a gesture as small and fragile as the tip of a hat can communicate the largest and most powerful of all realities—the love of God. Even actions as relatively insignificant as living in one place for more than ten years,[22] regularly buying produce from local growers,

---

20. Tutu, God 2000 Lecture.

21. Wilde, *The Complete Works*.

22. In his book The Unsettling of America, Wendell Barry writes that the average amount of time a North American lives in one place is five years, as compared with

supporting alternative energy,[23] and making socially responsible investments all have ripple effects. Perhaps the seemingly less significant acts, such as actively listening to a loved one just when it's most needed, creates the most life-changing ripples. When the ripples multiply they can change the world!

Fred Craddock relays the following sentiment . . . The mustard seed is easily dismissed or overlooked as inconsequential. We think it takes something impressive and large to grow a tree. Surely it takes more than we've got to make big things grow—more faith, more courage, more skill, more time. We turn our pockets inside out and say, "See, nothing here." To which God replies, "look again. There in the fold of the pocket, nestled in the dust, is a mustard seed that may remain tiny and of little consequence. But if we plant it, God can use it and it will grow beyond anything we can envision." The realm of God starts out small so we won't shrink from the enormity of the call.

We can no more bring about the dominion of God than we can make a tree grow. The parable of the mustard seed isn't a credo for the positive thinker. Jesus doesn't say we can do some big things, or big things with God's help, but that God can do big things, even establish dominion on earth, if we dare to plant the minute seed entrusted to us.

 My wife and I recently sponsored a thirteen year old girl named Delia from Bolivia through World Vision. This is no huge investment—only thirty-five dollars a month to sponsor a child—what amounts to approximately a dollar a day. Yet, somehow, in some minute way, we are adding one more drop of compassion to the parched earth of the developing world. All those drops add up and sustain families that otherwise would face more dire circumstances. It sometimes does feel utterly insignificant to make such a gesture. It's a drop in the bucket cynics would say . . .

It only takes a tip of a hat to inspire a life of service. May those who have ears to hear, hear.

---

forty years at the turn of the century. When we're only in a place for a short period of time, we aren't going to be that invested or care about the local politics, agriculture, environment, and community organizations. We're just passing through, so there's no motivation to care and to get involved. So, just committing to stay in one place for an extended period makes a big difference.

23. When it comes to alternative energy, it behooves the United States and other nations to look to Germany. Their utilization of wind and solar energy holds great promise.

DOWNWARD MOBILITY

"Jesus, being in very nature God, did not consider equality with God something to be used to his own advantage; rather, he made himself nothing, by taking the very nature of a servant" (Philippians 2:6–7a, NIV). Christian author, Henri Nouwen, popularized this gospel concept with the phrase "downward mobility." We're called to this same downward mobility, from whatever privilege we enjoy to solidarity with the least of these.

God came down to our level to be in solidarity with us. Downward mobility is characteristic of God's human incarnation. When downward mobility becomes characteristic of our lives, we accelerate our chances of seeing Jesus.

Mother Teresa's daily question to her sisters of charity was, "Have you seen Jesus today?" In a PBS Documentary on Mother Teresa, a sister relayed when she finally saw Jesus. She was bathing the wounds of one of the poorest of Calcutta's street urchins, then she met Jesus' eyes—the heart of Christ, which shatters all words and leaves them as dust. The sister was enchanted by the heart of the world looking back at her, disguised in the form of a hapless stranger.[24] This nun experienced transpersonal mystical awareness, which sees Christ in another person (Matthew 25:40).

Eastern Orthodox Writers, like Florovsky (d. 1979) and Kireevsky (d. 1856) assert truth isn't attained by the isolated individual relying solely on reason, but can be discovered primarily through shared experience and communion. According to these authors, "The knowledge of the truth is given to mutual love." Communion with others taps into our common humanity. Submission to relationships and their invisible lines of connection transform us.

The Eastern Church understands God is essentially about interrelationship and inter-being. Everything is in relationship with everything else. The reason I am who I am is because of all that's gone before me. If it wasn't for the statistic impossibility of the Big Bang, I wouldn't be here. If stars billions of years ago hadn't exploded and released their gifts of heavy elements, I wouldn't be here. Decisions people made hundreds of years ago profoundly affect who I am today. Invisible lines of connection through the ages bring me to this moment.

I'm defined by my relationships. My relationships create the reality I call "Amos," especially my relationships with my family and friends. I'm different because of these relationships. They all affect me. Beings from the

---

24. PBS, "Mother Teresa."

distant past and present take me beyond my isolated ego into an interconnected swirl of molecules larger than myself.

We experience God in relationship and Jesus tells us we experience him uniquely in relationship to "the least of these."

NOT TAKING SIDES

Most people I know have a subconscious aversion to the destitute. This is precisely why Jesus asks us to move in their direction, stretching our comfort zones. Most people have an innate aversion to visiting people in prisons, nursing homes, and mental institutions. Successful people have an innate aversion to the poor and to convicts and to racists. They may speak otherwise, but their gut and their actions lead them in the opposite direction.

In Jesus' time everyone had a profound aversion to lepers. Nobody in Jesus' time wanted to get anywhere near a leper. That's why lepers were banished to the outer limits of the cities. And if a leper came near, everyone turned and went the opposite direction at best, or picked up stones and pelted the leper at worst.

We naturally identify with successful, beautiful people who seemingly have their stuff together. We side with authority figures, even when their motives and actions are questionable. On the other hand we tend to dismiss people labeled convict, Klansmen, derelict, or poverty stricken.

A colleague in ministry named Dave came into my office one afternoon and said there was a member of my church named Jan whom he asked to lead a Bible Study. Jan wasn't paying him proper respect. She was independent and doing her own thing. Dave asked me to stand by his side when he confronted Jan and asked her to step down as Bible study leader. He thought for sure I would back up his position and his pastoral authority in this matter. After all, Jan was a member of my congregation who needed to be reined in and to accept his authority. Dave was exasperated when I told him I wouldn't take his side or her side in the issue. Instead, I would remain neutral.

Factions in one church I served were dead set against one another. The two opposing sides were always trying to get me to join their team. They would come into my office and start complaining about the other side. They were startled when I stopped them and said "Friend, please don't talk to me about this person. If you have a problem with the person you should talk to him directly. You see, I'm that person's pastor too." This was frustrating! And the misdeeds of the other side would then be pointed out more adamantly. Again, I would calmly say, "This is between you and him. It's not my problem."

We too easily take sides, assuming the fault of the more disreputable people in question. Yet, often social status and reputation are just a façade. We jump to conclusions too easily. Sometimes the people we would least expect are the ones most culpable. Sometimes the people who are the least respected in the community have the most wisdom. For, most often, public failure is followed by greater humility and honesty, which are the hallmarks of the saints.

I think Jesus emphasized reaching out to the poor, because in doing so, we let go of our shallow social scripting, which blinds us to the humanity of the least of these. Our culture has an unspoken callousness toward poor, obese, and homely people. This is obvious from watching television, where the stars are almost always wealthy, thin, and beautiful.

The surprising work of southern writer Flannery O'Conner (d. 1964) stands out here. By the end of her stories, through various plot twists, we end up siding with the derelicts and looking down upon the proud, impeccably dressed high society. The point is not to get in the habit of taking sides too quickly. The point is to probe continually behind appearances and check assumptions at the door. The point is to observe and ask as many clarifying questions as possible, opening the doorway to understanding. Otherwise, we go through life with blinders on, never seeing the humanity beneath the appearances. This is the unassuming, high-minded, and unbiased posture Jesus exemplified. It's as rare as it is healing.

By serving the least of these, we serve Jesus. As this mystical reality sinks in, it translates into practical service to the invisible sufferers. As we live in solidarity with humans on the margins, we live in solidarity with Jesus' humanity.

The closer we get to Jesus' humanity the closer we get to his Divinity. This is the holy mystery of the Jesus Paradox.

CONCLUSION

Jesus said "beware of the yeast of Herod (Matthew 8:15)." What did Jesus mean by this? He meant to be wary of all systems of domination, especially those that disregard the least of these. Disregard for the poor and oppression were the benchmarks of Herod Antipas' (d. 40) rule. Like yeast, which raises the loaf of bread, the toxins of aloof oppression have a way of infecting entire nations with violence.

Jesus' words are a wakeup call for us who were born into the middle and upper classes and into the privilege that followed. Jesus' words move us from entitlement toward solidarity with the least of these. His words move us from the assumption that our middle class experience is normative to understanding it is just one experience among many, with numerous blind spots.

May we attempt to "beware of the yeast of Herod (Matthew 8:15)." May we see the poor! And may we exclaim in solidarity, "Don't walk behind me. I may not lead. Don't walk in front of me. I may not follow. Walk beside me and by my friend." The Alexandrian Mystics were examples of this approach, renouncing material possessions and property and living in the desert, where their peers refused to live.

The Alexandrian Mystics had no interest in competing with their sisters and brothers for scarce commodities. They were content with a level playing field—a brotherhood of plain robes, simple dwellings, and plain bread. More importantly, they valued a state of mind that knew solidarity with God and neighbor, with Jesus as their exemplar.

QUESTIONS FOR REFLECTION AND DISCUSSION

1) Do you agree Jesus is present in the humanity of the hapless stranger we find by the roadside? Does this make sense to you? Why or why not?

2) Do you think God's solidarity with humanity in Jesus should translate into our solidarity with "the least of these?" Why or why not?

3) Do you think social justice is central to Christianity? Why or why not?

4) Can you give examples of how social justice can take place on a small personal scale?

5) What do you think of Jesus' words, "beware of the yeast of Herod?" Do you agree with the author's take on these words? Why or why not?

6) Application question: Have you been in touch with "the least of these?" If so, explain the experience. How did the experience affect you?

1 2

The Foreigner

For Christians, God is defined by Jesus; he is not confined to Jesus.
–HOUSTON SMITH

In God's house there are many rooms.
–THE GOSPEL OF JOHN

GOD'S VISION IS LARGER THAN OUR COMPREHENSION

THE BIBLE DOESN'T SAY, "For God so loved *the U.S.A.* he gave his only begotten Son." It says "For God so loved *the world* he gave his only begotten Son" (John 3:16, NKJV). As reiterated throughout the Bible, God doesn't show favoritism (Romans 2:10–11). God isn't interested in blessing one country above others or blessing one religion above others. God's vision is larger than our human comprehension.

Jesus gave the essence of his teaching—to love God and to love our neighbors. Then someone in the crowd asked, "Who is my neighbor?" Jesus answered with the story of a foreign Samaritan of a different tribe and religion who aided a Jew and saved his life (Luke 10:25–37). This response was a jaw dropper to all, because in Jesus' day loving neighbors meant loving actual neighbors. Actual neighbors were members of the same clan, country, and religion. Kith and kin neighbors were the people we're expected to love. The term *neighbor* didn't include Amalekites, Jebusites, Philistines, Samaritans. Certainly not! Ancient Israelites were not required to love these foreigners. They could slaughter them if they needed.

Jesus' interpretation of *neighbor* amounted to a revolution of the heart. Now the neighbors we're called to love aren't just from our same clan, religion, and nationality. Now our neighbors include the foreigner, even the detested Samaritan. And loving the foreigner requires respecting their religion and acknowledging their access to God.

JESUS' GRACE EXTENDS TO ALL PEOPLE

In Acts 10:1–16, Peter dreams of animals he's forbidden to eat by Jewish law. The passage doesn't get specific, but animals Peter must have seen are pigs, camels, rabbits, ravens, owls, etcetera. According to Jewish law, this assortment of animals wasn't allowed to be eaten. Then Peter hears a voice say, "Kill and eat." Peter's response: "No, these animals are nasty. I won't eat them." Then God says to Peter, "Don't call unclean what God has made clean." After this dream, Peter's ministry changes course. He begins to minister to "unclean" gentiles.

According to kosher laws all animals that have an abnormality are considered "unfit." Fish are meant to have scales and fins. So shellfish are unfit. Birds are supposed to fly. So, birds that can't fly are unfit. Land animals should have four legs. So, snakes are unfit. And the list goes on.

Jesus' inclusion of "unfit" people distressed his would-be followers and led to his execution. Like the Hebrew prophets, Jesus proclaims that God's realm comes on earth as in heaven when widows, orphans, homeless, and alcoholics are shown compassion. The world is thirsting to hear that through Jesus God's love reaches out to all. God's heart is bigger than we imagine. *Indeed!*

Could it be that God's vision includes other forms of revelation aside from God's human form? Is there salvation apart from faith in Jesus? Over the centuries Christianity's exclusive claim to salvation was accepted without question. But there's a conflict within the New Testament as to Christianity's relationship with other faiths. In Acts, Peter says of Jesus "There is salvation in no one else (but Jesus), for there is no other name under heaven given among mortals by which we must be saved" (Acts

4:12).[1] Later in Acts after Peter has the dream of the "unfit" animals he gives a radically different attitude toward non-Christian religions: "God has shown me I should not call anyone profane or unclean . . . I truly understand God shows no partiality, but in every nation anyone who fears God and does what is right is acceptable to God" (Acts 10:28b, 34–35). This Jewish view is also expressed in Romans, where Paul says righteous Gentiles will be judged by their own consciences when they meet their Maker (Romans 2:10–11, 14–16).

From Christianity's beginning there was a significant body of opinion that righteous, God-fearing Jews and pagans would be saved. Again and again in the Gospels Jesus' infinite grace extends to all people, including those of other religions.

GRACE TOWARD OTHER FAITHS

The Second Vatican Council and Mainline Protestant Christianity advocate graciousness towards other faiths. For example, many Catholics support a document entitled *Reflections on Covenant and Mission*, which pronounces, "Jews no longer have to convert to Catholicism. They have their own covenant with God."[2] Such affirmations offer hope.

In the New Testament Paul insists the covenant God made with Abraham and Israel can't be taken back: "For the gifts and the calling of God are irrevocable" (Romans 11:29). Paul's letter to the Romans also strongly suggests there are two separate covenants for Jews and Christians (Romans 11:25–36). It seems Paul turns his missionary efforts to the Gentiles and away from the Jews because God already honors a covenant with Israel.

God's vision goes beyond a select group of *chosen people*. It's not about God blessing a particular group. God's vision matches God's love shown in Jesus—it embraces the whole human family, even Gentiles, even foreigners of other religions.

Jesus has the audacity to claim God's preferential treatment is not always to Jews (Luke 4: 24–30). In fact, Jesus announces Elijah the prophet wasn't sent to one of the many Jewish widows of his time. Instead Elijah was sent to a foreigner, to a widow in the region of Sidon (vs. 25–26). Jesus then announces that the prophet Elisha didn't choose to cleanse one of the

---

1. This exclusive scripture is reiterated in John 14:6: "No one comes to the Father (God) but by me." And again in 1 John 5:12: "He who has the son has life; he who has not the son of God has not life."

2. Preston, "Catholics Will No Longer Seek to Convert Jews."

many Jewish lepers of his time. Instead, he healed the foreigner Naaman from Syria (vs. 27). These words infuriated Jews who saw themselves as the chosen people. "What? God's grace includes foreigners?! You crazy deluded Nazarene!" The Jews were so infuriated by Jesus' words about Elijah and Elisha that they tried to kill him (vs. 28–29).

To this day Christian fundamentalists are infuriated by claims that God shows favor to non-Christians. But throughout the Bible God is often revealed to foreigners—to non-Jews, to non-Christians. Another example is the foreign king Abimelech, who receives a vision from God (Genesis 20:3–7).

"My eye is not the only eye. My religion is not the only religion." These realizations mark the awakening from ego's stupor. At its best religion is the final frontier of the ego.

When Jonah realized the love of God is broader than the measure of the human mind and that God loves and cares for the entire human family, he became furious. In fact when Jonah realized God wasn't going to inflict wrath on the foreign people of Nineveh, as God had originally implied, Jonah became "so angry I wish I were dead" (Jonah 4:9–11).[3] Jonah, like many, was fixated on God's preferential treatment of a select few. When God's grace moved beyond the usual bounds Jonah became angry.

Mother Teresa served all, yet was personally ignited by the Gospel. This is the model for the contemporary saint. Mother Teresa adored her Catholic faith, which empowered her outreach to the poorest of the poor. She didn't insist the poor hear the Gospel and accept Jesus as their savior before she bathed and dressed their wounds . . . Jesus didn't say "When I was hungry you preached to me, and then fed me." He said "When I was hungry you fed me" (Matthew 25:35). Mother Teresa didn't care exclusively for people of her own faith, as some denominations do. She ministered to everyone she met in need: Hindu, Muslim, Sikh, Buddhist . . . This is the Gospel spirit of Christ. This is the Divine origin of Christian faith. Other exclusive attitudes are of human origin.

Walter Wink writes that God's work in the world is about "abandoning egocentricity not only as individuals, but as cultures, as nations, even as a species, and voluntarily subordinating our desires to the needs of the total life system."[4] I would add religions in general and Christianity in particular must abandon their egocentricities. The Jesus Paradox is a giant step in this direction.

---

3. Also see Jonah chapters 3 and 4.

4. Wink, *Engaging the Powers*, 97.

The Jesus Paradox, as defined by the Alexandrian Mystics, claims God isn't available to any human being in the unlimited and unqualified sense. As soon as God takes on form and/or language, God is limited. So, the language of religion is both necessary and limiting. In every religion there remains the ineffable unlimited essence that's only apprehended in silence and mystical experience. And every religion has forms of faith that require humor. When the forms become humorless, grace becomes sawdust in the mouth.

LOVE BEYOND CONVENTIONAL BOUNDARIES

Many will reject Jesus as understood by the Alexandrian Mystics. Yet Jesus' love does in fact move beyond the conventional boundaries, even those of religion. At some point religious traditions peek out beyond their accepted norms into the great mystery. Ironically, when religions loosen their rigidly held norms they become more powerful vehicles for transformation.

Jesus is my anchor. He's my true North. He's my point of departure and my point of return. I affirm Jesus' resurrection, not just as a tenet of faith, but as a reality in my own life. I have experienced the resurrection of the mind through centering prayer and it's made all the difference. The resurrection convinces me there's a power in the universe so great nothing can overcome it, not even death. Human beings try to put Jesus' infinite transformative power in a box. But ultimately the love of God in Christ transcends any and all limitations we try to impose. Jesus is at the center of my devotion and life. Yet I feel no need to take the next arrogant step and say any who don't claim Jesus as Lord are damned. And Saint Paul didn't say those who don't claim Jesus as Lord are damned.

Each day I reaffirm my love for my spouse. And each day I reaffirm my love for my Redeemer. It says in Romans 10:9, I am saved by faith in Jesus. This isn't a onetime thing but an ever-deepening relationship. My ever-deepening intimacy with Jesus through reflection and prayer is enough for me. Redemption for Christians is acknowledgement of Jesus' resurrection and lordship, followed by ever increasingly intimate relationship. Humility keeps me from making more superlative claims. I can't place limitations on God's grace. I can't presume to exclude foreigners from access to God. This may be easier on my egoist mind, but it is not true to the inclusive love of Christ found in the Gospels.

The fundamentalist mindset claims a hold on God in the ultimate unqualified sense, revealed exclusively to one group. If this exclusive picture of God is threatened, one feels God is being threatened. Yet, God's security is not so easily threatened. The Maker of heaven and earth can handle whatever we dish out.

At this point the Evangelical will step in and say, "Amos, I've been with you this far and pluralism is a great idea, but it's utopian. Ultimately, you're advocating watered-down religion that requires Christians to butcher the scriptures. There's no way interfaith dialogue can cohere with Christian scripture. Let's agree to disagree; I'm going my way and you go yours." I respect this stance. It has integrity. And "let's agree to disagree" is better than "burn in hell."

I acknowledge some scriptures, such as John 14:6, pose challenges: "I am the way, the truth, and the life. No one comes to God except through me." The Evangelical will point out the matter-of-fact clarity of those words "no one comes to God except through me (Jesus)." Yet, I maintain scripture isn't the problem. The narrow interpretation of scripture is the problem. The way I interpret John 14:6 is that the way of self-surrender, the way of joy, the way of forgiveness, the way of love, the way of suffering (the ways of Jesus), are the truth and the life. And people come to God through these ways of Jesus. At this point the Evangelical will ask what about Acts 4:12, John 3:3, and John 3:7? I concede my security doesn't ultimately depend on narrowly defined scriptures. My security depends on the spirit of Christ revealed in the Gospels, which is super-charged with God's all-inclusive love. Jesus as revealed in the earliest Gospels is the center of the tradition. Apostles like Paul, Peter, and John have a prominent place, but they're church builders. They're not God's human incarnation.

The New Testament authors were divinely inspired, yet culturally conditioned. Their intermittent exclusive claims reflect limited cross-cultural awareness. The current generation of Christian witnesses can have an emphatic love of Jesus, minus the narrow cultural conditioning and exclusive claims of our forbearers. In his book *Things Hidden: Scripture as Spirituality,* Richard Rohr talks about scripture in terms of wilderness wandering. For Rohr scripture is a "three steps forward and two steps back" experience.[5] The Gospel accounts of Jesus' life, death, and resurrection are three giant steps forward. The exclusive claims of later church interpreters are two steps back. Jesus as revealed in the earliest Gospels is my measuring rod for the New Testament and the Bible in general.[6]

5. Rohr, *Things Hidden.*

6. The Synoptic Gospels are Matthew, Mark, and Luke. The reason why Jesus, as revealed in the Synoptic Gospels, is my measuring rod for Scripture is because A) The Gospels most directly address the life, death, and resurrection of Jesus and B) They

Whatever conforms to Jesus in the earliest Gospels, I accept. Whatever doesn't, I question.

Jesus is the unique human form of God—one aspect of the Trinity.[7] Jesus isn't the whole ball of wax. As Houston Smith reiterates, "For Christians, God is defined by Jesus; he is not confined to Jesus."[8]

RESPECT FOR OTHER WORLD RELIGIONS

How broadly do we draw the Christian circle? Who is inside the circle? Who is outside the circle?

I have come to see these are the wrong questions. The right question is "Who is in the center?" If Jesus is in the center then draw the boundary lines wherever you please. The primary point is that Jesus remain at the center. Jesus will work with us wherever we are. And Jesus' circle includes the whole world, even if our circle is more limited.

Can we have an unswerving veneration for Jesus as understood by the Alexandrian Mystics, while exhibiting humble respect for other religions? Some have chosen this path, but their approach is so academic they lose the common reader.

Meanwhile the broad, folksy appeal of evangelicals continues to grow, even though evangelical foundations often lack introspection and depth. The truth is most evangelicals don't want to exercise healthy skepticism or question the assumptions of their faith. As author Mark Noll laments, "The scandal of evangelical mind is that there is not much of an evangelical mind."[9]

The characteristic lack of introspection among evangelicals gets scary when negotiations for a peace settlement between Israel and Palestine are viewed as a betrayal of end times prophesies. Such extreme distortions were prevalent in the highly publicized outrageous remarks

were written earlier than John and are thus closer to the source. I believe Matthew and Mark were most likely written by eyewitnesses. I base this observation on Carston and D'Ancona's book, *Eyewitness to Jesus*. John (The Mystical Gospel) has equal importance, but not as a measuring rod of historic faith in Jesus. John's unique authority is expressing the mysticism of the early church. The Gospel of John rockets us from "Jesus eats the Passover meal" to "Jesus is the Passover meal;" from "The Torah is the Word of God" to "Jesus is the Word of God."

7. See *Trinity* in glossary.

8. Smith, *The Soul of Christianity*, 16.

9. Noll, *The Scandal of the Evangelical Mind*, 3.

of Pat Robertson and Jerry Falwell. And the garden variety distortions are prevalent among uninformed evangelical pundits on television and talk radio today.

What we need is Christian faith with both passion and reason, where Jesus remains at the center, yet humility and tolerance are the operative words. In other words, we need tempered certainty or paradoxical certainty on the one hand and appreciation for mystery on the other.

FAITH WITH HUMILITY

I acknowledge I can't know God in God's entirety. No human mind can conceive the unlimited expanse of space, let alone the molecular complexity of a single mustard seed. So how can we presume to understand the God who breathed the universe into being? God in the ultimate unqualified sense can't be pigeonholed by human minds. I concur with The Eastern Church's widely held understanding . . . According to Gregory Palamas, God's essence always remains elusive—only God's energies (or forms) can be known.[10] The essence, which is beyond names and forms,[11] can never be pinned down in any way.

At their best, religions promote their beliefs and practices, without critiquing other faiths. As to which religion provides the most direct path, there's only speculation (Cain and Abel argued over whose offering was more pleasing to God and Abel wound up dead (Genesis 4:1–18)). Humility will keep us from postulating along these lines. It will keep us from arguing like school children: "My dad can beat up your dad!" It's enough to find our own path to God and to walk it with humility (Micah 6:8b). It is enough to find our own spiritual mothers and fathers, without intimidating other sojourners' spiritual parents.

In a recent poll taken in the United States, only seventeen percent affirmed the statement, "My religion is the only true religion."[12] So parishioners are drifting from Christianity's exclusive claims. This is a hopeful turn for interfaith dialogue. Yet our minds haven't caught up to this trend. The Jesus Paradox brings us up to speed, clarifying Christianity's place among world religions.

Jesus' most heinous crime to narrow-minded lawyers was his claim that people had access to God apart from the system of temple sacrifice.

10. Palmer, et al, *The Philokalia Vol. 4*, 376–77, 380–82.

11. Palmer, et al, *The Philokalia Vol. 4*, 414.

12. "Poll: Americans Shun Conversion Goals," 16.

Paul too was hounded and imprisoned for claiming Gentiles as well as Jews have access to God. Likewise, many Christians will claim The Jesus Paradox destroys the foundation of their faith by claiming people of other religions have access to God.

The lawyers of Jesus' day were blinded by spiritual pride. So too, many Christians today are deluded into thinking they alone have access to God—they alone are saved—that God's grace is limited. Jesus' inclusive love found in the earliest Gospels should be the measuring rod for Christian faith, not the letter of the law.[13] As Bill Coffin put it, "We worship the Word made flesh, not the Word made words." The Jesus Paradox is the most accurate lens I know for beholding the mystery. Of course, The Jesus Paradox is not the mystery. Jesus is.

Jesus claimed there's access to God apart from the temple and its system of sacrifice. Paul claimed that Gentiles have access to God. Can we acknowledge that people who don't confess Christ's sacrifice also have access to God? *Absalutely*

JUAN GARCIA

The story of Juan Garcia . . .

A school bus careened off the side of Miller road into a lake. Lake water rushed into open windows and the bus sank. The children locked inside franticly pushed the exit doors. But the weight of the water had sealed them. A truck driver happened to pass by and saw the half submerged bus. He squeezed the air brakes bringing the truck to a screeching halt. His heart hammered and a light went on in his head, "This is why I took the alternate route. This is providence." Without missing a beat he got out of the truck, turned around, and reached under his seat. His fingers went right to the crowbar as they had that late January night when he blew a tire and almost lost control. This time he was steady and sure. His fingers wrapped around the cold steel. And like the best sprinters in the NFL, he was down the hill and on the roof of the bus in a minute flat. He got on his stomach and peered upside-down through the windshield to see where the kids were located. They were all in the back as the engine slowly submerged under water. He didn't have much time!

---

13. Universal atonement is the hallmark of the theologian Anselm of Canterbury (d. 1109) and is considered by Christian historians as legitimate an atonement theory as any other. Incidentally, atonement was never clearly defined by the ecumenical councils of antiquity.

He climbed down onto the hood. The tread of his boots grabbed a sticky spot. The water came to his knees. He took a swing: strike. He took another swing: strike. He took one more swing with all his might. This time the crowbar carved through the water and hit the sweet spot. The glass shattered under water—slow motion shards sailed through the water. This time he was up to his waist. Then, with adrenalin high, he pushed his huge body (lighter since his wife got him off carbs.) through the jagged window.

From there it was a blur. The crowbar was whirling, glass was breaking, and children were climbing out of three windows, clamoring onto the roof if they could. Juan told the kids to get to land. Two brothers, James and John, were the only children who knew how to swim. They got to shore and found a huge fallen branch from a nearby Doug Fir. They managed to swing the branch onto the bus' roof. Miraculously, every last kid shimmied along the branch to shore: thirty-six total. On the shore they waited for the truck driver. Within fifteen minutes the bus was totally submerged. They waited a few more minutes. Light was fading on the horizon. They turned to each other speechless, chests heaving.

Within half an hour a helicopter was on the scene and cars were lined up along the shoreline. The kids didn't know whether they were coming or going and didn't know what they were saying into the microphones pushed into their faces. They were in a haze. That night they got into the laps of their sleepless bug eyed parents and watched the 11 o'clock news. They found out the truck driver's name was Juan Garcia. He had a wife and three children. Juan was on his way home after a long haul. The sheriff said he didn't understand what Juan's truck was doing so far from the interstate. But, apparently Juan didn't take the interstate home, which would have made the most sense. He took an alternate route. The reporter recapped the story of a bus coming back from a field trip to a remote ranch . . . Juan had valiantly risked his life to save the children. But, while shoving his massive body through the broken windshield, he had impaled himself on a long shard of glass. His adrenalin lasted until the last kid was safely out of the bus. Then Juan passed out from blood loss and drowned.

Three days passed. Then on the same Saturday night, James, John, and Mary all dreamed they saw Juan in the wee hours. Mary claimed Juan had walked into her room and laid his palm on her forehead. She even claimed Juan ate a sandwich in her presence. Her parents were concerned but the psychologist said such apparitions were normal after such a trauma.

In time with the help of their parents, James, John, Mary, ar others commissioned the school for a Juan Garcia Memorial Garden. Aₙ over the years, these twelve children honored Juan's memorial with flowers on the day of his death and on the third day when Juan had appeared to them. The other twenty-four kids all but forgot about Juan. Some school children remembered the name of the man who rescued them from their sinking bus. Other school children didn't remember the name of their rescuer, yet were saved nonetheless.[14] Years later, Juan's family humbly stated the memorial to Juan, and the eleven kids who honored it, warmed their hearts. They said Juan was a humble man and he would've been honored by their tribute. The fact that twenty-four kids forgot who saved them didn't seem to bother the Garcia family (Matthew 6:3).

JESUS' REDEMPTION NOT MOUTHED BY ALL

As John's first letter states, "Jesus . . . is the atoning sacrifice for our sins, and not for ours only but for the sin of the whole world" (1 John 2:2). When Jesus died he didn't die for a select few who acknowledge him as redeemer. He died for the transgressions of all.[15] Jesus is the redeemer of humanity, yet this truth doesn't need to be mouthed by all people the world over for its validation.

God showed infinite humility in becoming human. So it behooves the Christian community not to insist Christianity is the only way. Christians show humility by being content with the conversion of over one third of the world's population to Christianity.

Thomas Aquinas, the giant of Western theology wrote, "Simply and absolutely speaking, God could have freed us otherwise than by Christ's passion, for nothing is impossible with God."[16] Indeed, for God nothing is impossible. God has the power to reveal God's self to the human family in copious ways beyond our imagination.

Salvation isn't through Jesus alone. Salvation is relationship with God. I have a personal relationship with God through God's human form: Jesus. This is my redemption. Other world religions encourage relationship with God in other ways. Yet, it's foolish for me to try and speculate how God is revealed to other religions. It's up to believers of the world's

14. As Cyril of Alexandria put it, "Jesus graced everything under heaven with the economy of the incarnation" (Cyril, *On the Unity of Christ*, 132).

15. See Girard and Freccero, *The Scapegoat*.

16. Aquinas, *Summa Theologica*, Volume III q.46 a.2.

religions to define the particular ways God is revealed to them and to their respective faith communities.

The affirmation that all humans have access to God is the direct implication of Jesus' love in the Gospels—a love reaching out to Gentiles and Jews, slaves and free, men and women, Samaritans (foreigners), prostitutes, lepers, thieves, and extortionists (tax collectors). Also I'm convinced that denying others access to God is a giant step in the process of dehumanization, which leads to the justification and execution of violence.

ALL HUMANS MADE IN GOD'S IMAGE

Three Orthodox Christian monks were arguing about when to do the morning prayers. Traditionally the morning prayers are offered at dawn. But "dawn" was too vague. They wanted precision. They wanted to know which stage of twilight was appropriate for prayer. So the first monk said, "The time for morning prayer will come when you can tell the difference between the fig tree and the olive tree." The second said, "No, the time for morning prayer will come when you can distinguish a horse from a donkey." After a long pause, the third monk said, "The time for morning prayer will come when you look into the face of a stranger and see a sister or a brother . . ."

In our shrinking global village, we're all inter-dependent. To survive, we can no longer think in terms of "our clan, our kin, our religion, our circle." This is our death knell. Our ultimate concern is our whole planet and all its plants and animals.

Promoting peace is a job for the guardians of the world's sacred traditions who teach us each human being is made in the image of God (Genesis 1:27), and who teach us reverence and awe before a God too large to put into any corner or cubby.

CONCLUSION

In the prior chapter I ended with Jesus' words, "beware of the yeast of Herod" (beware of all thoughts and systems of domination). In this chapter I end with Jesus' words "beware of the yeast of the Pharisees" (Matthew 8:15). What did Jesus mean by this? He meant beware of any and all thoughts and systems of exclusion.

Beware of denying groups of fellow human beings access to God— the ultimate dehumanizing exclusion. Beware of the elitist Pharisees who want to separate themselves from common human beings and their common struggles, who worry about exclusive machinery like purity codes (Matthew 23:23–24) and the quantity of one's temple offering (Luke 21:1–4). What matters more is the condition of the heart.

Many outwardly appear to be inclusive. They say the right words and brandish the inclusive politically correct slogans. Yet in their heart of hearts they may reek of Ivy League elitism and haughty entitlement to exclusive privileges. I have nothing against the Ivy Leagues, except when they become a badge of entitlement and exclusion. The Religious Right may often argue for exclusive access to God. Yet beware of the numerous subtle gradations of exclusive yeast that infect our minds, inflate our egos, and prevent us from solidarity with our fellow human beings.

The Alexandrian Mystics were exemplars of inclusion. Their theology, rich in mystery, paradox, and humanity, perceived God's infinite breadth, which frustrates litigious exclusive dogma.

QUESTIONS FOR REFLECTION AND DISCUSSION

1) When we respect other world religions do we diminish our faith in Jesus? Why or why not?

2) Do you agree that for Christians God is defined by Jesus, but not confined to Jesus? Why or why not?

3) Do you think God's grace is limited to Christianity? Why or why not?

4) How does emphasis on God's human form humble Christianity and safeguard it against exclusive claims to God.

5) What do you think of Jesus' words, "beware of the Yeast of the Pharisees?" Do you agree with the author's take on these words? Why or why not?

6) Application question: Do you have a bone to pick with another religion? If so, why? Can the humility of The Alexandrian Mystics temper your judgments?

Part 6

The Christian Mystics' Love of God

13

The Holistic Mind of
The Alexandrian Mystics

The greater the tension the greater is the potential.
Great energy springs from a correspondingly great
tension between opposites.

–CARL JUNG

The intellect separates the inseparable.

–GREGORY PALAMAS

GOING BEYOND PAT, EASY ANSWERS

ONE YEAR I WORKED as a volunteer prison chaplain. I was assigned to juveniles who committed severe crimes that warranted adult trials.

While working with these juveniles I heard the same story over and over. The teens were brought up in single parent homes. Their mothers squeaked by from paycheck to paycheck. The lingering threat of being pushed out on the street was pervasive. There were no jobs available in the neighborhood. One day someone said "I'll give you fifty dollars if you deliver this package." Given their situation the lure was irresistible. Within months they were delivering packages regularly, carrying a gun, and caught up in the drug trade. Then they pulled the trigger and were convicted for murder.

By presenting these woeful circumstances, I'm not claiming these juveniles were innocent. They made bad choices and the appropriate consequence was prison. However, their situation is more complex than it appears and they're definitely not "all bad." They should've been able to resist the temptations. Yet their conditions exerted enormous pressures. And, as I now know, most crime is driven by the desperation of poverty.

These juveniles are criminals. But, they aren't criminals, period, end of story. They're also victims of poverty. There are U.S. neighborhoods where opportunities to better oneself through decent work are nonexistent; where liquor is sold on every other block. This is a social crime. Yes, these juveniles are guilty. But, our society is also complicit in its disregard for the poor.[1] This is a complex world. Either/or answers won't do.

One time Jesus' opponents sought to trap him in his words, so they asked, "Is it lawful to pay taxes to the emperor or not?" At the time, the oppressive taxes of the Roman state were vastly unpopular. If Jesus had said, "pay your taxes," popular sentiment would've turned against him. If he said, "don't pay your taxes," the State authorities would've charged him with sedition. So, Jesus asks for a Roman coin. They present him one and he remarks, "Whose head is this and whose title?" They respond, "The emperor's." Then comes the famous retort that confounded his detractors, "Give therefore to the emperor the things that are the emperor's, and to God the things that are God's" (Matthew 22:15–22).

 Jesus often evades direct answers because this isn't a yes or no world. When Jesus is asked by whose authority he teaches, he answers, "First let me ask you a question. Answer my question and then I'll present my credentials. About the baptism of John—who authorized it: heaven or humans? Tell me" (Mark 11:29–31, MSG). They were on the spot and knew it.

Whenever Jesus is asked a question in the Gospels he usually responds with another question. Jesus steers clear of litmus tests and ultimatums. Litmus tests include the question, "Are you born again?" It's a game

---

1. The fact that the United States spends more on its military than the next twenty-five countries combined shows our priorities. We would rather be the invulnerable superpower that controls history than the model society. We're more interested in power and control by any means necessary than with curtailing poverty within and beyond our borders.

of either/or politics that pins people down on single issues. The truth i more complex. We're in this world and the next. We belong to the Church and the State. Jesus is God and human with emphasis on the word *and*. For those with eyes to see and ears to hear we exist in both eternity and time. Either/or answers don't penetrate the truth. Jesus is God in human form with all the implied complications and subtle nuances.

One of my favorite Gospel stories illustrates Jesus' insight and holistic mind. It's the story of the adulterous woman about to be stoned to death. The authorities come to Jesus and say, "Rabbi, this woman was caught in adultery. What should we do?" The Law of Moses was clear: a woman caught in the act should be stoned. What was his response? Jesus' most reasonable response would be an argument against capital punishment: statistics prove it doesn't deter crime—the sixth Commandment states "You shall not kill," etcetera. Instead, Jesus begins scribbling in the sand. This may seem insignificant, but it speaks volumes. All effective leaders know how to step back from the fray and relax their reasoning faculties. In that meditative space, intuitive answers come forth that surpass reason. It amazes me that in the middle of such an intense macabre scene of angry men with stones in hand, Jesus had the wherewithal to step back and doodle. Then the brilliant flash of insight and the response comes . . . "Let he who is without sin cast the first stone." This is an answer that's so true it hurts. It sears the hearts of the would-be assailants, many of whom had visited a prostitute in their youth. One by one they put down their stones and leave the grisly scene.

The simple truth was she was caught in adultery and Moses' law sanctioned stoning. The deeper truth was more complex: compassion is the ultimate seal of God's action in the world and the men weren't guilt-free. This paradoxical understanding saves the day (John 8:3–11).

LOOSENING OUR GRIP

When we take our social role too seriously the first thing we lose is our sense of humor.

For ministers, wearing a robe or a stole on Sundays provides ritualistic breathing room. The role of priest can be put on for worship, baptisms, weddings, funerals, and then taken off again. I know some ministers who, figuratively speaking, wear their robe all week long—they can't pull themselves out of the role. Just think if, when you put on a pair of gloves, you couldn't take them off again. That would be horrible. The beauty of gloves is we can put them on when dealing with roses, then set them aside when we're massaging our spouse's back. Our roles are like robes or gloves that can be set aside.

Some of the most well-balanced and joyful people I know are multidimensional. They don't subscribe to just one role, but several. Sometimes these roles seem contradictory. I have a friend in New York who's a corporate lawyer by day, dressed in starched shirts and patent leather Italian shoes. On Friday and Saturday nights he's the drummer for a blues band, dressed in a t-shirt and torn jeans. I have another friend who is a straight-laced Christian minister during the week and a Harley Davidson riding leather-clad mamma on weekends. She looks up New Testament Greek for her sermons on Wednesdays and polishes her hog on Saturdays.

Jesus is multidimensional. He's the laughing Jesus, who reclines at table with misfits and oddballs (Luke 7:36–50). He's the fiery-eyed prophet who overturns temple tables and drives out moneychangers with a whip (Matthew 21:12). He's the compassionate one who weeps at the death of his beloved friend Lazarus (John 11:35). He's the ecstatic desert mystic who fasts and prays forty days and nights (Luke 4:1–2). He's the God-man who walks on the stormy sea (Mark 6:48). He's the healer whose electricity flows from his robes—one touch of the robe's hem and you'll come away whole (Luke 8:44). He's the baby born of peasants lying in the damp hay among barn animals (Luke 2:16). He's the young man who amazes scholars with his profound knowledge of Hebrew scripture (Luke 2:46–47). He's the wordsmith with the exquisite combination of words that evade the legalistic Pharisees (Matthew 22:15–22). He's the son who, at the point of death, thinks first of his mother's welfare (John 19:26–27). He's the self-disciplined master of nonviolence (Matthew 26:52).

Jesus was comfortable with all of these roles because, like God, he had a sense of humor. Spaciousness and humor characterize supple minds. They're also the traits of bending green branches. It's the hard brittle branches that snap. Hardened minds take extreme measures lacking all humor—jettisoning planes into buildings and bombing abortion clinics.

Humor is about widening the gap between stimulus and response. It's about creating space where there is no space. It's about juxtaposition. The Jesus Paradox says, "Yes, Jesus is God in human form," while leaving enough space to acknowledge the possibility of God's revelation in other forms. This is the magic of The Alexandrian Mystics, as comfortable with paradox as a giraffe in tall trees. This is the legacy of spacious minds, which see past the persistent dualisms to the creative tensions that hold opposites together.

I worship a God who is as broad as the outer limits of the expanding universe and as tiny as a mustard seed. I worship a God who plays with labels like sacred and profane and ultimately dismisses them in the woman at the well.[2] I adore a God who is beyond words yet contained in the word *Jesus*. I worship a God who doesn't take her different roles too seriously. I worship a God who whispers the infinite in one ear and the finite in the other. I adore a God who ascended into heaven and walked the earth. I worship a God who shatters my limited conceptions and opens me to awe and wonder.

SHADOW PSYCHOLOGY

Some of the most brilliant work of psychologist Carl Jung was on the human shadow. Shadow psychology illuminates religion.

Essentially the thirst for God is the pursuit of the everlasting, unchanging absolute. This thirst for God has a profound shadow side, unleashed in grotesque proportions on September Eleventh. The human psyche also has a vast shadow, which is its self-centeredness and skepticism.

So how do we take the edge off absolutist claims, which smother religion's torch and its torch bearers? And how do we take the edge off unbridled skepticism, which loiters in the human psyche? For me the answer is *Miaphysite* theology's exquisite symmetry, which tempers the extremes.

Author John O'Neil says even the most cherished strengths of character have a shadow. Dedication can become workaholism . . . Sympathetic joy can degenerate into compulsively drawing comparisons . . . Firm resolve can become blind rigidity . . .[3] Even the most cherished aspirations of the human soul can turn back on themselves and become twisted beyond recognition. This reminds me of the spiritual teaching, "Where angels are most, devils are most." This is certainly true of religion. The angel of passionate dedication to selfless service can turn into the devil of intoxicating absolutist zeal stopping at nothing to obtain its objectives. How do we

---

2. Jews of first century Palestine considered Samaritans unclean "half-breeds" who were the result of marriages with non-Jews. And in first century Palestine men generally didn't converse with women aside from their wives. Jesus broke these social conventions in his conversation with the Samaritan "woman at the well" (John 4: 5–42).

3. O'Neil, *Success and Your Shadow*.

keep the angel from growing fangs and horns? The answer is remaining anchored in Jesus according to The Alexandrian Mystics.

Jesus is the ultimate shaman, bridging the material world and the spiritual world. He's the nonviolent master who spoke the three most revolutionary words of the Bible, "Love your enemies" (Matthew 5:44, Luke 6:27, 35). He's the dynamic One, who shatters the false dichotomies of sacred and profane, us and them. The genius of the Alexandrian Mystics is their center of gravity: The Jesus Paradox.

The primal impulse toward absolutism is hardwired into human beings. When humans are consumed by base absolutist instincts they use anything, including religion, as tools to justify their obsessions. The travesty of religion is it's often twisted by domineering and controlling personalities. On the other hand, the unparalleled beauty of religion is its refinement by artists of the soul, sensitive and subtle, who touch holiness and fill the world with light.

Isaiah proclaims "Every valley shall be raised up, every mountain and hill made low; the rough ground shall become level, the rugged places a plain" (Isaiah 40:4). This is the power of the incarnation. The Divine Christ is brought low, taking the form of a servant. The human Jesus is glorified as no human being has ever been glorified—raised from the dead and venerated by roughly one third of the world's population.

Jesus did what the early guardians of fire did. The torch bearers took a raging force beyond human reckoning that flattened forests . . . They took this force and tamed it, domesticating it just enough to work for them, so it cooked their food and warmed their caves. The acquisition of fire raised humanity above other mammals in every way. Human pioneers took control of what every animal innately fears. When human beings acquired fire, its primal other worldly power was brought low. Fire was harnessed by humans: God became human!

Jesus tempers limited human inquiry and skepticism. He also tempers the all-consuming finality of God. Jesus zigzags between them. He weaves a tapestry that brings warmth and comfort to our frail humanity, and friction to challenge us to reach beyond ourselves toward God.

All things create a shadow. Fire warms our homes and cooks our meals. When untended it flattens forests, devours neighborhoods, and burns children alive. The greatest shadow is created by God. The Alexandrian Mystics understood this. Their genius understood The Jesus Paradox and its exquisite balance between Divinity and humanity which harnesses the shadow. In Jesus, the all-consuming fire of God found a human vessel where the families of the world could come and warm their souls. From there the mystics took some fire, lit their torches, and found pathways through labyrinths of existential darkness.

TEMPERED RELIGION

The Jesus Paradox tempers religious hierarchies with universalism, reminding us that ultimately God isn't limited or qualified in any way. This allows for mutual respect among world religions. This prevents us from taking hierarchical thinking to its tragic totalitarian end. This prevents us from thinking our race, class, gender, orientation, nation, or religion is superior.

The Jesus Paradox tempers universalism. It reminds us that the religious form handed to us has a built-in primal orthodoxy that can't be tampered with, without the risk of unraveling the whole tapestry. If we tamper with the basis of God's particular testament to Christians (God's human form), we twist our faith into something no longer recognizably Christian. The Jesus Paradox tempers God's universal eternal essence with God's distinct human form revealed in time. The Jesus Paradox tempers the infinite with the finite, the absolute with the relative. It sets rocks around the holy fire. It sets a human cloak upon the Great Mystery. It reveals eternity in time.

Only foods that meet certain nutritional standards are edible and nourishing to the human body. That's why the father advises his four year old not to drink paint. In the same way only ideas that conform to certain bare-bones standards of faith are nourishing to a faith tradition. That's why the mystics advise against both absolutism and relativism. If Christian faith loses sight of the central Paradox, Jesus, then our tradition is vulnerable to corruption. Then greenhorn Christians will drink the kerosene of fundamentalism and the paint of the new age. The mystics are clear. We can't undermine the relationship between Jesus' *full* Divinity and *full* humanity. The Jesus Paradox protects the two aspects, while loosely defining their dynamic interplay.[4]

4. Christ's Divinity and humanity are the key to the fundamentalist/new age debate. The economy of the incarnation keeps fundamentalism in check by always qualifying Jesus' Divinity with his humanity. The economy of the incarnation also always keeps new agers in check by qualifying Jesus' humanity with his Divinity . . .
This is precisely the point that will provoke fundamentalists and will incur their wrath. Because for most fundamentalists, Jesus is God, end of story. (Some Fundamentalists may take to a variation on the same theme—that Jesus is the only way to God.

Fundamentalism says Jesus is the ultimate reality. New age says God, who is beyond all names and forms, is the ultimate reality. The Jesus Paradox says God, who is ultimately beyond names and forms, came to us in human form.

utterly Divine AND utterly human

COMPLEX DYNAMISM

Miaphysite is dynamic, moving. This point caused ancient theologians to stumble. Many in the fifth century thought *Miaphysites* made Jesus out to be a fixed identity somewhere in between God and human, compromising both in the process. But the *Miaphysites* were actually talking about a dynamic interplay that doesn't diminish either aspect. The two aspects of Jesus are in creative and dynamic union, which can't be pinned down by the human mind. Jesus is a moving target. As soon as he does something utterly Divine (heals the woman who touches the hem of his garment) he turns around and does something entirely human (he curses the fig tree) (Luke 8:43–48; Mark 11:12–14).

The creative dynamism of the incarnation encourages creative thinking and doesn't succumb to this or that camp. *Miaphysite* encourages us to weave together the important points found in the extremes . . . Strings of thought are only imprisoned within this faction or that if we give our consent. I'm not sure why so many consent to being locked into *either/or, yes or no* pigeonholing. This dualistic standard of primetime newscasts divides us. As the great historian Jacob Burckhardt (d. 1897) was fond of repeating, "beware the terrible simplifiers." An example of this terrible

---

And here they will quote the passage from John, "I am the way the truth and the life, no one comes to the God except through me" (John 14:6)). Yet, this scripture shouldn't be taken out of John's context. John's second century church was trying to define itself over and against the Synagogue. There were many hard feelings because John's church was persecuted by the Synagogue. So, passages such as this reflect animosity toward the Jews, particular to the context of John's Gospel . . . "Hey, if you don't accept Jesus, you're damned! How do you like that?!" This passage is not in sync with the all inclusive love of Christ, reflected most clearly in the Synoptic Gospels: Matthew, Mark, and Luke.

Miaphysite gives the balanced view, which is more in keeping with the Synoptic Gospels—that Jesus is God in human form, not God in the unqualified sense. And here is where *Miaphysites* turn to Paul's words—that Jesus "emptied himself" in order to be "born in human likeness" (Philippians 2:7). The idea here is the second person of the Trinity must have laid aside some powers and activities in order to take human form. This isn't to say that God divests God's self of any Divine properties in Jesus (God's full Divinity remains in him). God simply limits God's own activities in the incarnation. This is referred to as "the economy of the incarnation."

simplification is that we are fond of blaming "the perpetrator." Yet, most often the response to the original offense is as egregious as the offense itself. A case in point are cop killings, when a police officer gets trigger happy and does as much or more damage than "the offender."

Here are some examples of simplistic either/or thinking that doesn't account for the complexity of a situation . . .

The well known writer Steven Covey gives the following story. One time Covey was on a train with a man whose children were completely out of control. The children were disturbing passengers, running up and down the aisle, pulling papers from passengers' bags, and wreaking havoc. Covey was disgusted that this man wouldn't lift a finger to take control of the situation or to discipline his children. He made some quick judgments: this man lacked personal accountability; he didn't accept responsibility for his children's behavior. Finally Covey said to the man, "Your children are out of control. They're bothering me and other passengers. Can you please take control of the situation?" The man replied, "They just came back from the hospital where we learned their mother died. She didn't make it through surgery. The rug has been pulled out from under us." He sighed . . . "That's why they're acting out. But, I know you're right. I need to rein them in." This man's response disarmed Covey and completely shifted his perspective. He no longer responded to the situation with annoyance and anger, but with sympathy and compassion. His perception was instantly transformed.

Here's another story about a basketball star. The star and a reporter were walking along a Chicago street when a homeless woman asked for some money. The reporter mechanically put his right hand into his pocket to pull out some change. Then the star stopped the reporter's hand and said, "Don't do that." He continued, "If the beggar can ask 'spare change please' she can also say, 'welcome to McDonald's. May I please take your order?'" The star's turn of phrase is clever but it's too quick. It is also dismissive of the complexities of homelessness. The star's response doesn't account for the fact that according to a group called Access (a campaign for mental health care) about forty percent of homeless people are mentally ill. In other words, there could be many reasons the person was homeless and begging, not just apathy or a lack of initiative. Mentally ill people can't hold a job at McDonald's or anywhere else until they get treated.

It's easier on our minds to make quick judgments. Then we're spared having to wrestle with complex issues of homelessness. It makes dealing with the homeless easier.

We so easily jump to conclusions about people's character, especially when tragedy strikes. Sometimes our worst assumptions are correct. Sometimes people make terrible choices that have tragic consequences. But things aren't always as they seem and I've found my assumptions are sometimes wrong.

Are our perceptions accurate? Self awareness and scrutiny will reveal that often the answer is no. Most people have distorted vision. I have distorted vision—inaccurate perceptions. I think I understand when I don't.

Often times problems in marriages and other relationships are a result of not listening deeply enough and not asking enough clarifying questions. We make quick judgments and assume we're right, when all the while there are gaps in our understanding.

I've come to realize that the most objective people are those who soberly acknowledge their own subjectivity, then take careful steps to compensate for their subjectivity (asking numerous clarifying questions, for example). The most dangerous people in our communities and world are those who are certain of their own objectivity—that they are right and everyone else is wrong.

BALANCE PLEASE!

The Jesus Paradox profoundly changes the way I think. After wrestling with The Jesus Paradox, the crown jewel of the mystics, I now acknowledge what I know while remaining humbly aware of all I don't know. I resist playing the role of judge and jury and bringing down the gavel. I also resist throwing my arms up in disgust. Like Jacob I wrestle the angels of truth (Genesis 32:23–34). Wrestling means I no longer settle for easy answers expressed in sound bites and either/or propositions beginning with yes or no. And I no longer settle for quick fixes, which only scratch the surface.

I don't think the political landscape is a labyrinth of gray areas, where ambiguity is so great that the jury is out indefinitely. Distinctions can and must be drawn in order to achieve personal and collective integrity. There's a temperate position in most theological and political debates that achieves balance.

People tend to see Jesus as either human or God, but not both at the same time. So too, people tend to swing from one side of a political pendulum to another. Finding the center is elusive, not only in relation to Jesus, but in relation to a broad range of political issues. There are black and white thinkers to the right and fuzzy grey area thinkers to the left. For the former, arriving at a centrist position that holds extremes in tension somehow admits defeat. It's a compromise of integrity. "We can't have it both ways." The grey area thinkers are more at ease when the jury is out and precise analysis and decisiveness is put off for another day; meanwhile issues affecting the planet's future are tabled. The endless gathering of data becomes another addiction, which puts off having to make the difficult decisions. Balance please!

Mystic theologians emphasize Jesus is fully God and fully human, not partially one and partially the other. Yet, in order to come to a centrist position, sometimes we're partially in favor of one polar political position and partially in favor of its antithesis. In this idealistic search we take the best of both worlds and try to weave them together. If integrated, the ideal of balance and symmetry will bear fruit in practical social and political debates, helping to weave creative solutions. It's not your way or my way. It's a creative alternative neither of us has thought of yet.

I'm not interested in wishy-washy slack positions. I'm also not pushing for one position to the total exclusion of the other. I want to weave the best threads from the one with the best threads of the other. Everyone does this. We can't be liberal in all areas of life. We conserve some traditional aspects of life to foster stability. We can't be conservative in all areas of life, without being in total denial of changes in the social, political, and environmental landscape.

Weaving a tapestry with the best threads of two opposing positions is often unrealistic, not because it's irrational—it is the most balanced and rational approach. The reasons it's often unrealistic are first, the center, which always carries a sense of creative tension and mystery, is less easily defined than the extreme positions. Second, many people won't budge on their entrenched positions.

The Jesus Paradox is about seeing past narrow and limiting positions to the shared interests behind those positions. My favorite example is Jane and Beth's fight over an orange. When clarifying questions are asked it turns out that Jane only wanted the orange peel to make marmalade jam. And Beth only wanted the flesh of the orange to eat. So they could stop fighting over the orange and they could each get what they wanted.

The Jesus Paradox is about looking beyond either/or binaries of the left brain, to the holistic vision of the right brain. Western civilization is hell bent on the dualistic left brain, which is careening over a precipice. It's the right brained holistic thinking of The Alexandrian Mystics which can heal the divide. It's always easier to stay in the comfortable scripting of a left brain biased society, which frames reality in terms of winners and losers, perpetrators and victims, guilty and innocent. It is easier to take sides, burn bridges and polarize issues. Likewise, it's easier to point an accusatory finger than to turn the searchlight inward. It's easier to fault-find and blame than to humbly confess one's own part in the problem. The road less traveled is mutual confession, expressions of regret, introspection, dialogue that models active listening, and bridge building. The road less traveled is idealism with teeth, love coupled with strength.

HYBRIDIZATION, COMPROMISE, RECONCILIATION

Cross-pollination and hybridization create resilient strains of thinking that hold up to the onslaught of Twenty-first Century challenges . . . Innovative and courageous thinkers help solve Twenty-first Century problems. Innovative people don't get sucked into red states versus blue states nonsense. They think for themselves.

If we're able to look at multi-dimensional issues from a number of angles, conceding the merits of seemingly opposing views, there's hope for the future. Beyond the dualistic quagmire there's a third way that transcends and includes the dualisms. Both diplomacy and peace require supple minds and dynamic faith. Entrenched views and static faith won't do. We long for a dynamic holistic approach. We long for the freeing and transformative Jesus Paradox.

The road to peace is often thwarted by unbridled nationalism. The Hindu nationalist who killed Mahatma Gandhi believed the Mahatma had given up too much to the hated Muslims during partition. The Israeli nationalist, who killed Israel's Prime Minister Rabin (d. 1995), believed Rabin was conceding too much to the hated Palestinians. Hardliners oppose collaboration—give and take. Yet collaboration is the road to integrity, wholeness, and peace. Adept and sensitive souls are capable of creative synergy reaching beyond mere compromise to collaborative solutions better than either party could conceive on their own. The one plus one of the incarnation, doesn't produce two. It produces an ineffable dynamic unity far greater than two! *Synergy*

Saint Paul advocated a ministry of reconciliation with God and with neighbor (2 Corinthians 5:19). Like Paul we're called to rely on words and dialogue instead of military arms. Essentially, Paul's conversion is a transformation from militant to preacher, from reliance on force, to reliance on written and verbal persuasion; from lethal finality to verbal communication and process (Acts 9:1–22).

The ministry of reconciliation starts with eyes that see God in all people. How can we behold other human beings with awe unless we first behold their divine origin? Human beings are created in God's image (Genesis 2:27). This is the starting place for mutual respect and respect's higher form: reverence. This divine origin or original nature keeps us from writing people off. Obviously this thinking has its limits, when dealing with lawless, boundary-less, and immoral people, like Hitler. Yet even the most reactionary and repugnant organizations have a shred of truth, if not in their ideology, then in the vehemence of their reaction to a perceived threat. There's always something to be learned when we dig beneath the surface of any personality, ideology, or organization.

We're called to love our enemies (Luke 6:27). Loving enemies means granting our political enemies their humanity. This was Gandhi's example when he shared tea with English military brass who were directly responsible for gunning down unarmed Indian civilians. This was Martin Luther King's example when he sat at table with avowed racists and segregationists.

The other day a colleague of mine said "We never know the burden someone is carrying." Beneath the layers of every person there's an unspoken load. There is an abusive parent, a scandalous secret, an unresolved conflict, a lingering loss. When we realize this, patience and gentleness naturally arise. Tyrants harbor the unconscious pain of estrangement from their own selves. Otherwise they wouldn't need to dominate others. Martyr personalities often harbor some form of self-hatred. Smooth and calculated control freaks suffer from deep unconscious insecurity. All people— sadists, masochists, control freaks, rich and poor, you name it, are afflicted. The Hindu saying is apropos: "The poor suffer on the street. The rich suffer in luxury."

ESSAY INFORMED BY THE JESUS PARADOX: EVOLUTION VERSUS CREATION

I hope the following essay jogs your own creative synergistic thinking. I don't necessarily want you to agree with my point of view. My hope is you'll creatively apply The Jesus Paradox's dynamism to your own thought process. Here I appreciate John F. Kennedy's sentiment: "It is better to debate an issue and leave it unsettled than to settle an issue without debating it."

Evolution versus Creation

There's a rift between *Creation* and *Evolution* in U.S. society. For many this rift spells the permanent departure of religion from science. Yet, I think there's the possibility for synthesis of *Creation* and *Evolution*. Either/or thinking is limited and problematic. Albert Einstein (d. 1955) once said, "Religion without science is lame, science without religion is blind." So let's sketch a synthesis of creation and evolution.

First, a number of authors have mentioned that the sequence of organisms in Genesis concurs with the sequence of evolving organisms as understood by evolutionary science. There's a bit of a discrepancy in the time factor. What Genesis tells us took seven days took billions of years according to evolutionary science. Yet, for me this isn't much of a discrepancy. It's easy to imagine that days for God can be interpreted as millions of years on the solar calendar. Second Peter says: "With God one day is like a thousand years, and a thousand years are like one day" (2 Peter 3:8). Isn't God ultimately beyond limitations of time and space?[5]

A Bible scholar in the seventeenth century calculated the beginning of time according to Biblical genealogies. He concluded the earth began at the year 4004 BCE.[6] Well, we know it takes longer than six thousand years to explain seashells in mountaintops or the dynamics of Grand Canyon erosion. So, it's impossible for a reasoning mind to maintain the medieval faith-fact that the earth began six thousand years ago.

Here, we come to an important question. Is the Bible a book of facts? Some would say, yes. But, I believe it's a book of poetic truth, not facts. Why else would the psalmist exclaim, "Let the floods clap their hands; let the hills sing together for joy" (Psalm 98:8). Did the floods literally clap their hands or the hills actually sing together? Why does Jesus say "If your eye causes you to sin, gouge it out" (Matthew 18:9)? Is this to be taken literally? If so, I'd expect to see more people with their eyes gouged in church!

For me, science can answer questions of how and when well. But it can't answer the question, "why?" Only religion can do that.

Back to evolutionary science . . . Currently, the field of evolutionary science is being blind-sided by one simple fact. If evolution followed laws of probability, we would still be at the amoeba stage now. In order for

5. In Genesis chapter 1: 14–19, the Sun and the moon, and consequently the "days and the years" were not created until the fourth day. So, obviously the first three "days" and probably the last four don't pertain to chronological time.

6. James Ussher, Archbishop of Amagh, Church of Ireland (d. 1656).

evolution to have taken place as fast as it did, there had to be numerous occurrences of up to seven catastrophic mutations in a single generation of species. The odds of one catastrophic mutation occurring in a single generation of a species' development are one in over a hundred million. The odds of having three or more catastrophic mutations in a single generation defy all laws of probability. Evolutionary scientists now realize there's a mysterious principle beyond chance pushing species to transcend themselves—to make quantum evolutionary leaps forward on a regular basis. Many evolutionary scientists such as Fred Hoyle and F.B. Salisbury[7] have shown that twelve billion years isn't enough time to produce a single enzyme by chance, let alone our current world with all its diversity. People of faith call the self-transcending guiding principle of evolution/creation God.

One final observation . . . In a biography of Charles Darwin I was struck by the fact that Darwin didn't have a crisis of faith on the basis of his observations in *The Origin of Species*. His crisis of faith had to do with his inability to reconcile himself with the death of his children. He simply couldn't fathom a God who would allow his children to die, for no good reason, before his eyes. How could a benevolent God allow this? Whenever I see a bumper sticker exaggerating the rift between Darwin and the so-called Creationists, I wonder how things would be different if Darwin hadn't lost his children and thereby lost his faith in the God of Christianity. We can't know the answer to this question, but I'm sure there would be less of a rift between science and religion today if Darwin's children had lived.

So I, too, lament the death of Darwin's children. I, too, don't understand why they died young. I also don't understand why religion and science had to part ways. As Teilhard de Chardin (d. 1955) and so many others have pointed out, each has so much to offer the other.[8]

---

7. Hoyle, *Mathematics of Evolution*.

8. The "Intelligent design" debate is another example of the polarization between creationists and evolutionary biologists. It's a more sophisticated polarization, yet a polarization none the less. The Intelligent design folks don't give enough credence to the irrefutable basis of evolutionary science. And they don't give credence to God's ability to work within the parameters of evolutionary science. For me, this is where the juice is—the scientifically unexplainable series of catastrophic mutations which allowed complex life forms to evolve so quickly (See Hoyle, *Mathematics of Evolution*). What's behind these quantum evolutionary leaps forward? My answer: The Holy Spirit!

MOVING BEYOND HAIRSPLITTING DIVISIVENESS

In Southern states during slavery days some African American churches separated members with a comb. If someone wanted to become a member they were required to run a comb through their hair. If someone's hair was fine they could run a comb through and passed the litmus test. Then they were allowed membership. If their hair was too kinky to run a comb through, they were sent to the church down the street.

Some Southern churches also employed the brown bag rule. If someone's skin was lighter than the brown bag, they were allowed membership. If their skin was darker than the bag they were barred. Such practices created ever more subtle divisions among an already divided people. This pernicious divisiveness is the hallmark of the infamous Jim Crow laws (1879–1950).

Divisions take place among people as a result of the most insignificant details. For instance, the Bosnian Muslims and Croats use the Roman alphabet and the Serbs use the Cyrillic alphabet. Otherwise the languages they speak are virtually identical. This insignificant cultural divide was a pretense behind Serbian violence and ethnic cleansing.

There were two Russian German churches in the town I served as minister. I asked why they worshiped apart. They were both Russian German churches after all. I was told one church had Germans who emigrated from Northern Russia and the other had Germans who emigrated from Southern Russia. Due to this regional variation, the German language they spoke was slightly different. So the two churches worshiped separately.

On any given day groups of people can exacerbate their differences and stereotype and demonize one another. Every day most married couples can find reasons to start divorce proceedings. It's easy to pick a fight. It is harder to humbly ask forgiveness, swallow our pride, acknowledge our fault, find common interests, and seek reconciliation.

I remember the story of a white minister in the South who marched in the Civil Rights Movement. After a lynching, this minister visited the widow of the man who'd been lynched. He held the widow's hand, read her Psalms, and they wept together. The next day that same minister visited the Klansman pending trial for the murder. An incredulous newspaper reporter waited outside the jail house for the minister. When he emerged the reporter asked the minister, "How on earth can you visit both the white supremacist murderer and the widow of the man murdered." He responded colorfully: "I am a Christian, God damn it!"

WITHHOLDING JUDGMENT
—HEARING THE OTHER SIDE

Polarizations and strict either/or propositions breed competition and violence. Solutions are found in complex thinking and bridge building.

May wild-eyed liberals, who've rejected all organized religion, become more conservative in the best sense of the word—conserving community, not just families in all their diverse forms, but communal faith. May wild-eyed conservatives loosen their grip on their convictions and withhold judgment long enough to debate the issues and leave room to be surprised, even astonished.

If we can withhold judgment long enough to hear the value in an opposing rant. If we can strain our ears for the cloaked truth, we've become ministers of reconciliation. If we can make room for the leper, the prostitute, the extortionist, the gang member with face tattoos, the arthritic uncle, and the beamer driving sorority sister, the sacred heart of God has seized us. It has taken us beyond the compulsive and tedious sibling rivalry that plagues churches and communities.

Often, people who're outwardly open and liberal, when pressed on deep-seated issues, are in fact rigid and uncompromising. And often people who're outwardly more structured and intolerant, when pressed, are in fact open-hearted. People who seem outwardly neurotic and broken often actually have it together. And people who seem outwardly pressed, plucked, and put together are often barely holding together their fragmented selves. People have numerous layers and when the layers are peeled back I'm often surprised.

My most fanatic friends have overreacted to growing up in extreme environments. One peer became reactive to his hippie parents whose radical openness (to everything from recreational drugs to an open marriage) threatened his sense of stability and security. In reaction he became ultra-conservative. Another peer is the opposite. Her extremely conservative background in Houston, Texas compelled her to swing to the opposite extreme of misguided utopian experiments, a strict vegan diet, and unbridled Northern California whims, which include giving all of her disposable income to her guru.

Balance prevents backlash. When sojourning down a particular path, there's a tendency in all of us to overdo. When I started riding an exercise bike three times a week, I started out going for half an hour each session and overexerting. I dreaded the workout fatigue in my thighs that followed. So, my good intentions waned, and then I abandoned the exercise.

When I began silent prayer I practiced an hour every morning. Soon I burned out. It was too much. Since then, I've gotten back into regular exercise and silent prayer, but now I give myself slack. At present I often exercise for short bursts, realizing the main point is habitual exercise. The same is true of Centering Prayer. I started with twenty minutes every morning and didn't worry if I occasionally overslept. Because of the moderation at the outset, now both practices have become habits as familiar as breakfast or brushing teeth. And as the months and years pass I periodically do longer prayer and exercise sessions. There's beauty and poise in temperance.

A friend of mine has a variation on the theme of moderation in meditation. When she can't bring herself to practice, she goes to her cushion and tells it her excuse for not meditating. When she does this, sometimes she is struck by how lame her excuse is, so she follows through with her intention to meditate after all. The breathing room she gives her practice contributes to habituation.

The Alexandrian Mystics convince me balance is the greatest wisdom. Passion is best expressed in a vital and energized state of mind, not in extremism and excess.

I'm glad I've lived in Berkeley, in the Seattle and Portland areas, in rural Montana and Washington, and in Tucson, Arizona. I've taken in the best elements of these liberal cities and conservative rural environments. And now, my home isn't primarily geographic. It's spiritual. My home is Jesus according to the Alexandrian Mystics. That root system anchors the entire tradition for me. It's the plumb line that sifts the many layers. It also happens to be the hard won root system of the Oriental Orthodox Church today.

With the crown jewel of The Jesus Paradox at my center, I no longer succumb to polarization. Beneath the numerous issues and platforms I see human beings, with many of my same vital needs and struggles.

The Alexandrian Mystics move us from excess to moderation, from extremism to balance, from dualistic consciousness to holistic consciousness. This doesn't mean settling for some status quo middle. As Leonard Sweet eloquently wrote me in an email: "Mystic roots don't meet in the middle; they hold the ends together, which ignites the fireworks."

The mind of the Alexandrian Mystics points to God, who transcends and includes opposites, who holds contradictions in creative tension.

QUESTIONS FOR REFLECTION AND DISCUSSION

1) What do you make of Smith's emphasis on moderation and balance?

2) Do you accept Smith's synthesis of Creation and Evolution? Why or why not?

3) What do you make of Smith's use of the phrases "holistic thinking" and "creative tension?" Do these phrases do anything for you? Why or why not?

4) Do you think when the dualism between Jesus' Divinity and humanity is reconciled in our minds that we're better equipped to reconcile divisions in society?

5) Application question: Is there an issue that needs creative resolution in your life? If so, can you think of ways to resolve it that are informed by The Jesus Paradox?

14

The Silent Prayer of
The Alexandrian Mystics

Practice stillness and know God.

–PHILOKALIA RENDERING OF PSALM 46:10

*Silence is God's first language and everything else is a poor
translation.*

–JOHN OF THE CROSS

THE MEADOW

W HEN I WAS GROWING up in Virginia, there was a large open meadow up the hill from my childhood home. Even though most of the
acreage in my neighborhood was well developed, the meadow was left
wild. After I climbed over a dilapidated wood fence and made my way
through a thick barrier of trees, tall green grass sprang, resembling an
overgrown alpine meadow. At night the sky above the meadow opened
into the great expanse. The distinct stars illumined the darkness as though

I was far from habitation. In the summer the fireflies added lights to the deep blue.

The meadow gave me the space I needed when my little house and family began to close in. As with all families, sometimes things got claustrophobic. At those times I headed out the back door and started the slow walk toward the meadow. When adolescent insecurities mounted and there was no outlet I started the slow walk . . .

After I pried through the wall of trees I would walk several paces then lie back against the thick grass. At first my thoughts raced, as they had throughout the day. Then, slowly my thoughts settled like particles of dirt floating to the bottom of a glass of water. If I stayed there the water became still, all the dirt settled, and the murky water of my mind cleared. Space between thoughts lengthened. My breath slowed. And a homesickness I struggle to articulate softened.

I was only yards from home, yet I had another home akin to silence.

EXCUSES TO DO NOTHING

A number of my peers are devoted to fishing and sailing.

I'm convinced the primary motivation for these activities is an excuse to do nothing—to just sit waiting for a bite—to just get carried by the wind. Rarely, in our industrialized world, are we afforded the time required for our minds to still—to settle into the desert quiet that fertilized the minds of the prophets—the minds of shepherds like David who wrote "God leads me beside still waters. God restores my soul" (Psalm 23:2–3).

Christian tradition, especially Protestant tradition, emphasizes revelation from scripture. Yet, at its root, revelation in scripture begins with silence. Silence is the fertile soil where God's word originates. To discover the revelations of scripture we expose ourselves to scripture. To discover the revelations of silence, we expose ourselves to silence.

In silence there is revelation—revelation about ourselves. We come to the frontiers of silence and we find a number of things. Some feel discomfort, some anxiety, some feel tension in their bodies, and still others feel emotional turmoil. And most will discover above all else the wandering monkey-mind and how difficult it is to still it. What we experience reveals something about our nature. The revelation of the wandering monkey-mind is itself a great gift of awareness.

When our mind finally stills and enters deep silences we come to understand more and more about ourselves.

CREATOR'S SIGNATURE

Our Maker leaves a signature, ever so subtle, in all of creation. For those willing to press beyond the uncomfortable frontiers of silence the letters of God's signature become more legible.

Silence can reveal our God-given name, the signature etched in the depths of our being. Silence is unique to each. No two people experience God's pregnant silences the same way, just as no two snowflakes share the same shape. Yet silence opens windows into the mysterious power that can transform all things: God in whom "we live and move and have our being" (Acts 17:28a).

Silence leads us into transformation and toward knowledge of God. God whispered a word in our ear at the beginning of time and continues to whisper it. If we listen long enough, that word will become audible. Then after fording river after river that word may even become embodied—embodied in our thirsty bones.

The prophet Hosea invites us into silent places where God's presence is most palpable: "I will entice you into the desert and there I will speak to you in the depths of your heart" (Hosea 2:14, NRSV). The desert symbolizes stillness and silence. It's free of the buzz of numerous organisms and habitation. The desert symbolizes freedom from thoughts and words.

The deserts of silence await us as they awaited Jesus, the saints, prophets, and apostles. "Be still and know that I am God" (Psalm 46:10). Be still and peel off the layers of who you're not, of who you thought you were. Find out what The Alexandrian Mystics call your *original nature*, unencumbered with images, words, thoughts, props. Your original nature is satisfied with the present moment and desires nothing that it does not already possess. Free from clothing and all artifice we can return to the Garden of Eden and walk hand in hand with God in the cool of the day (Genesis 3:8–9). We can let go of our habitual and compulsive clinging to sense objects, because we have something more luminous and deeply satisfying to behold.

SILENT PRAYER'S BIBLICAL ROOTS

Many Biblical scholars acknowledge that Jesus most likely followed in the Essene footsteps of John the Baptist. The height of Essene practice is to fast and pray for forty days and nights in the desert. The Essene fast requires not just fasting from food, but fasting from thoughts and resting in silence.

In fact, the only way a person can survive forty days without sustenance is to rest in silence. This conserves precious energy to sustain life throughout the fast.

It takes vigorous training to build up to a forty day desert fast. If we tried it cold-turkey we'd die. Those who fast for health reasons today understand if they fast too long, before their body is prepared, they can easily lapse into acidosis.[1] Essene practitioners built up to the forty day fast after years of preparation and training.

Jesus fasted (from thoughts as well as food) in order to build up to the forty day fast (Matthew 4:1–11, Mark 1:12–13, Luke 4:1–13). This fast is the central departure point of Jesus' ministry. After his fast from all food, sensory stimulation, and thoughts, Jesus was "filled with the power of the Holy Spirit" (Luke 4:14). We could say the Holy Spirit's presence is contingent upon this kind of fasting. Of course this insight has precedent throughout the Bible in the prophets of the desert, many of whom, like Elijah, were hermits. John the Baptist, Anthony of Egypt, and the Desert Fathers and Mothers of the third century were essentially hermits.[2]

Many Christians who practice silent prayer are aware of its ancient precedent within the tradition. Yet most Christians are not. This is unfortunate because silent prayer is where the high voltage electricity is that awakens and enlivens the nervous system.

Most don't realize Christianity has rich contemporary resources for the deepest forms of silent prayer. Thanks to the work of Thomas Keating, Basil Pennington, William Meninger, Thomas Merton, William Johnston, Joan Chittister, Richard Rohr, Cynthia Bourgeault, and others, many have been turning back to the roots of silent prayer in Christian tradition. My hope is that more and more will connect the dots of contemporary devotion to silent prayer and the mystic theology of The Alexandrian Mystics.

SABBATH TIME

The ancient Hebrews knew the importance of un-programmed relaxation time—time to refrain from all conventional work. In order to insure sacred time free from usual work the ancient Hebrews established a holy day; The Sabbath.

---

1. Faulty metabolism causes fat to produce acids which are released into the bloodstream. For more on fasting in contemporary context see Bragg, *The Miracle of Fasting*.

2. Jesus is different from all the prophets. He is God's unique human incarnation.

In American culture, Sabbath observance is the most ignored of the ___ Commandments.

What did Jesus say about the Sabbath? He said the Sabbath was created for people, not people for the Sabbath (Mark 2:27). He meant we don't have to get legalistic about it. If someone's ill, by all means care for them on the Sabbath. If a cow is caught in a fence, by all means, release it, even if it's the Sabbath. But, (and this is the point) Jesus never did away with the Sabbath. Jesus observed and honored it (Matthew 5:17–18).

In recent North American history, business owners closed shop and refused to conduct business on Sundays. Throughout the last century Sunday was treated as a Sabbath day. People spent Sundays with their families, had brunch, went to church, and relaxed in a hammock with a cold glass of lemon spritzer. On Sundays people spent leisure time in the garden, tending to their tomato vines and flower beds. It was a day for picnics and barbeques, for walking the pooch, and splashing in the pool. It was a time to hear a familiar Psalm or a song on the ukulele.

Now most businesses keep their doors open on Sundays. Clubs and schools hold meetings and galas on Sundays. Few are bothered. The conventional sense of Sabbath vanished. It has lost its hold throughout American cities, suburbs, and ranch lands. If we want a day of rest we'll have to create it. We'll have to value it enough to carve it out of our busy lives and hear the protests from family and business partners.

I strive for at least one half day a week for centering prayer, devotions, reading, and writing—no other commitments.[3] This day of rest is a lifeline. It's a key to holistic health—a time to counteract the incessant activity.

On the Sabbath the ancient Hebrews read Torah and rested from all physical work. The Hebrew notion of Sabbath made a profound impact on Western society. The two day weekend practiced by all industrialized countries has its roots in the Judaic Sabbath.[4]

Sabbath reconnects us with the burning desires of our lives. It puts our lives in perspective, and helps us discern what we in truth want to do with our time. "What are my priorities?" "Am I happy?" "Are my choices in line with my faith?" "What am I on fire about?" "Do I take time to serve?" "Is my life caught up with numerous insignificant details?" "Why am I doing what I'm doing?" "What is my life's mission?"

3. I carve this sacred time out of a very busy schedule, with a working spouse, children, and a more than full time job. I carve the time out because it's essential to my relationship with God, and it regenerates my spirit.

4. Cahill, *The Gift of the Jews.*

If we don't take regular time to cultivate our human endowments and get perspective, we may become ensnared in numerous commitments out of sync with our core values. Sabbath reconnects us with our most profound human endowments: conscience, self-awareness, creative imagination, and independent will.

Sabbath time is the Mary part of the Mary and Martha story (Luke 10:38–42). Martha was busy, multitasking to make it all happen. Mary simply sat at Jesus' feet, absorbed his words, and listened in stillness and rapture.

The fourth commandment is just as important today as it was to the ancients. The commandment is, "Remember the Sabbath day, by keeping it holy" (Exodus 20:8).

CENTERED, CALM, STABLE

My profession as pastor of a progressive church is demanding, to put it mildly. My vitality depends on daily, weekly, and yearly Sabbath time. My daily Sabbath is to use half of my lunch hour for centering prayer. My weekly Sabbath is setting aside a half day a week for prayer, reflection, reading, and writing. And my yearly Sabbath is a six to ten day Centering Prayer retreat. We all need daily, weekly, and yearly Sabbath time to recharge.

What Sabbath time teaches is we're more important than what we do. We're primarily human beings, not human doings. Are we a prayerful presence when things get stressful or are we bouncing off the walls like those around us? Are we a calming presence or an anxious one? We gravitate toward people who keep a sense of internal poise, who stay calm in the midst of life's storms. Centered people of faith inspire—people who are stable and anchored. Many minds are swept to sea when life gets unmanageable. We need rooted, grounded presence. Christians don't make disciples by evangelism and charity alone. They make disciples by the quality of their being—by the quality of their presence. "Are we centered?" "Are we calm?" "Are we stable?" "Are we always running around (often with little awareness) or do we have a sense of Sabbath?"[5] I don't think any of us can maintain a sense of Sabbath all the time. Yet the more we marinate in pregnant silences, the more thoroughly the flavor of that silence will permeate.

---

5. It's possible to maintain "a sense of Sabbath" even in the midst of a very hectic life, yet this is the graduate course in "a sense of Sabbath." First we simply need to slow down, take on less, and do everything with more attentiveness.

In the following pages I explore rest not just in the conventional sense, which has value in and of itself. Rather, I explore rest in the most profound sense—what early Christian mystics referred to as "resting in God." Through training we can attain complete respite from all thoughts and enter into an abiding and healing calm. Advanced stages of relaxation in silent prayer are far deeper and more therapeutic than sleep. I know this thorough personal experience, which is now gaining support through scientific experimentation.[6]

Silent prayer is the best way that I know of to experience profound healing rest, which eventually releases deep tensions stored in the body's nervous system and muscles. This healing rest is always available and calling us home to our *original nature*.

SILENT PRAYER

When I discovered deep collective silences in Quaker meetings, I knew I'd come upon something as profound and vast as the ocean. I wanted to go deeper into silence than the prescribed hour of silent worship allowed. So I practiced silent worship every morning for progressively longer periods. In the process I made numerous discoveries, which eventually led to my love affair with silence. Thomas Keating refers to silent prayer sessions as "heavy dates" with God. A "heavy date" with a spouse usually involves physical intimacy. A "heavy date" with God involves intimacy with God's most essential and primal being, stillness and silence.

Silent prayer is practiced by Quakers, Centering Prayer Practitioners, Prayer of the Heart practitioners, and monastic Christians from East to West. Western Christian tradition refers to silent prayer as the prayer of faith, the prayer of simplicity, the prayer of simple regard, and silent worship. It is also referred to as blessed stillness, watchfulness, and noetic stillness in the writings of the Eastern Church. Resting in God's pregnant silences is the mystics' common ground.[7]

"Resting in God" is a phrase Gregory the Great (d. 604) used to summarize the essence of silent prayer. This was the classical meaning of contemplative prayer for Christianity's first sixteen centuries.

Thomas Keating writes:

6. See Motluk, "Meditation Builds Up The Brain."

7. In all the world's religions silent prayer exists in various forms. These prayer forms are the foundation for deep and recurring mystical experiences, and for deeper and deeper intimacy with God.

Contemplative Prayer is the opening of mind and heart—our whole being—to God, the Ultimate Mystery, beyond thoughts, words, and emotions. We open our awareness to God whom we know by faith is within us, closer than breathing, closer than thinking, closer than choosing—closer than consciousness itself. Contemplative Prayer is a process of interior purification leading, if we consent, to divine union.[8]

Silent prayer begins with Jesus. Jesus says "Go into your room and shut the door and pray" (Matthew 6:6). In Jesus' day homes were simple, usually consisting of two rooms, with no closets or closet doors. The two main rooms of the house were usually bustling with the activities of a large family. So, in Matthew 6:6 Jesus isn't referring to an actual room with an actual door we shut.

"Go into your room and shut the door and pray" is a metaphor about closing the doors of the senses (not engaging senses of smell, touch, sight, hearing, or taste). Jesus speaks of closing the door to all sense activity including thoughts and imagination, to wait for God who is beyond thoughts, words, and emotions. This interpretation of Matthew 6:6, passed down through generations of mystics, is centering prayer's scriptural basis. In Matthew 6:6 Jesus gives basic instruction on prayer, which he invariably elaborated to his disciples. We wish we knew what the elaborations were. The Gospel of Thomas gives us clues.[9] Other scriptures say Jesus "prayed all night" or "retreated to a lonely place to pray" (Mark 1:45b; Mark 6:31, 46; Luke 5:16).

The writer Kathleen Norris tried to get some kids in a classroom to sit in silence. When asked to sit silently a second time one fifth grader retorted, "I don't want to!" He continued "It's like we're waiting for something, it's scary."[10] Silent prayer is not only scary. It's exceedingly difficult. On the surface, it seems simple, yet anyone who's tried it will attest to its difficulty. It's perhaps the hardest thing I've undertaken. Yet, it's also the most rewarding.

The nature of the untrained mind is like a wild monkey, jumping from branch to branch. The mind's always clinging to one thing or another. Rarely, will it let go of the numerous stimuli and settle into silence. Because of its distracted nature, the mind has to be trained to focus. This training takes time. A challenge is that training the mind is less tangible

8. Keating, "Method of Centering Prayer."

9. See *Gospel of Thomas* in glossary.

10. Norris, *Amazing Grace*, 17.

than training for a marathon or practicing a musical instrument. Training the mind is more primal and less concrete than other kinds of training. Because it's insubstantial and doesn't produce any immediate measurable results, the Western mind usually dismisses it as "navel gazing" or "self hypnosis." "Don't you have something better to do?" Yet, the mind is the root of our existence and our experience. Our state of mind is everything. So changing habits of the mind is powerful! At times it may seem insignificant—as if anything else is a better use of time. Yet, mystics the world over tell us this kind of training is the key for dismantling hidden addictions and is the key to freedom.

The Alexandrian Mystics retreated from all worldly affairs. They sojourned into the desert to behold blessed stillness. And Quakers (The Religious Society of Friends) through the ages have written that deep listening to God requires stillness and silence. We can't pray unless we pause and listen for the "still small voice of the Lord" (1 Kings 19:12b, NKJV).

GATHERED MEETINGS

From experiences of deep collective silences, Quakers are often led to speak to the needs of congregants at silent meetings for worship. Regular attendees to silent meetings for worship are often amazed at how Quaker elders can accurately speak to the circumstances of those present. When there's what Friends call a "gathered meeting" there's a visceral sense of God's presence. When a seasoned Friend is able to channel God's presence with some well placed words it can pierce the heart. During meetings for worship, a Friend's words have often spoken to my condition in a fresh and startling way. Sometimes all my games and pretenses fell away in an instant and the naked truth jabbed me in the ribs.

During these revelations, it's not the spoken words that open windows of perception and shed new light. Another person in the meeting may hear the exact same words and get a different message. The only way I can explain the nature of revelation in a gathered meeting is *Holy Spirit*. Something about the way the words coincide with a memory or the light through the window or the tingle in the arm sets off a particular train of thought that would derail under any other circumstances. At gathered meetings there's a sense of expanded consciousness—of piercing pre-rational intelligence. Sometimes all the points of light in the meeting converge to form a dense beam that lays bare an aching problem that's begged resolution for weeks, months, years.

Pre-rational expanded awareness at gathered meetings can put a finger on exactly what needs redress. These lightning flashes of insight are a revelation of God's word for us, which is "living and active, sharper than any two-edged sword, piercing until it divides soul from spirit, joints and marrow; it is able to judge the thoughts and intentions of the heart" (Hebrews 4:12).

CENTERING PRAYER PRACTICE

To expand awareness and insight in silent meetings for worship, Quakers are encouraged to deepen silences on their own, to train their minds through habitual silences.

Centering prayer is my preferred method of training.[11] During centering prayer we sit comfortably with back straight. Then a sacred word is introduced, which is a symbol of our intention to enter into silence in anticipation of God's presence. The sacred word is a gentle reminder to return to our still and silent center. Whenever distractions arise during centering prayer, I gently and inaudibly recite my sacred word to redirect focus to the blessed stillness. This ancient prayer form has roots dating

11. See *Centering Prayer* in glossary.

back to the third century. Centering prayer is made contemporary today by the work of Thomas Keating, Cynthia Bourgeault, and many others.[12] The point of silent prayer in all its various forms is to achieve naked awareness/stillness of mind.

In the beginning, the untrained mind will get distracted every few seconds. With training, our level of concentration gradually lengthens. The length of distracted periods gradually shortens. During periods of extended relaxed awareness free from distractions, spaces between thoughts get longer until minutes can go by without a single thought entering the mind.

An analogy for silent prayer practice is training a puppy to sit in the center of a circle.[13] At first the puppy can't sit still for even a moment. It habitually wonders off again and again. The point is to gently and repeatedly bring the puppy back to the circle's center. This process is tedious. But, with much practice, eventually the puppy sits still for a few moments without wandering—a triumph. Finally, with months and years of practice, the puppy sits in the center of the circle for two, five, ten minutes . . .

One last analogy . . . The cumulative practice of centering prayer is like a cloud—a cloud of unknowing. Every day we practice is a drop of water that adds to the cloud, until eventually the cloud expands to include all the activities and relationships of our lives.

FREEDOM FROM DISTRACTIONS

It's amazing how much of our energy is wasted on distracting thoughts and daydreams. These distractions are habitual, recycling our same thoughts and reactions over and over. Habitual distractions of mind are a part-time job for most people—something which keeps us preoccupied for countless hours. This waste of energy stymies our full potential.

Once we're able to still the mind, amazing things begin to happen. Old tensions from long ago held in our spine, jaw, or shoulders begin to dissipate and we experience renewed vigor in all aspects of our lives. Our minds get sharper and concentrate more easily for longer periods of time. Our ability to drop pet projects at will and to take up despised projects

---

12. My particular practice is Centering Prayer, yet there are other practices based on the same principles that go by other names such as Prayer of the Heart, so I don't make the mistake of using Centering Prayer as a blanket term for all silent prayer in Christian tradition. See glossary.

13. This is an analogy of Buddhist author Jack Kornfield.

with the same ease is another benefit of this training. Tedious proj[ ]
become more and more effortless. The mind experiences liberation—
longer compulsively drawn to pet projects or repulsed by despised ones.
Habitual aversions to cleaning the bathrooms or facing conflict slacken.
What freedom!

In the beginning, the point is to repeatedly bring the mind back from
distractions to stillness and primal silence. [14] This gradually habituates
the mind to naked awareness, free from auto pilot stimulus and response
conditioning. I've heard corporate executives speak of "unplugging" from
the frantic pace by vacationing in Hawaii or Tahiti. But the ultimate unplugging possible is through centering prayer, which reverses years of
stimulus-response conditioning and enables new levels of awareness and
freedom.

Another way to think about centering prayer is to visualize all in-
coming thoughts as boats coming down a river. Some boats (distracting
thoughts) are exciting and alluring. Others are mundane. Yet we get carried away by each and every boat coming downstream. The point of silent
prayer is to get less and less caught up in the various boats coming along
the stream of consciousness. As we become more detached from the boats,
the boats become less frequent with more space between them. Then
eventually we enjoy complete quiet with no boats, just the calm, energized
water, which carries every boat.

With fewer and fewer thoughts we're able to rest in pure being: God
in whom "we live and breathe and have our being" (Acts 17:28a). This is
the fulfillment of Jesus' first commandment: "Love the Sovereign your God
with all your heart, and with all your soul, and with all your strength, and
with all your mind" (Luke 10:27, Matthew 22:37, Deuteronomy 6: 4–5).

How can we love God with our entire mind when we're distracted?
First we need to still our minds. Then we can experience what God wants
to impart. Deep communion with God requires our full undistracted attention. Perhaps Saint Maximus puts it best: "He who truly loves God prays
entirely without distraction, and he who prays entirely without distraction

---

14. The sacred word is the tool to bring the mind back to the pregnant silence. A
sacred word is usually chosen from the Bible. Yet, any word that effectively brings your
mind back to its intention to wait for God with undistracted awareness can be used.
Some common sacred words are Emmanuel, Mary, Jesus, *Shalom*, Peace, *Maranatha*
("Come Lord Jesus" in Aramaic), Holy Spirit . . .generally the fewer syllables, the better. For the word is simply a tool to arrive at naked awareness. You don't want the word
to become a distraction in itself.

loves God truly. But he whose intellect is fixed on any worldly thing does not pray without distraction, and consequently he does not love God."[15]

DIVINE UNION

Christian mystical experiences of union in prayer are referred to as Divine Union. One elementary question people may ask: Divine Union is with whom? My answer: Jesus is the paradoxical depth of silence. When we emerge from the silence "Jesus" is the sound of one hand clapping! Jesus is our *koan*, our Paradox with a capital P.

Union is a derivation of the word communion, which for Christians is about partaking in the body Christ. Through silent prayer, intimacy and communion with Christ go deeper.. Through prayer we are united to Jesus' Divinity and humanity. His exquisite symmetry of Divinity and humanity is mirrored in us. He becomes our all-in-all. In him, through him, and with him, everything belongs, particularly the broken places, which are transformed in his light. Jesus isn't about fixing things gone wrong within us. Jesus is about finding us in our brokenness and calling us home. Our broken humanity and our glorious original nature unite to reflect his risen nature, broken, yet glorified.

In the Paradox we find our deepest security and refract its everlasting light, which echoes from the caves of the desert hermits, which echoes through the ages. In the state of union we are transfigured by his luminous darkness. Then we realize the entire cosmos and its spinning planets bear his glorious imprint.

The Christian spiritual journey is ever deepening relationship and intimacy with Jesus. First, we get to know Jesus through the Gospels. Then we experience Jesus in the sacrament of Holy Communion. Finally, we experience Jesus in supraessential paradoxical silence. Silence and Holy Communion become our two sacraments: the sacrament of solitude and prayer on the one hand and the sacrament of beloved community on the other.

During prayer we don't name the silence. It's beyond names. But when we return from the luminous silence, we exclaim the holy name: Jesus. The Jesus Paradox becomes the best phrase we have for penetrating the silent mystery. Jesus has two aspects, absolute God and relative human. In the deepest forms of prayer we move beyond the bodily fatigue, various distractions, and pain to experience the absolute or non-dual aspect of

15. Palmer, et al, *The Philokalia Vol. 2*, 65.

Jesus (Jesus' Divinity). When we return from prayer we experience the relative or dualistic aspect of Jesus once again (Jesus' humanity).[16] These are the two aspects of The Jesus Paradox: absolute consciousness beyond names and forms and relative consciousness steeped in language.

QUESTIONS FOR REFLECTION AND DISCUSSION

1) Do you think our society has a problem with anxiety, tension, and stress? If so, how extensive is this problem?

2) Do you think silent prayer has a place in our culture and society? Why or why not?

3) What do you think of Smith's claims that silent prayer relieves stored-up tension in the body and enables deep relaxation and peak mystical experiences?

4) Application question: Do you need a sense of Sabbath in your life? Why or why not?

---

16. How does the Trinity fit in here? Well, Jesus is "at once God and human." The Trinity is "at once One and Three." The same Greek word, *hypostasis*, describes both. See *Hypostasis* in glossary. Also see appendix B.

15

Understanding The Silent Prayer of The Alexandrian Mystics

Believing in God is the easy part. Waiting for God is the hard part.

–ANNE LAMOTT

CLARITY ABOUT SILENT PRAYER IN CHRISTIAN TRADITION

UNADDRESSED TENSIONS IN OUR nervous systems produce uncon-scious anxieties that keep our minds distracted. When our minds are repeatedly trained to quiet and focus, the unconscious anxieties begin to surface and dissipate.

The deep stillness of the mind allows profound relaxation far beyond what is possible through sleep. This profound relaxation releases stored-up tensions in the nervous system and in the muscles of the body. The release of these tensions can come in the form of sharp pains, tears, or strong feelings of fear or grief. In the centering prayer community this is called "unloading."

As a result of unresolved tensions in the body most minds are tense, even in a so-called relaxed state. Most minds are like tense muscles, not relaxed muscles. This problem can be overcome through silent prayer. In other words, on the most basic level centering prayer teaches the mind to relax. When the mind learns how to relax and release stored tensions, the whole nervous system and the muscular system relaxes. Eventually this process invites the practitioner into a peak experience, summed up with Paul's words: "the peace of God, which surpasses all understanding" (Philippians 4:7).

I've addressed the effects of silent prayer on the mind and body. Now, let's clarify what we mean by silent prayer in the Christian context. The experience of deep silence is so universal there's a danger of getting too broad and abstract in our approach. Silence is the broadest and most abstract experience we can have. But I believe our approach to silence, when integrated, is deeply rooted in particulars of our faith tradition.

There is the silence itself, which John of the Cross (d. 1591) refers to as "God's first language." Yet our approach, understanding, and way of holding silences are particular. Silent prayer and our Christian container for holding the silences are equally important. We need both for balance.

In the Christian context, silent prayer is always understood as prayer. Prayer is conversation with God. Most Christians understand prayer as a one-way conversation or monologue. A person inaudibly utters to God what is on their heart. However, as the Quakers point out, prayer as it's popularly conceived is a one-way telephone conversation with few pauses to listen for promptings from the other end of the line.

Silent prayer balances the mistaken understanding of prayer as a one-way conversation by focusing on what's most important: what is being communicated from the other end of the telephone line. When we sit in silence waiting for God's presence, our minds experience distraction. No matter the intensity of distraction, we wait. And when the chatter finally subsides, God can give us what we desire most: experiences of God's self. The deepest experiences of prayer are sheer silence, which echo a primal peace beyond understanding, beyond conditioning, beyond choosing.

A Montana rancher spoke eloquently of this silence. He said his favorite part of the day is the stillness at dawn when the sun peeks over the hills. Then he feels God's presence. As he walks on the open field in the dawn's light to feed his cattle he feels spaciousness—a lightness and clarity of mind that echoes freedom.

The centering prayer tradition is informed by the fourteenth century spiritual classic, *The Cloud of Unknowing*, contemporized in William Meninger's book, *The Loving Search For God*. "The Cloud" refers to Jesus' transfiguration in a cloud on Mount Tabor and God's appearance to Moses in a cloud on Mount Sinai (Luke 9:28–36, Exodus 34:29). When we go deeper into silent prayer, God becomes less tangible and distinct. There's an unknowing in God's presence . . . visceral, real, yet indefinite like a cloud. The unknowing quality of silence makes it mysterious and scary. Yet, the inexplicable silences give an instinctive feeling of benefit. After silent prayer I feel the same way I do after a run: healthy and good. Many mainstream health enthusiasts, like Doctor Andrew Weil, now teach the therapeutic effects of silent prayer.

The author of *The Cloud* teaches us to be "unclothed" in our approach to God. In other words, to be naked of all thoughts, concepts, perceptions . . . We can only come before God nude, stripped of all knowing and all images (Exodus 20:4). This is complete surrender. Nakedness was Adam and Eve's state in Eden before separation from God.

In Centering Prayer we allow whatever comes up in prayer to run its course. We surrender to the present moment as it is, without trying to alter it, patiently waiting for God. Waiting for God requires infinite patience. "Believing in God is the easy part. Waiting for God is the hard part."[1]

Eventually all arising thoughts and images fade into the background. Then we experience fullness, spaciousness, and liberty from the hidden addictive process deep within our minds. This is God's intent. For God is all vitality and goodness, radiating from the center of every cell, every earthworm, every cheetah, and every sycamore.

Meditation and contemplation are misleading terms. Meditation implies Eastern meditation and everything associated with it. Contemplation implies thought. To avoid confusion in this chapter, instead of the terms contemplation or meditation I've used *silent prayer*. Unlike meditation, the term silent prayer never loses sight of relationship with God. The self never dissolves into God. The self is always in relationship with God.[2] The term *prayer* always implies relationship and intimate conversation. That's why Christians carefully retain the word *prayer* to distinguish Christian silent prayer from other forms of meditative practice.

---

1. Lamott, *Grace Eventually.*

2. In Mystic Christianity the distinction between us and God is never completely obliterated. The veil gets thin, transparent, and even blows wide open occasionally, yet the veil remains. Again we come back to balance. To lean toward total absorption into God or total distinction from God is just more extremism and isn't in line with the spirit of *Miaphysite* (The Jesus Paradox).

SILENT PRAYER'S PURPOSE
IN CHRISTIAN TRADITION

Westerners most often have an aversion to silent prayer. Most see silent prayer as irrelevant to the enormous political and social problems of our times or as a luxury for the middle and upper classes. Along these lines all forms of mysticism, Christian included, are shrugged off as sensuality, self-hypnosis, or luxury. These dismissive caricatures ignore the powerful link between silent prayer and social activism, epitomized by the Quakers and The Church of The Savior.[3]

In order to overcome aversions to silent prayer in the West many have couched silent prayer's benefits in terms of higher efficiency. So, it's argued if we practice silent prayer we will be more productive members of society. Although increased effectiveness is one of the characteristics of the life of prayer, it's not the purpose. Likewise, stress reduction isn't the ultimate purpose either. The purpose of silent prayer is intimacy with God, the source of our being, who comes to us in Jesus' non-dual essence—who heals our souls, uniting the disunited self.

It's true that minimizing distractions creates better efficiency in our work, less stress, and better problem-solving ability. But we can't reduce the profound depth of silent prayer to a technique for increased effectiveness. Nor can we rely on teachings about meditation from other traditions.

Carl Jung was enthusiastic about Zen and yoga. But in a famous line he said, "The West will produce its own yoga, and it will be on the basis laid down by Christianity." For me centering prayer and its equivalents are this yoga, built on the foundation of The Alexandrian Mystics.

Another distinction between Christian silent prayer and disciplined silences of other Eastern religions . . . In the Christian context, silent prayer can only be taught by the great teacher, which Augustine calls the *Magister Internus* (Latin): the Master Within. This is the Holy Spirit—the aspect of God available to us at all times, nudging us and prompting us into deeper and more consistent relationship with God. This is different from non-Christian Eastern forms of meditation, where sometimes emphasis ultimately rests on one's self or one's teacher. In the Christian context emphasis may briefly be placed on one's self or a teacher, yet the focus always returns to relationship with God. It's not up to us or our teacher to work in centering prayer. It is Jesus' Paradoxical essence and grace that ultimately

---

3. See *Quakerism and Church of the Savior* in glossary.

heal us. This focus on Jesus, not our own effort, is unique to Christian prayer and is in line with Paul's theology of grace, not works.

Silent prayer is about what Jesus does for us, not about our efforts. Of course, to increase depth in centering prayer we need to maintain designated times for prayer and we need to leave behind our distractions, waiting for God in naked awareness. Yet, in centering prayer there's no goal we're working toward step by step, as with some spiritual practices. Centering Prayer is an effortless, passive prayer form. To progress, we have to show up habitually for prayer (daily prayer has a cumulative effect). And we need regular time for retreat.[4] So we need to take initiative to show up. Then, after we show up, it's up to Jesus to transform us.

EMPHASIS ON EXPERIENCE

Historically, Western Christianity has approached personal experience with suspicion at best and wholesale repression at worst. Mystical experience was considered dangerous, and so relegated to out-of-the-way monasteries, which were kept under close watch. Fundamentalists today are threatened by direct experience, which is sometimes labeled demonic. And for all their fetishizing of personal experiences, new agers usually don't offer deep-rooted and disciplined forms of it.

Leaving our religious tradition for a new age experiment isn't the answer. Theological assumptions void of deep personal experience are also not the answer. We can't settle for authoritarian experience bashers on the one hand or unscrupulous experience fetishizers on the other. The Jesus Paradox isn't about dogmatic certainty and political control and it's not about shirking tradition for new age experiments. It's about experiencing God in silent prayer and having a language for the experience, a language rooted in The Alexandrian Mystics. That language is The Jesus Paradox.

THE JESUS PARADOX INFORMED BY MONASTICISM

The Desert Fathers and Mothers are often celebrated as repositories of Christian spiritual wisdom. Yet few look to the roots of that wisdom—to the theology that informed their monastic life. Few realize they were in

---

4. People who do regular daily practice of silent prayer and periodic retreats are said to be a part of a contemporary movement, variously called Neo-monasticism, New Monasticism, and/or Lay Monasticism. See *Neo-monasticism* in glossary.

fact *Miaphysites*. These monks and hermits clung to *Miaphysite* theology as interpreted by the Alexandrian Mystics.

Athanasius of Alexandria in particular, won the hearts and minds of the desert mystics as no other bishop. And, yes, Athanasius embraced *Miaphysite* theology in its root form, which was later developed by Cyril, Dioscorus, and others. The Alexandrian Bishops from 312 to 454CE represent a unified lineage of teachings about the incarnation, which is Mystic Christianity's definitive core.

The desert monks vehemently clung to *Miaphysite* even when faced with persecution, torture, and death. A primary example of this is Samuel of Kalamun of the Seventh Century, who was repeatedly tortured within inches of death for not recanting his *Miaphysite* faith.[5]

The desert monks and hermits were passionately *Miaphysite* because *Miaphysite* (The Jesus Paradox) makes more sense of Christian mystical experience than any other theology. The synthetic minds of the Desert Fathers and Mothers experienced the underlying unity of the cosmos— going back to the supraessential unity of the Big Bang. At the same time they acknowledged the source's human form: Jesus. *Miaphysite* is the only theology high enough and broad enough to transcend and include both dual (human) and non-dual (Divine) awareness, without dissecting, without interjecting the scalpel of reason where it doesn't belong.

Silent prayer eventually takes us beyond the realm of names and forms to rest in God's ineffable peace. There, unqualified experience of the living God lavishes ultimate meaning and inexpressible joy. *Miaphysite* affirms that God's first language is this mysterious and quickening undifferentiated silence.[6] *Miaphysite* also affirms the human form in which the unlimited became limited, the absolute became relative, and the high-voltage electricity became grounded.

---

5. Alcock, *The Life of Samuel.*

6. "Silence is God's first language and everything else is a poor translation." This is a well known quotation from John of the Cross . . . Some may find this quotation pretentious and off-putting. So I want to acknowledge that God's communication isn't limited to one language or another. For one friend of mine God is most present in the wilderness. Her peak experiences of God happen on mountain tops of oxygen thin air and panoramic vistas. Another friend of mine finds her most exhilarating encounters with the Divine during child-birthing. She is so awed by the sacred dimension of child-birth that she has become a licensed homebirth midwife. John of the Cross uses the phrase "Silence is God's first language . . ." to emphasize the unequivocal primal power of undistracted silence in spiritual transformation, which is usually accompanied by stillness. Yet, the power of God can penetrate a broad variety of human experiences.

The monks experienced ultimate reality beyond words, then moved back again into the particular forms of Christian tradition that Jesus set into motion. They didn't come out of deep silences with nothing to say. They found language for their experience—the language of *Miaphysite*. The *Miaphysites* staked their lives on the Paradox of the incarnation. They balanced the contemplative life with life in the world. They balanced silent prayer with theological utterances. They balanced Jesus' Divinity and humanity.[7] They beheld The Jesus Paradox.

If we can still our minds long enough, we can glimpse the holistic nature of Jesus beyond the persistent dualisms. The mystics claim when we acclimatize to habitual stillness and quiet, Jesus' Divinity and humanity can't be talked about separately. Likewise, the life of prayer (communion with God) and the life of service (solidarity with humanity) are complementary. They're a dynamic unity.

THOMAS KEATING

I remember when I met Thomas Keating for the first time at his monastery in Snowmass, Colorado. In that moment I knew I had met a spiritual master. Spiritual mastery is a rarity, because unlike other disciplines, abiding spiritual wisdom requires the convergence of numerous circumstances outside our control. It also requires tremendous sacrifice.

Spiritual mastery isn't something we can will, as with other disciplines. And we cannot congratulate ourselves when and if spiritual mastery begins to dawn. Spiritual masters speak, above all else, of a sense of wonderment . . . "Really?!" "You mean that after all my stupid mistakes and all the messes I've made, you (God) are going to bestow these spiritual gifts on me?!" The spiritual gifts that come with mastery are completely undeserved. They're not based on our credentials, will power, or stamina. Even if they were somewhat based on these character traits, who bestowed the traits upon us to begin with? Any way we slice it, we can't take any credit for spiritual gifts.

After meeting Keating tears came to my eyes. I had finally found a master in my own tradition. I didn't have to travel to the Himalayas or to *Dzogchen* Monastery in Tibet. There in Snowmass, at the foot of the Rocky Mountains, in a monk's garb, I stumbled on that lanky iceberg

7. This pencil sketch was drawn by Rev. Bill Tibbs, a UCC minister who lives with his wife in Billings, Montana.

called Keating—an iceberg with untold depths . . . A presence that expanded beneath the surface—thousands of feet wide and deep—touching the ocean floor.

I spoke with an Australian named Ethan shortly after a ten day retreat he had with Keating. This is his account . . . Ethan shuffled down a windowed hall toward a large sunlit room. Before he entered the room he was asked to take off his shoes. Ethan recalled the verse, "Take off your shoes, you're standing on holy ground" (Exodus 3:5, Acts 7:33). He dismissed the random thought and crossed the threshold where Keating was seated.

Immediately, Ethan noticed the difference . . . "The atmosphere was luminous," he said. When he came into Keating's presence, his mind suddenly stilled. He felt profound clarity and peace as though he had been sitting in silent prayer for an hour. But, he hadn't been praying, he had simply come into Keating's presence. Ethan felt "light and buoyant," he told me with a thick smile. To Ethan, the room where Keating sat seemed disproportionately bright, as though everything was back-lit.

Ethan said the truth of his experience was two-fold. One, he had just completed a ten day centering prayer retreat and was in a different frame of mind—much more open to the Holy Spirit. Two, according to Ethan, the glow of Keating's presence is what Hindus refer to as *darshan*—a Hindi word that means "the experience of blessing in the presence of a spiritual master." Thomas embodied what Ethan had been looking for all his life—a realized master in his own tradition. Ethan had heard of the spiritual mastery of Thomas Merton, Anthony De Mello, and some obscure Christian hermits of Ethiopia. But, he wanted to experience such a master first-hand. He finally did in Keating.[8]

After the encounter Ethan realized that if the raw spiritual power he encountered in Keating that day was magnified exponentially, it could heal the sick, restore sight to the blind, and generate other wonders. Ethan explained that his experience in the presence of the Benedictine monk was a minute portion of what Jesus' disciples must have experienced when they were drunk on the Spirit at Pentecost (Acts 2). The experience buckled his innate skepticism. It was a profound gift—an experiential window into the Gospel miracles. Before his experience with Keating Ethan didn't have an

---

8. Westerners are familiar with stories of spiritual geniuses and lineages of spiritual masters that have emerged in the Himalayas or along the Indus river valley. Yet, few are aware that such a legacy of masters also existed within Christian tradition in the Egyptian desert, most distinctly among the Alexandrian Mystics in the fertile period between the fourth and fifth centuries.

entry point into the supernatural phenomena of the New Testament. He had no related personal experience.

After the encounter with Keating the Gospel miracles made more sense to him. So did select written accounts of the Desert Fathers and Mothers . . . Some of the hermits of the Egyptian desert, like Saint Anthony, were said to be luminous and to shine as if encompassed with light, as Moses shone when he came down from Mount Sinai or as Jesus shone when transfigured before the disciples on Mount Tabor (Exodus 34: 29–35; Matthew 17: 1–2; Mark 9: 2–3).[9] Saint Anthony was widely known for his luminous presence, which healed many. People flocked to the desert to bathe in his light. Orthodox Christianity refers to Anthony's profound purity and holiness as deification.[10]

Unlike Ethan, most Westerners haven't encountered genuine spiritual power. And they don't have any reference point for it. Because there is no personal experience to back it up, many discredit the possibility of spiritual power altogether. Because of a lack of a reference point, many reject Jesus' profound spiritual power witnessed in the Gospels. Ethan's encounter with Keating gave him a reference point for understanding previously inexplicable aspects of the Gospels. The experience opened his mind to the reality of spiritual power.

For me the most important aspect of religious experience is Divine presence (Holy Spirit). This presence is available at all times and in all places to all people. The second most important aspect of religious experience is the receptivity of the hearer. Others who saw Keating that day experienced a nice old man. They didn't experience what Ethan did. And others may have experienced that same presence but at other times and to varying degrees. The third most important aspect of religious experience is the teacher. It is tempting to elevate the teacher to the first position, but this is always dangerous and not in line with Christian tradition. The Holy Spirit shining through the vehicle of Keating is most revered, not the vehicle itself. *Exactly*

Spiritual masters like Keating represent the pinnacle of human transformation—what is possible through lifelong practice of silent prayer and regular retreats. Through silent prayer contemporary spiritual masters incarnate some small fraction of Jesus' transforming presence.

---

9. See *Tabor Light* in glossary.

10. See *Deification* in glossary. Also see the index of Lossky, *The Mystical Theology*.

WILDERNESS

Most of us live in glorified boxes and rectangles in cities, ride boxy subways to work, work in cubicles, and stare at square screens all day. To compensate we need the grandeur and freedom of wide open spaces—places like Glacier Bay in Alaska and the Grand Canyon in Arizona.

Like the boxes that dominate most of our lives, our mindsets are predictable, our world views are prone to stimulus and response conditioning, pervasive cultural scripting, and cookie cutter text book approaches to problem solving, heavy on reason and analysis—light on imagination and mystery. In this context the mystics of the Egyptian desert and the contemporary mystics are equivalent to the pristine Alaska wilderness. To cultivate the mystic state of mind and teach it to coming generations is the interior equivalent of preserving Alaskan wild lands for posterity.

We need to know that wilderness exists. It frees our minds from the tedious boxes in which we live, drive, and work. In the same way we need to know there are those who have tasted the human minds' liberated primordial state or *original state*, written about in *The Philokalia*.

There is beauty in the wild lands that are beyond the reach of commercialism and development. There is also beauty in freedom from the pervasive monkey-mind and the attachment and aversion conditioning that dogs us all. There is beauty in liberation internal and external! The beauty of the Alaskan wilderness and the holistic mind of the mystics is that they are beyond category. They are untouched, luminous, eternal . . .

Philokalia (Greek) is translated "Love of the Beautiful" in English. May we revere the majesty and stillness of the wide open spaces of pristine wilderness! May we revere the luminous minds of the mystics who know freedom in the deepest sense—untouched by desire for anything they don't already possess. "Love of the beautiful." Yes!! Finally a love affair that brings the deepest fulfillment and purpose, that echoes eternity, that nothing can take away, not even death.

QUESTIONS FOR REFLECTION AND DISCUSSION

1) What is the purpose of silent prayer in Christian tradition?

2) How are silent prayer and The Jesus Paradox related?

3) What do you think of Smith's assertion that the life of prayer and the life of service are a dynamic unity?

4) What do you think of Smith's assertion that Keating, Merton and others incarnate some small fraction of Jesus' transforming love?

5) Smith equates the internal pristine mind of the mystics to the external pristine wilderness. Does this work for you? Why or why not?

6) Application question: Have you ever met a holy person? If so, please describe the experience.

Part 7

Conclusion

16

Anchored in Jesus According to The Alexandrian Mystics

God (is) in the flesh.

–CYRIL OF ALEXANDRIA

In Jesus the unity of creature and Creator is realized.

–CORNELIUS A. BULLER

The treasure of Christ is hidden in earthen vessels.

–THOMAS MERTON

AVOIDING THE INCARNATION

MANY CHRISTIANS SHY AWAY from Jesus' name since it has been used to exclude. In the process, they completely disregard the center of Christian faith. There are liberal churches where I've been told, "We don't use the J word here (Jesus). Too many people have been burned by it."

If this is really my stance, I should become Unitarian or Baha'i. But, to remain within the Christian tradition and not mention Jesus is ridiculous.

Some current theologians refer to Jesus as a Jewish mystic, a healer, a wisdom teacher, a social prophet, and a movement initiator. Yet they never explicitly refer to Jesus as the human incarnation of God, which is the most important belief of Christianity's two thousand years of witnesses.[1]

Generations of witnesses have claimed that with Jesus something unique and unprecedented happened: God's human incarnation. Disregarding this unique claim of Christian tradition is an unprecedented break from historic faith (1 Corinthians 3:11).

Many broadminded theologians today reflect the words of Don Cupitt: "The critical historian no longer sees both natures displayed in Jesus' life. He sees a purely human Jesus, a first-century man of God in the Jewish tradition."[2] This new age Jesus becomes a pattern for human life, but is no longer the incarnation.

Most broadminded theologians miss Thomas Merton's sentiment in *The Seven Storey Mountain*,

> Jesus Christ was not simply a man, a good man, a great man, the greatest prophet, a wounded healer, a saint: He was something that made all such trivial words pale into irrelevance. He was God. But nevertheless He was not merely a spirit without a true body, God hiding under a visionary body: He was also truly a man.[3]

Contemporary theologians say Jesus was "God embodied in a human life."[4] But, Jesus wasn't just God embodied in a human life like other prophets. Jesus was utterly unique: God's human incarnation. This affirmation of generations of witnesses differentiates Christianity from all other world religions. Some claim "His life incarnates the character of God."[5] But, "Jesus incarnates the character of God" evades the bold affirmation of the ages: God incarnate; "God in human form" (Philippians 2:8, Colossians 2:9).

---

1. Borg, *The Heart of Christianity*, 89–91. A number of people I've talked to have concurred that they appreciate Marcus Borg's *The Heart of Christianity* as a corrective to imbalances in the Christian faith, but that it's not a definitive work because it gives away too much that is uniquely Christian. Christian author Houston Smith agrees with this assessment. See Smith, Lecture.

2. Goulder, *Incarnation and Myth*, 43.

3. Merton, *The Seven Storey Mountain*, 209.

4. Borg, *The Heart of Christianity*, 88.

5. Borg, *The Heart of Christianity*, 88.

"The Word (God) became flesh (human)" (John 1:14). This is the difference between God's human incarnation and God's prophetesses and prophets. In Jesus God didn't dwell within a human like Moses, Elijah, and Deborah. God became human. This is the unique legacy of the Christian testament.

Some recent theologians have suggested the incarnation is a metaphor.[6] This is completely out of step with generations of Christian witnesses beginning with the apostles. The incarnation is no metaphor. The incarnation is the foundation of Christian faith. Reducing the incarnation to metaphor squashes Christianity's power. Tens of thousands of apostles and martyrs wouldn't have risked everything and died for a metaphor.

Many broadminded theologians reduce Jesus to the status of another prophet.[7] For them the Word has no longer become human, but has merely inhabited a human. Cyril of Alexandria dealt with this very idea in the fifth century. Cyril's response to the claim "God dwelled in Jesus:" "If he became a worker of wonderful signs because the Word was within him, are they not simply saying that he was one of the holy prophets?"[8]

I've heard new age Christians say we can become like Jesus. This may be true to a degree, but no matter how blessed we are and no matter how much spiritual practice we do, people will never heal their terminal diseases by touching the hem of our garments (Luke 8:44, Matthew 14:36). The sheer power Jesus radiated is unique to the incarnation. For Christians, Jesus is the only person who could say to God "I am that." For the rest of us, the spiritual journey is characterized by ever-deepening relationship.

---

6. Unless well defined, I shy away from the terms Christ Symbol, Cosmic Christ, or Christ as Metaphor. If Christ becomes relegated to one of these three terms, then what differentiates Christ from Krishna, Krishna Consciousness, or some other nebulous term co-opted by the new age? Not much in my estimation.

7. Some recent interpreters of Christianity, such as Marcus Borg, go as far as to say that Jesus' designation as son of God was not remarkable—that a number of Jewish healers were referred to as sons of God. (In a 1997 lecture in Berkeley, California, author Houston Smith concurred that Borg had "given away too much that is uniquely Christian"). This signifies that Jesus is just another Jewish mystic or another prophet. But in actuality the Greek term *huios theou*, which applied to "sons of God" in the plural ordinary sense, was only used in reference to Jesus three times in the Gospels (Mark 1:1, 15:39, and Romans 1:4). Usually Jesus is described as *ho huios tou theou*: not just a "son of God," but "the son of God." So Borg and others navigate a slippery slope, which doesn't reflect authentic incarnational Christianity . . . The Oriental Orthodox Church knows the incarnation is where the power is. Otherwise, they wouldn't have fought over it so vehemently, sustaining tremendous losses to preserve its pure essence: *Miaphysite* (The Jesus Paradox). See Borg, *The Heart of Christianity*, 88. Also see Appendix G.

8. Cyril, *The Unity of Christ*, 97.

The emphasis on Jesus' humanity and denial of Jesus' full Divinity permeates liberal churches and obliterates Christianity's power.[9] Author Houston Smith warns, "Liberal churches, for their part, are digging their own graves, for without a robust, emphatically theistic world-view to work within, they have nothing to offer their members except rallying cries to be good."[10]

When the fully Divine Christ is not at the center, then a charismatic leader, conservative sensibilities, liberal sensibilities, or some other less worthy candidate takes the center. Then our faith is no longer about devotion to our transcendent higher power. Then the agenda of the current leadership becomes central. Then the church has no generations-old anchor and becomes vulnerable to the whims of congregation and culture.

As Christian author Eugene Petersen has reiterated, people need two things from worship: transcendence and fellowship (Divine connection and human connection). The Christian Right is all about transcendence, often tolerating community in order to praise God. The Christian Left often enjoys fellowship and tolerates God so they can be together. We need both!

We need vigorous faith that is ultimately not about rights, devotions, and know-how. It is not about knowing something! It is about knowing someone! That someone is Jesus, who mysteriously holds the fullness of Creator and creature in his very being! That someone is transcendent God beyond the bounds of science or any other limited human framework. That someone is also immanent human being, who shares our human limitations!

RE-ENVISIONING TWENTY-FIRST CENTURY CHRISTIANITY

Those re-envisioning Twenty-first Century Christianity are in crisis. Progressive theologians seem oblivious to the crisis, which is that theologians are straying further and further from the mark: Jesus.

In order for progressive theologians to make enduring contributions to Christianity, they need to be rooted.[11] Jesus is the root from which all

9. Another ancient theologian, Arius, taught "once Christ was not," meaning that Jesus' nature was not eternal—that Jesus was essentially human. This was considered heretical by the early church, yet many who profess Christianity today maintain this belief. The eternal aspect of Jesus, which existed before the historic incarnation and after the incarnation, is *The Word* (*Logos* in Greek). See *Logos* in glossary. Also see more on Arius in Appendix F.

10. Smith, *The Soul of Christianity*, xx.

11. Process theology's essential idea "that we are 'in' God" has ancient antecedents

Christian theology stems (1 Corinthians 3:11). If we're true to Christian faith and stand within it, then we are rooted in Jesus, "the pioneer and perfecter of our faith" (Hebrew 12:2). If we're not rooted in Jesus, then we're outside the two thousand year old tradition.

Jesus isn't new age. Jesus is old age!

I'm not advocating for freakish fixation on Jesus. If some want to call me a *Jesus freak* I will shrug and add, "There is a reason generations of witnesses revere the name. If you want to discount them all for another fetish, go ahead. I will stand with the tried and true that's weathered the generations and the counter arguments of numerous geniuses." Yes, Jesus defines God's unique revelation to Christians. So Jesus is our starting place, our unique testament, our departure point and point of return.

The source of the ancient Christian river is Jesus. We acknowledge the source in order to keep Christian faith real. We never step into the same river twice; the river is always changing.[12] But, the source of the river doesn't change: "Jesus Christ is the same yesterday and today and forever" (Hebrew 13:8). As long as we name Jesus as the source of the Christian river, we can forge ahead through the Twenty-first Century and beyond. If we're not rooted in Jesus, then we stand in a different river and should call our faith by a different name.

When Christianity drifts further and further from its source, importing a little of this and a little of that, it becomes new age. These shifts from Christianity's source will eventually lead to the river drying up. And if the banks of the river cave, so will many values buoying up society.

I get that Jesus is not in vogue in many hip circles. When Christian author Anne Lamott ,converted some of her friends and family questioned her judgment, to put it mildly. I also get that Jesus has been nauseatingly misrepresented and politicized. Yet the Jewel of the Nile (The Jesus Paradox) exists! And it has the potential to resurrect the mind and heart!

FROM DISUNITY TO UNITY

Spirituality easily becomes subjective and amorphous. Jesus keeps our spirituality powerfully specific. He is our window, which focuses the rays of light. He is our *koan*.

in the New Testament, where God is the one "in whom we live and move and have our being" (Acts 17:28).

12. In the Gospels Jesus never heals the same way twice.

There are numerous Jesuses. There is the Vatican II Roman Catholic Jesus (culled from Thomas Aquinas and Thomas Merton, to scratch the surface), the Eastern Orthodox Jesus (filtered for the West through Tolstoy and Dostoevsky), the Nonviolent Jesus (gleaned from The Peace Churches, Jesus' Third Way, and French Philosopher, Renee Girard), the Jesus of the oppressed (from mainline churches emphasizing justice and from liberation theologians like James Cone), the liberal Protestant Jesus (from historical Jesus scholars like Marcus Borg and John Dominic Crossan), and the neo-feminist Jesus (culled from Elizabeth Schussler Fiorenza and the multitude of feminist theologians since). And the list goes on . . . The primal revelation about Jesus that is broad enough to undergird them all is the incarnation as understood by the Alexandrian Mystics.

Jesus may be elusive and mystifying. Jesus may be obscured by centuries of calcified interpretations. Yet he remains Christianity's fulcrum. And at one point or another, if we take our faith seriously, we have to submit to one authority or another on the person of Jesus. Here I resonate with the words of the desert mystic Evagrius: "He who prays is a theologian; and he who is a true theologian truly prays."[13] What convinces me of the monastic authority of these Alexandrian Mystics? What convinces me that they are the true theologians? I am convinced because they truly prayed. They experienced God firsthand, not secondhand through books, classes, and workshops. Mystics like Athanasius of Alexandria swam in the ocean of God. They didn't read about God perched in their recliner (not that there's anything wrong with that). They ardently watched over their souls in desert solitude. Athanasius wasn't only a bishop, he was also a monk. And his identity as a monk came first! This is evident from early images of Athanasius with a monk's hood. In the fourth century only monks wore hoods. The unique genius of the Alexandrian Bishops from Athanasius on is they were monks and theologians first. The clerical titles were secondary.

The Alexandrian Mystics plumbed the depths of theology. They also plumbed the depths of self knowledge through ardent training of the mind. Athanasius and the Alexandrian Bishops who followed him were scientists of our greatest human endowment: our conscience (also known as God). They conducted original firsthand experiments. They came away from these experiments radiating the power of God's Holy Spirit. This gave them the authority to lead the churches and monastic communities of their time with passion and zeal.

13. Ponticus, *The Praktikos*.

From the principles of Greek philosophy, to psychology's *collecti* *unconscious*, to the God of the world's wisdom literature, there is a con mon thread. This common thread is the appropriate exaltation of our greatest human endowment: our conscience, and its innate desire to reach toward its Maker. Dedication to the recognition and development of our conscience is what inspired The Alexandrian Mystics to leave everything and enter the laboratory of the desert. They weren't bearded madmen, although it would be easier on us to dismiss their genius. They were the true athletes of the soul.

After generations of soul spelunking, The Alexandrian Mystics came up with The Jesus Paradox, which has the power to heal divisions in the Church. The Jesus Paradox, sifted through and thoroughly understood, can bring primal cohesion to worldwide Christianity. The Nicene Creed brought cohesion to the early church. But now mainline Protestant churches in particular have drifted miles from The Nicene Creed. They need a primal anchor, more basic and more far reaching than creedal statements of the past.

The church schism between Rome and Alexandria at the Council of Chalcedon (451) and all subsequent church schisms point back to our essential understanding of Jesus. If we can at least come to common ground about Jesus, there's hope for deeper ecumenism in the coming centuries.

May The Jesus Paradox of The Alexandrian Mystics and of the Oriental Orthodox Church today be the yeast in the loaf. It will take time to knead it through the dough (Matthew 13:33). But eventually it will gain prominence, because it conforms to the Spirit of truth more than the partial truths that now abound.

A BARE-BONES MYSTICAL THEOLOGY OF JESUS

Today religious people are plagued by too narrow a pursuit of orthodoxy on the one hand or dispensing with orthodoxy altogether on the other.

If the theologian defines orthodoxy too narrowly she succumbs to exclusive trains of thought, which are subtle forms of violence. If, on the other hand, the theologian throws her hands up and claims ultimate unknowability, she betrays her faith tradition and leaves the gate open for any imposter.

If there's no measuring rod of faith, no banks to the river—that faith, that river, will begin to become indistinguishable from the surrounding landscape. And eventually the river will be no more. This is the ultimate threat of new age phenomena—that culture will influence faith for the worse, rather than faith influencing culture for the better.

Over time, progressive Christianity has been less and less interested in creedal statements. If this isn't tempered, if there isn't some orthodox standard around the person of Jesus, the whole progressive enterprise will succumb to questionable innovations. Theology of Jesus is the measuring rod of orthodoxy. Once there's resolution about Jesus, then there's a foundation upon which to anchor the Twenty-first Century Church, in all its breadth.

My hope is the emerging Christian paradigm will learn from our Oriental Orthodox sisters and brothers. My hope is that theologians won't deviate so far from orthodoxy so as to become unrecognizably Christian. The Jesus Paradox is the anchor for the Oriental Orthodox Church. It is also the anchor for contemplative Christianity and progressive Christianity.

If Christianity is going to be remade it can't be remade around hot-button political issues, political correctness, environmentalism, trends in philosophy, an inclusive mind-set, or a charismatic leader. It has to be remade in the image of Christ conceived in the minds of The Alexandrian Mystics. Nothing substitutes for firsthand experience of the person of Jesus through prayer. Yet, that experience needs an accurate lens, leaving room for both conviction and mystery. The Alexandrian Mystics temper conviction so it becomes *paradoxical certitude*. They also temper mystery, helping us to understand that mystery isn't the result of missing data. It's the result of a fullness we can never fully comprehend. The foundation of The Jesus Paradox is the hope for Christianity's future and for its enduring post-modern legacy.

Orthodoxy as it's usually understood (especially in the West) defends five fundamentals: virgin birth, biblical inerrancy, substitutionary atonement, the bodily resurrection, and the imminent return of Jesus. Yet, this orthodoxy hasn't served to unify Christians—far from it! Why? Because few agree on these particulars. We need a more primal mystical root drenched in transcendent unity. We need a more basic orthodoxy which can heal the abscesses in the worldwide communion.

The Jesus Paradox articulates a primal orthodoxy while respecting other religions. It acknowledges Christianity's unique root—the incarnation. At the same time it humbly acknowledges that God is available in other forms aside from the human form. The time has come for authentic faith in Jesus that acknowledges pluralism as part of God's plan—as part of God's revelation in history. This is the root insight of The Jesus Paradox and The Trinity. The alternatives to this balanced approach are religious fascism on the one hand or eclectic new age experiments on the other.

THE CULMINATION OF THE SEARCH

Distilled Christianity is the knowledge and love of Christ. The knowledge and love of Christ includes theological knowledge. After my two-decade-long international search I finally found the anchor I was looking for—the theological rock of Jesus.

My core truth about Jesus isn't rooted in mainstream Western Christian tradition. It's rooted in Jesus' essence. It's about the deep stillness of silent prayer and a theology big enough to give that blessed stillness words. The psalmist says, "Be still and know that I am God" (Psalm 46:10). The container for this stillness and intimate communion with God is Jesus. The Alexandrian Mystics give us words that encompass infinite God and finite humanity, that reverberate in heaven and on earth.

The Jesus Paradox is about a core theology rooted in mystical experience and it is about experience rooted in a life giving mystical theology.

The Jesus Paradox is the distilled essence of the Alexandrian Mystics—the resolution of the Jesus tug-of-war. Its truth convicts my soul, yet doesn't require me to leave my reasoning mind at the door. This word stretches my reasoning mind to its limits and makes room in my heart for the world. For "God so loved the world" (John 3:16a). The Jesus Paradox doesn't stop short of the world, its many people and religions. It's broad like the mystics, making room for the sacred heart of God and for the rough and tumble world rife with despair, brokenness, and war.

Our thinking is only as large as our vocabulary. There were no English words for *non-violence* or *non-dual* until after World War II. Before then these concepts didn't exist in English. The East has had words for *non-violence* and *non-dual* for hundreds of years. But only recently did these words appear in the English lexicon.

The word *Miaphysite* is virtually unknown in the West. Yet, it holds the key to unlock doors in our minds, which can return depth and breadth to our theology. Non-violence, non-dual, and *Miaphysite* are all connected. All these terms introduce a new mind. It's not an either/or mind. It's not a win/lose mind. It's a holistic mind with untold depths, ultimately apprehended in what The Alexandrian Mystics call *blessed stillness*.[14] When the mind is still and focused beyond any sensory distractions it plumbs the mystery of our pre-fallen state in Christ—of our original nature. And for Christians that mystery has a word: *Miaphysite.*

---

14. There are references to "blessed stillness" throughout *The Philokalia*. For example, see Palmer, et al, *The Philokalia Vol. 2*, 317.

Miaphysite, also known as The Jesus Paradox, changes the way we see. It takes us beyond the limitations of conventional religion into a larger world of imagination and possibilities. It takes us beyond dualistic thinking and the subtle and gross forms of violence that follow. It takes us into the light of Christ, which excludes no one, not even lepers, and whose parables turned either/or dualisms on their head.

The Jesus Paradox, if we really absorb it, catapults us out of the complacent risk-averse numbness of suburbia into the mysterious harmony of the desert coyote's howl. Along with Richard Rohr, I think Jesus was the first prominent non-dualistic thinker in the West. And, generally speaking, the West hasn't known what to do with him. The West doesn't understand his essence or his thinking. The East apprehends Jesus' Paradoxical essence. The East understands the incarnation with more depth and subtlety than the West's dualistic "in two persons" theology.

Our tradition needs a fulcrum. We need something we can trust in an ultimate sense, somewhere to turn when our health fails, when our job falls through, when our marriage disintegrates. The mystics affirm there's no relationship, community, belief, or form of prayer we can completely trust. Nothing is worthy of our trust, nothing but the person of Jesus. In *The Philokalia*, Gregory of Sinai (d. 1346) puts it well: "Behold your liberation, which is Jesus Christ, the redemption and salvation of souls . . . who is both God and man (human)."[15] Jesus: God's dynamic human form—the game changer—paradoxical, active, a moving target.[16]

Parker Palmer said "truth is an eternal conversation about things that matter." The intent of my work isn't to conclude the conversation about Jesus, but to keep it alive in the most vital sense. Teachers know that just as every cell has a wall, every subject has authentic boundary lines. Staying within those lines protects the sacred conversation. These parameters don't confine us. They liberate us to plumb the depths and get to know our subject with greater intimacy. Every committed relationship has responsible boundaries, which allow the relationship to deepen and blossom. Conversation about Jesus also has parameters. When respected, these parameters draw us deeper into the mystery. The mystics know all the magic happens in the interplay between the Divinity and the humanity.

Progressive Christianity celebrates diversity, but there needs to be unity within the diversity. Otherwise, we risk a fractured tradition.

15. Palmer, et al, *The Philokalia Vol. 4*, 234.
16. May, *The Awakened Heart*, 189, 198.

Diversity is wonderful. It's what makes progressive Christianity compelling and vital. Yet, that diversity needs an anchor.

Jesus' person as understood by The Alexandrian Mystics is our Twenty-first Century anchor for contemplative and progressive Christianity. The anchor's rope is long enough to plumb the pluralistic Twenty-first Century ocean. The anchor's rope is thick enough to weather postmodern storms. It is our mystical legacy. It's our heritage passed down through centuries of clerics, monks, monastic orders, and Oriental Orthodox Tradition, dating back to the fourth century. It is Christianity's mystic root, which has the power to heal the divide!

The Jesus Paradox's profound primal power changes our frame of reference. It changes our paradigm. And as many teachers point out, the most powerful changes we can make as human beings are not changes in our attitude or in our habits. The most powerful changes we can make start with a shift in our frame of reference, a shift in our paradigm. This will indirectly affect our attitudes and habits more powerfully than if we were to work on attitudes or habits.

The Jesus Paradox gets us to see that God is more of a verb than a noun, more of a process than a conclusion, more of a dynamic relationship than a static idea.

May we recover the integrating holistic vision of The Alexandrian Mystics, which has the power to heal our souls and our communities! May that paradigm shift celebrated by the mystics shed its transforming light on our hearts and minds! May this book fall into the right hands and bear much fruit (Matthew 13:3–9, 18–23).

QUESTIONS FOR REFLECTION AND DISCUSSION

1) Does the standard exclusive model of Christianity work for you? Why or why not?

2) What do you make of the numerous Jesuses the author refers to (Nonviolent, Catholic, Progressive, etcetera)? Can The Jesus Paradox of The Alexandrian Mystics undergird and unify these disparate theologies of Jesus?

3) If Christian faith is primarily a relationship with Jesus, is theology about Jesus relevant? Why or why not?

4) Application question: Is The Jesus Paradox as understood by The Alexandrian Mystics life-giving to you? Why or why not?

17

Filling in the Trenches, Healing the Divide

I believe in the resurrection of the mind.

–ANNE LAMOTT

I lived in the virtue of that life and power that took away the occasion of wars.

–GEORGE FOX

TRENCH WARFARE

THE MOST DESTRUCTIVE TRENCHES and foxholes are not necessarily in the war torn regions of the world. At least those trenches are visible. The most destructive trenches and foxholes are the invisible ones we silently dig in our own hearts and minds.

This is where the trench warfare begins that tears apart relationships, families, churches, communities, and the world. Here we dig defensive lines against science or religion, against conservatives or liberals, against feminists or patriarchs, as the case may be. Here we dig defensive lines against people who bring up our childhood wounds or our other baggage, which we refuse to acknowledge and so project outside ourselves. Here we dig defensive lines against illegal immigrants. And the list goes on.

One of the primary functions of the Gospel is to fill in these trenches and call a cease fire. Jesus' parables most often address our mental and emotional state—our underlying value system, biases, and prejudices. But, the trenches in our hearts and minds are dug so deep and they have such a long history in our family of origin and culture that sometimes the Gospel isn't enough to fill in the trenches or to call a permanent cease fire. When trenches have been dug in early childhood and reinforced by cultural scripting over and over for decades, dismantling them requires varied means.

The Alexandrian Mystics knew the Gospels are an excellent start on the road to integration and wholeness. They are an excellent start to dismantling self-serving cultural paradigms. Yet, in order to call a permanent cease fire between dualistic factions within, we need as many tools as possible. A combination of The Gospels, the root mystic theology of The Jesus Paradox, and spiritual practice, can keep our minds and hearts open and supple. This combination has the greatest potential to vanquish the trenches for good and to slowly pry the implements of war from our hands one finger at a time. The Gospels are an antidote to individualism and prejudice. Silent prayer is an antidote to relentless activity and the addictive process. The Jesus Paradox is an antidote to dualistic thought and absolutism. Combined they spawn brilliant synthetic genius, which can sift through even the most subtle divisive thoughts in our minds and the most calcified cells in our bodies, churches, and society.

Getting rid of trenches in our minds is like trying to get rid of weeds. We need to come at the weeds from numerous angles. To get rid of weeds in my lawn I start by digging them out by the roots, then I apply an environmentally friendly yet tenacious "weed and feed" fertilizer. Finally, for the persistent weeds, I spray a little heavy duty weed killer directly on them. This analogy works for weeds in our minds. For difficult people the following analogy is more appropriate. In his book, *Friedman's Fables*, Rabbi Edwin Friedman writes about a Tiger who wants to live in "the friendly forest." The tiger resorts to bullying and manipulation and doesn't know how to spell *boundaries*. Finally after one boundary transgression too many, the other animals in the friendly forest are faced with the necessity of caging the tiger. Elements of our communities (friendly forest) and society, which cannot regulate themselves (i.e. Hitler, Stalin, and the most immature and negative elements in our communities) must be contained.

...ction (weeding out the divisive thoughts in our minds) needs to ...d with social realism (containing the tigers).[1]

...n permanent cease fire and lasting peace in our hearts requires numerous skillful methods, including dynamic gospel teaching, a sound theology of Jesus, and dedicated spiritual practice. Otherwise, as soon as we think we have vanquished the trenches, just like those persistent weeds, they'll reappear. Fragmentary and dualistic thinking have taken hold of the Western mind. Reconciling painful and messy divisions within and in our society requires deep faith and diligence.

To heal the divide requires shedding ego enough to hear and absorb the brutally honest truths about ourselves. It requires radical humility. It also requires the courage to "speak the truth in love" (Ephesians 4:15), not only to ourselves, but to our loved ones, and to our communities. On this path, Jesus is the great healer, whose Spirit guides us generation after generation, who calls us to a "ministry of reconciliation" (2 Corinthians 5:18), who has the power to heal divisions wherever they exist.

SOWING SEEDS OF NONVIOLENCE

I talked to my friend Susan about this book. She said, "It sounds like the book promotes nonviolence." I said, "Yes, but not conventional nonviolence. This book doesn't necessarily address activists or soldiers in the field. It focuses in on the mind and heart of the community organizer in her office before the rally is planned. It addresses the mind of the general in his study before war is declared."

It's said wars are won or lost in the general's tent. So too, war can be prevented in the general's tent. Divisiveness can be healed in the tent of our own minds. That's the source of the river we call our life, which flows out to our children, families, and communities. Holistic consciousness and the seeds of reconciliation begin in our minds. It is there that we wrestle in the trenches. It is there that the trenches are filled in or reinforced according to our choices . . . "Let there be peace on earth and let it begin with me." Another way of putting this: Let the violence end with me. What does this mean? It means that we acknowledge that offender and offended have an equal part in a conflict. If we are the offender we ask forgiveness. If we are the offended we grant forgiveness. We move beyond the dualistic mind to the new mind. We don't take sides. This requires inner strength and deep integrity—the integrity of The Jesus Paradox.

1. Friedman, *Friedman's Fables*, 25–28.

This book addresses the mind and heart of the general and the general's spouse, who talks things over with him the night before war is declared. It addresses violence in its most primal and subtle forms: ideas as they take shape in our minds and lodge in our hearts. This is where the seeds of violence or nonviolence germinate.

Prayer, absorbing the values of the Gospel, and understanding Jesus according to the mystics, heals the divide. These practices make us less likely to scapegoat others. They help us see the enemy within, instead of labeling an enemy "out there." These practices will open us to the paradoxical and multi-dimensional quality of human beings and their circumstances. These practices will leave us open to ambiguity and to living the questions. These practices ground and stabilize the law of love (Mark 12:30–31). The monks of the Egyptian desert from the third to the fifth century knew this. It's time we understand it too. May we absorb it on deeper and deeper levels. The combined strategy of the mystics empowers us to "live in that life and power that takes away the occasion for all wars," as George Fox puts it. A supple mind not prone to taking sides, to quick-fixes, and to unilateral absolutist whims, is fertile for sowing seeds of non-violence.

The compulsion toward violence is deep in our mammalian brain. It is in the roar and aggression of the lion. It's the strategy of the mystics, not psychoanalysts, or pop-culture quick fixes, which has the primal power to reach these deep sub-conscious layers . . . That has the power to tame the lion (1 Peter 5:8). My favorite mammal is the whale—free from the more regressive violent instincts of the reptilian brain and so large and expansive that it's no longer threatened by the primeval sharks.

HOW WE IMAGINE ULTIMATE REALITY

How we imagine ultimate reality is of ultimate significance and influences everything in our lives. Humorless finality and absolutistic thinking squash creative collaboration and shared power. Paradox spawns creativity, encourages experimentation, shares control, and opens up myriad possibilities!

If our image of God is stagnant, our theology, preaching, teaching, and worship will be sluggish. If our image of God is informed by experimentation, personal experience, and dynamism then all aspects of our faith will become vibrant! The Alexandrian Mystics' fertile imaginations conceived of God's human form in the freshest way. Now we can catch that holy spark and set our souls aflame.

If people have a fixed dualistic understanding of God, faith becomes rigid. The truth is we're baptized in a flowing river. And we never step into the same river twice. The river is always morphing. Jesus' mystical essence is a moving target. If our ultimate truth (The Jesus Paradox) is a moving target that can't be pinned down, then we're less vulnerable to enticing absolutes. Then our faith will safeguard us from fixations, ultimatums, and violence. Then our faith will have breadth worthy of the mystics and worthy of the Twenty-first Century. The Jesus Paradox calls a cease fire; it halts trench digging. It keeps our minds pliant—able to come up with creative solutions on the spot, to create space where there is no space, to find humor in the humorless situation.

May the cease fires be called! May the trenches be filled! May dynamic union and Paradox win the day, not absolutes! May the body of Christ be cured of its excesses and be restored to wholeness!

May Evangelicals loosen their grip on various certainties and behold Mystery. May progressive Christians behold a primal orthodoxy or *paradoxical certitude* (The Jesus Paradox) to protect the mystic epicenter of Christian tradition. May solidarity with Jesus' humanity produce ever-deepening commitment to service and social justice. May solidarity with Jesus' Divinity produce life-long commitment to Christianity's deepest prayer forms.

If I were to sum up the Christian path it would be devotion to Jesus as understood by the earliest lineage of Christian mystics (The Alexandrian Mystics) and commitment to justice. Sentimental devotion to a narrow Jesus without wholehearted commitment to justice is not the answer. Commitment to justice and to the political allies of justice without devotion to the paradoxically Divine and human Jesus is also not the answer.

Our human nature needs transcendence and immanence. We need robust intuition and reason. We need silent prayer and vocal communal worship. Our hands need to hold onto the prayer beads. Our hands also need to hold on to the recently bereaved widow by the hospital bed. We need Jesus and we need justice!

Our society needs monks, neo-monastics, pastors, and social prophets. We need more people with the courage to take extended silent retreats. We need robust families broadly defined. We also need faith communities enlivened and broadened by the creative tension of the Jesus Paradox.

May Christ's united nature shatter our violent paradigms and lift us from the ashes into a new paradigm, into a new mind. Roll away the stone (John 11:39)! Prepare for the resurrection of the mind. Like the risen

Christ, the resurrected mind will create ripples in our relationships and communities, which will have numerous practical applications, such as conflict-mediation,[2] deeper listening, greater honesty, and stamina in the face of messy real world debacles, not to mention affirmation against the odds that yes, life is good (Genesis 1:31)!

May we heal divisions in our hearts and world by absorbing the Gospel on deeper and deeper levels! Through Gospel marinating, sound mystical theology, and deep forms of prayer, may we experience ever-deepening intimacy with God. Through service to the beings who share our planet, including foreigners, "the least of these," and devastated forests, may we experience ever-deepening intimacy with our neighbors (plant, animal, and human). Then the mystic heart of Jesus will beat in our chests and in our communities.

> Teach me your way, O God,
> that I may walk in your truth;
> give me an undivided heart to
> revere your name. (Psalm 86:11)

FROM PERSISTENT DUALISMS TO UNITY

If our ultimate reality is dualistic, then we have succumbed to the idol of mere knowledge. Binary thinking is the basis of conventional knowledge, which divides and conquers. Dualistic knowledge is fool's gold, which traps us in this visible world of the senses.

On the other hand, if our ultimate reality is holistic, then we kneel at the golden throne of wisdom—the golden throne of Jesus. Then "we walk by faith, and not by sight" (2 Corinthians 5:7)—a faith beyond the visible persistent dualisms, which spawn attachment and aversion. Then the cross and the resurrection are spoken in the same succession of breaths. Then we no longer cling to the resurrected Jesus or run from the cross in horror. Then we glimpse the divine union of the mystics. Then the dichotomies of religious and secular, heaven and earth, fall away like scales from the eyes (Acts 9:18). Then freedom is within reach—primordial liberation from the tight shoe of our selves—blissful abandon into the arms of God. To

---

2. Blackburn, Lombard Institute Mediation Skills Training, April 4, 2012 (According to the conflict mediation skills training offered by the Lombard Institute, "right" and "wrong" are misnomers that contribute to dispute grid-lock. Both the party who committed "the original offense" and the "offended" party play equal roles in a conflict).

move beyond mere glimpses and occasional rapture will take discipline and patient endurance, not unlike the persistence required to learn to play the violin or to attempt an assent on Denali. The union of the mystics is a rare achievement beyond the scope of other disciplines, yet within our potential. This potential for divine union is our greatest human endowment. And it is undergirded by a unified theology of Jesus.

The value of holistic wisdom and the interior freedom that follows is unsurpassed (Proverbs 4:7). Wisdom is the gateway to Gospel healings, to The Jesus Paradox, to the sacred heart of God. If through prayer and insight we can behold hidden wholeness, then Holy Communion reaches beyond sanctuary rites and our digestive tracks into our souls, beyond the confines of the senses and even science. Then the incarnate word peeks through the shutters of our eyelids and sees through our pupils![3] Then the scales fall and dross slinks away. Then the spark of the mystics emanates from our eyes and sets a wonderful fire to the world. Then the theological Jewel of the Nile is no longer entombed in the past. Then, like Peter, James, and John, we behold the radiant unity transfigured on Mount Tabor (Matthew 17:1–9, Mark 9:2–8, Luke 9:28–36). Then like Mary Magdalene, we are the first to behold the risen Christ (Mark 16:9, John 20:14). Then we reach past the divisions and trenches to the summit.

The apple slices and walnut pieces and partial visions of the managers have their place. We all see only a small part of the path when we're climbing the mountain. But, when we reach the summit only the whole walnut in the shell, the whole apple with skin and stem, and the panoramic vista on the cloudless day . . . Only they will do!

In the end the transfigured Jesus, whose light shines in the hermitages of the desert monasteries and the countless prayer rooms in cities and towns, takes our breath away and fills us with new wine. Jesus, resplendent on Tabor, gives us what we're starving for—the spiritual food that satisfies the depths of our souls (Matthew 17:1–9, Mark 9:2–8, Luke 9:28–36). The mystic vision of Jesus integrates Divinity and humanity, Creator and creatures, eternity and time! Dedication to the meditation cushions and to the spouses who encourage us to drop the feverish goal orientation and let the moment unfold . . . They save the day.

All of us have the capacity to see the whole! We had it as children. And it can be cultivated in adulthood. The wide-eyed wonderment of a child at play, at one with the universe, at one with the self and its unique

---

3. The incarnate Word (*Logos*) is available to us through insight and prayer. See *Logos* in glossary.

blemishes, can and will break in on the denizens of a highly litigious left brain society!

The path of the Alexandrian Mystics was not naïve daydreaming.[4] It was finally satisfying the veracious thirst for ultimate meaning—for ultimate purpose and fulfillment—for Joy! It was about beholding the electric Jesus Paradox, which fills the trenches and heals the divide, which "has made both groups into one and has broken down the dividing wall" (Ephesians 2:14). It was about interior evolution and rebirth.

Einstein often reiterated that "imagination is more important than knowledge." The future depends on the imagination of synthetic minds, free from the divisiveness that stalks our communities and world. The future of the planet depends on the imagination of the mystics. The Alexandrian Mystics and the Jesus Paradox anchor the vision of Mystic Christianity, carefully winding us through the creative tensions to the panorama at the top.

QUESTIONS FOR REFLECTION AND DISCUSSION

1) Is the shift from dualistic thinking to holistic thinking important? Why or why not?

2) Is paradox the antidote to absolutism? Why or why not?

3) What is the difference between binary knowledge and holistic wisdom, as described by the author?

4) Do you agree that imagination is more important than knowledge? Please explain.

5) Application question: Where are the trenches and foxholes in your mind and heart? Please explain. How can you begin to fill in these trenches?

6) Application question: What is a summit experience in your life, when a panoramic transforming insight changed your life's direction? Please explain.

---

4. There is a simplicity on this side of complexity, which is generally naïve and ignorant. There is a *supraessential simplicity* (Palamas) on the other side of complexity, which is the distilled essence of holistic minds. They are two completely different states of consciousness.

BOOK OVERVIEW QUESTIONS

1) Who is Jesus for the most long standing lineage of early Christian Mystics?

2) How does renewed understanding of Jesus (The Jesus Paradox of the Alexandrian Mystics) change . . .
   a. Our faith?
   b. Our approach to prayer?
   c. Our relationships with neighbors?
   d. The life of the church?
   e. Our relationship with other religious communities?

3) If you were to rank the book: *Healing the Divide* on a scale of 1–5 (five being highest), what would you rate it and why would you give it that rating?

4) What part of the book spoke to you the most, and why? (If you can find it please read it)

5) Are there any quotes in the book you like? If so, which ones? Why?

6) What part of the book confused you the most or created the most questions? Why did you have a hard time with that part?

7) What are some things *Healing The Divide* says about Jesus, faith, and life that you disagree with?

8) What parts of Smith's description of Jesus differ from your understanding of Jesus? How do they differ?

9) What parts of Smith's description of Jesus resonate with your understanding of Jesus? How do they resonate?

10) Did your understanding of Jesus change as a result of reading this book? If so, how?

11) What was your favorite illustration in the book? Why?

12) The author says a relationship with Jesus is about intimacy (silent prayer) and responsibility (rooted mystical theology). What do you make of this?

13) Do you think a bare-bones mystic theology of Jesus is needed? Why or why not?

14) Do you think The Jesus Paradox safeguards Christian tradition from excesses and eventual demise? Why or why not?

15) The balancing act of The Jesus Paradox is a high bar. How do you think you measure up?

16) Did you refer to any of the Appendices? If so, did it/they speak to you?

17) Application question: Has this book impacted your thinking? If so, how?

18) Application question: Has this book impacted your life? If so, how?

Afterword

YOU HAVE BEEN LED on a dazzling journey—and it could well lead to dazzling results. I deeply admire Amos Smith's courage and study set forth in this book. This is a foundational work written in a style that will be respected by scholars—yet easily accessible to ordinary Christians and would be seekers—where such wisdom has been long awaited, much desired, and desperately needed. I believe the Jesus Paradox is needed for the foundational reform and reformulation of the Christian message itself, and especially now for its very *hearability*.

The dynamic union of opposites that the Christ Mystery *is* surpasses, undercuts, and has the power to resolve so many levels of denominational argument and even political theory that have divided and re-divided us in Christian history. We did not realize how large and reconciling our own Christ was, despite being told that "God wanted all perfection (*pleroma*, fullness) to be found in him, and all things to be reconciled through him and for him" (Colossians 1:19).

Instead of The Great Reconciler, we made Jesus into a mere tribal god, who then had to compete with other world religions (even with his own Judaism!), and with our very humanity—which was now very hard to sanctify or liberate. "That which is not incarnate, is not redeemed" said St. Irenaeus. Without the dynamic terms of incarnation being absolutely clear, Jesus remained *only* Divine, and we remained *only* human, thus confusing and diminishing the very process of redemption itself. We missed the major point which was that God had put the two together in a very dynamic way for all to see and trust, but we did not know how to even *imagine* that either in him or in ourselves. Yes, we had the will and the desire, but did not trust the extraordinary incarnational method that God used, nor its Exemplar.

Further, there has been little appreciation of the cosmic role of Christ and his very purpose in history up to now, which is much larger than a mere "religious" or doctrinal statement (Ephesians 1:3–14). Although I must humbly remind readers that my own Franciscan school always had a cosmic notion of Christ through Francis' own intuitive genius.[1]

Truly great ideas, like Miaphysite theology, are invariably slow in coming, because the normal mind thinks in static dualisms and even prefers to. It allows us to take clean sides and argue from supposedly pure positions. Only "prayer," and especially prayer of quiet, can overcome such splits and such artificial separateness. Only inner stillness can absorb and comprehend paradoxes and seeming contradictions, which the Eastern Fathers seemed to understand much more than the Western.

Many of you are surely saying, "Why have others not seen this?" or "Why are others not teaching this?" I have often asked this myself when teaching on contemplative prayer or the Cosmic Christ, and I still do not have a fully adequate response. I do know that the very nature of a religion is that it often sees itself as "too big to fail" or "too right to be wrong." Otherwise normal critical faculties seem to be suspended in favor of some unconscious notion that "All the smart people ahead of me could not have failed to ask every good question." And yes some surely did, but most were willing to parrot back practiced creedal formulas without unraveling either the untested *assumptions or the implications* of the simple formulas.[2] Amos Smith helps us see how we even did this with the Nicene Creed and the Council of Chalcedon.

We now know, if we are humble and honest, that most of our churches and even most of our leaders have not consistently read the Gospels from the contemplative mind, which I believe is another word for "the mind of Christ" (1 Corinthians 2:16). Without it, we severely limit the Holy Spirit's capacity for inspiration and guidance. We had arguments to win, logic to uphold, and denominations to hold together, after all. Without the contemplative mind, humans, even Christians, revel in dualisms and do not understand any dynamic unity between seeming opposites *as the Jesus Paradox was meant to teach us and precisely exemplify for us.*[3] The separate

1. Francis' genius was soon built upon by the philosophical theology of St. Bonaventure and John Duns Scotus, who rightly saw the Christ as the template of creation.

2. We did the same with "substitutionary atonement theory," which we Franciscans never agreed with either.

3. I might call the Jesus Paradox imaginal causality, Scholastic philosophers would call it exemplary causality, science today might call it morphogenic fields.

self fears and denies paradoxes instead—which is to deny our own self, of course, which is always filled with seeming contradictions.

"Until the single grain of wheat dies" we see everything as a mirror of ourselves—separate and split—and we cannot see in wholes. As Jesus put it, we "will not yield a rich harvest" (John 12:24). Maybe we cannot even see holiness? We are then unable to comprehend that *Christ is our own wholeness* and not just his own (1 Corinthians 1:30)—*set forth for all to imagine, trust, imitate, and comprehend—through him.* He is the Exemplar of Reconciled Humanity, the Stand-In for all of us. At this wondrous level, Christianity is hardly a separate religion, but simply an organic and hopeful message about the nature of Reality itself. Who would want to fight that? Who would need to defeat it?

Amos Smith takes brilliant advantage of our newly found capacity for non-dual consciousness to point out that we have some important and once central ancestors, the Alexandrian Mystics, who already recognized the power of Christ to overcome the dualisms, dichotomies, and divisions that seem to be the preferred mode for the non-prayerful mind. I do think this is an evolution of consciousness for most of the West and even for most of the world! Now much of the East has lost its older wisdom too, and can be quite dualistic. As Augustine said, we are being offered something "forever ancient and forever new." It is revolutionary because it is so traditional and yet so hidden, and it is traditional teaching that can still create a revolution of mind and heart—and history itself.

It bears repeating what Amos Smith wrote toward the end of this important book (223): *"My core truth about Jesus isn't rooted in mainstream Christian tradition. It's rooted in Jesus' essence. It's about the deep stillness of silent prayer and a theology big enough to give that blessed stillness words."* That is the whole book beautifully summarized, in my opinion.

Jesus has always been so much bigger than our ideas about him, our readiness to surrender to him, and our ability to love and allow all that he clearly loves and allows in human history and all of creation. He is the microcosm of the macrocosm. He is the Great Coincidence of Opposites, as St. Bonaventure taught. Only the Jesus Paradox gives us the permission and the freedom to finally and fully love the paradox that everything already and always is.

Receive that permission and freedom here.

—Fr. Richard Rohr, O.F.M.
Center for Action and Contemplation
Lent, 2013 in Albuquerque, New Mexico

Appendix A

Glossary

Alexandrian Bishops

The legacy of the Alexandrian Bishops (also known as The Holy See of Saint Mark) began with the apostle Mark, who wrote the Gospel of Mark, and who brought Christianity to Egypt. The Alexandrian Bishops claim an unbroken line, beginning with Mark in the first century. This line has continued through the ages to the current Alexandrian Bishop, who resides in Cairo, Egypt (instead of the historic seat of Alexandria). A distinguishing characteristic of the Alexandrian Bishopric is its emphasis on monastic experience. From the beginning, the Monastic Authority of the Alexandrian Bishops was not based on title or clerical hierarchy. It was based on direct experience in prayer in a monastic setting. To facilitate this direct experience in prayer, Alexandrian Bishops are required to have a monastic background. It is significant to note that before Cyril VI (d.1971) became the one hundred sixteenth Bishop he was a hermit of the Egyptian desert with deep experience in silent prayer. Cyril VI was a profound mystic, to whom many miracles were attributed. Because of the monasticism infused in the Alexandrian Bishopric, I sometimes refer to the Alexandrian Bishops as monk-bishops. See *Alexandrian Mystics, Athanasius of Alexandria, Cyril of Alexandria, George Fox* (in the context of Monastic Authority), *Monastic Authority,* and *Neo-monasticism*. Also see Appendix B. For a complete list of the 117 Alexandrian Bishops, which have spanned two thousand years, see Meinardus, *Two Thousand Years of Coptic Christianity*, Appendix B.

Alexandrian Mystics (Alexandrian Fathers)

The Alexandrian Mystics are so named for their association with Alexandria, Egypt. The Alexandrian Mystics were the Christian monks, nuns, and hermits of the 4th through the 5th century (312–454 CE) who resided in the Egyptian Desert, near Alexandria. They are also the Alexandrian Bishops who resided in Alexandria during that time period. Some of the monks and hermits of the Egyptian Desert outside of Alexandria are better known as The Desert Fathers and Mothers. The Alexandrian Mystics were predominantly Miaphysite (which was fully developed by Cyril of Alexandria). They were also hesychasts. These monks and monk-bishops predate the split between Roman Catholicism and Eastern Orthodoxy (1054). They also predate the Oriental Orthodox split that eventually followed The Council of Chalcedon (451), so they rightfully belong to the Church universal. Scholars of patristics will prefer the more well known term "Alexandrian Fathers (312–454 CE)" to "Alexandrian Mystics (312–454 CE)." This is of course admissible. I prefer the less precise and broader term "Alexandrian Mystics" because it presses the point that the entire city of monasteries that flowered in the Egyptian Desert outside of Alexandria between 312 and 454 were predominantly Miaphysite in their experience, beliefs, and theology. And, like my sisters and brothers in the East, I cannot separate theology from mysticism. So, if the theology of the Egyptian Desert was predominantly Miaphysite (a mystical non-dual theology), they were Miaphysite in their experience and beliefs too. Hence the term, "Alexandrian Mystics." See Alexandrian Bishops, Anthony of Egypt, Asceticism, Athanasius of Alexandria, Cyril of Alexandria, Desert Fathers and Mothers, Hesychasm, Miaphysite (The Jesus Paradox), Monastic Authority, and Mystic Christianity.

American Friends Service Committee

The American Friends Service Committee (AFSC) is a peace and social justice arm of the Religious Society of Friends (Quakers). The AFSC was founded in 1917 to assist civilian victims of World War I. From the beginning the AFSC has provided those who object to war with constructive alternatives to military service. For their efforts, in 1947 the AFSC received the Nobel Peace Prize on behalf of Quakers throughout the world. See *Catholic Worker Movement, Church of the Savior,*

Glos

Emergent Church, George Fox, Jesus' Third Way, Liberation Theology, Peace Churches, Progressive Christianity, and Quakerism.

Anthony of Egypt (Anthony the Great, Saint Anthony)

Anthony, also known as Antony (d. 356), was the foremost monk of the Egyptian Desert. His journey is the prototype for all of Christian monasticism that followed him. He is called "Father of All Monks." Athanasius' biography of Anthony's life, *Life of Antony* (360), helped spread the concept of monasticism, particularly in Western Europe, through Latin translations. Shortly after Anthony entered the Egyptian desert he went into seclusion in a cave for a number of years, where he diligently practiced silent prayer. When Anthony emerged from seclusion he was transfigured and radiant. Many flocked to the desert to bask in his light and he was reported to have healed many. After Anthony monasteries began appearing all over the Egyptian desert. See *Alexandrian Mystics, Asceticism, Centering Prayer, Deification, Desert Fathers and Mothers, Divine Union, Hesychasm, Monastic Authority, Silent Prayer,* and *Tabor Light.*

Arius (Arianism, Arian Controversy)

See Appendix F.

Asceticism

Asceticism has gotten a bad reputation in Western Society, yet rightly understood, it's the key to restoring balance to our lives and communities. Asceticism is retreat from the senses, because God in the most profound mystical sense is beyond the senses. As scripture tells us, "we live by faith and not by sight" (2 Corinthians 5:7). Asceticism affirms that our deepest and most treasured life (that treasure in a field or pearl of great price Jesus spoke of in parables (Matthew 13:44–46)) is not of the senses. Its first language is silence. In order to make room for silence, other less important priorities are set aside. This laying aside of sense attractions, is asceticism rightly understood, which is not repressive, but liberating. We deny our senses, for a greater reward that is waiting in the pregnant silence. The extreme deprivations associated with asceticism in the past need to be recast. Yet, the primary insight that periodic abstinence from sensory stimulation (solitude), from auditory stimulation (silence), from food (fasting), from sex (abstinence), from incessant activity (stillness), etcetera, is liberating. The compulsive addiction to sense objects is what is actually repressive and

243

enslaving. See *Anthony of Egypt, Buddhist/Christian Dialogue, Centering Prayer, Cloud of Unknowing, Desert Fathers and Mothers, Dionysius The Areopagite, Dispassion, Essenes, Hesychasm, Monastic Authority, Mystic Christianity, Neo-monasticism, The Philokalia, Qumran, Silent Prayer,* and *Unloading.*

Athanasius of Alexandria

Athanasius (d. 373) was the twentieth monk-bishop of Alexandria. He was bishop for forty five years, with over seventeen years spent in five exiles ordered by different Roman emperors. He had a leading role against the Arians in the First Council of Nicaea, arguing that Jesus is "of one being" (the Greek for being: *hypostasis*) with God (a precursor to what Cyril of Alexandria called *Miaphysite*). Athanasius was also the main contributor to the Nicene Creed. He had a profound interest in promoting monasticism, which included his book, *Life of Antony,* which became the best seller of his time and promoted Christian monasticism throughout the world. See *Alexandrian Bishops, Alexandrian Mystics, Cyril of Alexandria, Monastic Authority, Neo-monasticism,* and *Nicene Creed.*

Buddhist/Christian Dialogue

Buddhist/Christian Dialogue is bearing promising fruit today. Excellent titles in this area are *Living Buddha, Living Christ* and *Going Home: Jesus and Buddha as Brothers* by Thich Nhat Hanh, *The Good Heart: A Buddhist Perspective on the Teachings of Jesus* by the Dali Lama, and *Jesus and Buddha: The Parallel Sayings* by Marcus Borg and Jack Kornfield. Various schools of Buddhism have deep kinship with Christian monasticism. Hence, Thomas Merton's well known comment: "Thich Nhat Hanh is more my brother than many who are nearer to me by race and nationality." Merton and Hanh had a deep monastic kinship and both deplored the Vietnam War. See *Asceticism, Centering Prayer, Cloud of Unknowing, Dionysius the Areopagite, Dispassion, Hesychasm, Jesus Prayer, Monastic Authority, The Philokalia, Prayer of the Heart, Silent Prayer, Unloading,* and *Vatican II.*

Cappadocian Fathers

See *Hypostasis* and *Trinity.*

Catholic Worker Movement

The Catholic Worker Movement was founded by Dorothy Day (d. 1980) and Peter Maurin (d. 1949) in 1933. It strove to embody Jesus' social justice emphasis by reaching out to those on the margins of society, especially the homeless. There are over 213 Catholic Worker communities that provide various social services. Catholic Worker houses are diverse according to the needs of their particular communities. The houses actively oppose war as a viable solution and promote nonviolence and a more equitable distribution of wealth. The Catholic Worker house in New York City publishes a paper called *The Catholic Worker*, which sells for one cent. See *American Friends Service Committee, Emergent Church, Jesus' Third Way, Liberation Theology, Peace Churches, Progressive Christianity*, and *Quakerism*.

Centering Prayer

Centering Prayer, a term first coined by Thomas Merton, is a method of silent prayer with deep historic roots, preserved in Western Contemplative tradition, most notably in *The Cloud of Unknowing* and in the teachings of John of the Cross and Teresa of Avila. Centering Prayer has been made contemporary in recent decades by Basil Pennington, Thomas Keating, William Menninger, Cynthia Bourgeault, and others. Perhaps the seventh century monk, John Climacus, gave the best description of Centering Prayer: "the shedding of thoughts."[1] Another way to think about Centering Prayer is training the mind to become free from distractions so it can "rest in God."

The evangelical arm, so to speak, of contemporary Centering Prayer tradition, is Contemplative Outreach, Ltd, which produces numerous resources, organizes Centering Prayer retreats worldwide, and administers a website, etcetera.

The best advice about Centering Prayer that I've received from seasoned practitioners over the years: A) Do Centering Prayer at least twice a day for at least twenty minutes each time (the second time exponentially increases the long term healing effects) B) Do Centering Prayer at the same times every day on an empty stomach C) Daily silent prayer has a cumulative effect and requires years of steady practice for deep healing to take place. Give it time! D) A regular exercise program speeds up Centering Prayer's long term healing process E) Do at least one extended six to ten day Centering Prayer retreat yearly. This too,

1. Palmer, et al., *The Philokalia Vol. 4*, 278.

catapults progress. See *Asceticism, Buddhist/Christian Dialogue, Cloud of Unknowing, Deification, Dispassion, Divine Union, Hesychasm, Mystic Christianity, The Philokalia, Prayer of the Heart, Silent Prayer,* and *Unloading.*

Christian Mysticism

See *Mystic Christianity.*

Christology

Christology is theology about Jesus, primarily concerned with Jesus' nature and personhood (Jesus' Divinity and humanity and the relationship of the Divinity with the humanity). *Monophysite, Dyophysite, and Miaphysite (The Jesus Paradox)* represent a primal progression of depth and breadth in theology about Jesus: a progression from simple union (drop in the ocean), to separation (dissect), to dynamic union (behold). See *Dyophysite, Historical Jesus, Jesus Seminar, Logos, Miaphysite (The Jesus Paradox),* and *Monophysite.*

Church of the Savior

The Church of the Savior is a network of nine independent faith communities based in Washington D.C, which has over forty ministries that advocate an alternative approach to conventional church. Their emphasis is Christian discipleship, which tries to reflect some of the vigor of the early church. The Church of the Savior has informed contemporary movements such as The Missional Church, The Emergent Church, and Neo-monasticism. Like the historic Quakers, the Church of the Savior tries to keep an exquisite balance between contemplation and social activism. Church of the Savior members are required to devote at least an hour a day to a spiritual practice and are required to volunteer (at least weekly) for a charitable service organization. See *American Friends Service Committee, Catholic Worker Movement, Emergent Church, Neo-monasticism,* and *Quakerism.*

Cloud of Unknowing

The Cloud of Unknowing was a spiritual guide for silent prayer practitioners in the latter half of the fourteenth century. It was written anonymously in Middle English and has proven a classic of the Western Contemplative Tradition. See *Asceticism, Centering Prayer, Deification, Dispassion, Divine Union, Hesychasm, The Philokalia, Prayer of the Heart, Silent Prayer,* and *Unloading.*

Contemplative Christianity

Most of what I have written in this book could be labeled Contemplative Christianity. Yet, I steer away from this term, because when people hear it, the first thing they think of is contemplating a sense object of some kind, such as a word, thought, or image. This is how I experience Contemplative Christianity. I think it's important to identify Mystic Christianity as the core within Contemplative Christianity. To get away from the fixation on words and contemplating I also think it's important to clarify that Christian Mysticism or Mystic Christianity, is ultimately not about contemplating (formation), but about beholding (deformation). In its highest form Mystic Christianity is not about "contemplating" any sense object. It is about basking in the freedom of primal undifferentiated silence, or what Gregory Palamas calls "God's supraessential simplicity,"[2] from which profound energy and creativity flow. It is about beholding the paradox at the center of our being in communion with Christ. This element of depth is what's missing from Christianity today, especially in the West. We are overloaded with information. We don't need any more cornucopias for the senses, even if they are of a contemplative variety! What we desperately need is to consistently and thoroughly behold the mystery at the center which, as *The Philokalia* continually reminds us, is beyond anything we can apprehend with the senses! See *Logos, Monastic Authority, Mystic Christianity, The Philokalia, Progressive Christianity,* and *Quakerism.*

Council of Chalcedon

The Council of Chalcedon is the fourth ecumenical church council that met in Chalcedon (Asia Minor) in 451, which condemned the "one united dynamic nature" or *Miaphysite* nature of Jesus, which was the spiritual legacy of the Alexandrian Mystics. Instead, Chalcedon, under pressure from Rome, proposed the dualistic theology that Jesus was "in two natures" (*dyophysite*). In my estimation, the crux of the dispute at Chalcedon was that The Roman Catholic Pope, Leo (d. 461), had no knowledge of Greek. As a result, he misinterpreted the *Miaphysite* theology of Alexandrian Bishop, Dioscorus (d. 454), which was passed down to Dioscorus from Cyril and Athanasius.[3] Because Leo had no knowledge of primary Greek concepts, such as *hypostasis,* he confused the Greek term *Miaphysite* (The Jesus Paradox). He

---

2. Palmer, et al., *The Philokalia Vol. 4*, 423.
3. Sellers, *The Council of Chalcedon*, 227.

and Rome's misunderstandings of *Miaphysite* (Greek) were labeled *monophysite* (Latin) and condemned at Chalcedon. The unfortunate power struggle between the Roman See and the Alexandrian See for supremacy in Christendom played an integral part in the dispute.

The Council of Chalcedon led to the separation of the Church in the Eastern Roman Empire—the first and most significant Church split. For the most part, those who rejected the Council of Chalcedon eventually identified with the Oriental Orthodox Church. Those who accepted the Council of Chalcedon identified with the Roman Catholic and Eastern Orthodox Churches. There were many exceptions. See *Christology, Dyophysite, Miaphysite (The Jesus Paradox),* and *Monophysite*. See Appendix G. Also see Samuel, *The Council of Chalcedon Re-examined.*

Cyril of Alexandria

Cyril (376–444) was Alexandrian Bishop from 412–44, when Alexandria was at its height of power and influence in the Roman Empire. His predecessor, Athanasius of Alexandria, had refuted Arius' *dyophysite* theology. Cyril followed some of the same lines of argument in his refutation of Nestorius' *dyophysite* theology at the Council of Ephesus in 431. Cyril was the champion of *Miaphysite* theology—that Jesus is "at once God and human." This was contrary to Arius and Nestorius, who in various ways denied the dynamic unity of Divinity and humanity in Jesus. If only Cyril had lived to see the Council of Chalcedon (451), the first church split may have been prevented and authentic *Miaphysite* (The Jesus Paradox) theology may have been preserved by the Church as a whole. The healing medicine of Cyril was his ability to keep the balance. Before the incarnation Cyril could accept the two separate natures of Jesus' Divinity and humanity. After the incarnation Cyril emphatically insisted on the one united dynamic nature. This appeased both sides of the Christological dispute for a time.[4] Then, after Cyril died, the disputes all erupted again at Chalcedon, with no one able to effectively keep the delicate balance.

Readers familiar with Cyril's biography will note that the first half of his life was characterized by some unfortunate violence. The redeeming message, confirmed by witnesses, is that Cyril experienced a transformation in the second half of his life. Along these lines, I am

---

4. Sellers, *The Council of Chalcedon*, 299–300.

reminded of these words of Mohandas Gandhi: "There is hope for the violent man to become nonviolent. There is no hope for the coward."

See *Alexandrian Bishops, Alexandrian Mystics, Athanasius of Alexandria,* and *Miaphysite (The Jesus Paradox).*

Deification

Deification (*theosis* in Greek) is the culmination of profound dedication and diligence to the decades-long process of purification (usually through silent prayer), whereby practitioners enter into a deified or glorified state of consciousness. This state of consciousness is variously referred to in *The Philokalia* as incorruptible, immortal, and eternal. It is accepted that Saint Anthony of Egypt realized complete deification. As a result, he lived to be at least 105 years of age and was widely known for many miraculous healings. A famous quotation of the Eastern Church is "Jesus became human so humans could become divine (divine with a lower case d)." The best summary of deification I have seen is from Gregory Palamas in *The Philokalia.*[5] The scriptural basis of deification, which *The Philokalia* refers to, is 1 Corinthians 6:17. See *Anthony of Egypt, Centering Prayer, Cloud of Unknowing, Dispassion, Divine Union, Hesychasm, Original Nature, The Philokalia, Silent Prayer, Tabor Light,* and *Unloading.*

Desert Fathers and Mothers

The Desert Fathers and Mothers were hermits, ascetics, and monks who lived in the Egyptian Desert between the third and sixth centuries. By the year of Saint Anthony's death in 356, thousands of monks had flocked to the Egyptian Desert, primarily in Scetes, to follow Anthony's example. Although sayings of the Desert Fathers have recently been popularized, most don't realize that the Desert Fathers and Mothers were first and foremost mystics and that they were predominantly *Miaphysite.* See *Alexandrian Mystics, Anthony of Egypt, Asceticism, Contemplative Christianity, Miaphysite (The Jesus Paradox), Mystic Christianity,* and *The Philokalia.*

Dionysius the Areopagite (Pseudo-Dionysius, Pseudo-Denys, Denys)

The writings attributed to Dionysius the Areopagite (an Athenian convert of Saint Paul in Acts 17:34) in *The Philokalia* and elsewhere,

5. Palmer, et al., *The Philokalia Vol. 4,* 421.

were later discovered by scholars to be wrongly attributed. This writer is appropriately referenced today as Pseudo-Dionysius, Pseudo-Denys, or Denys, who was a theologian and philosopher of the fifth and sixth centuries. Regardless of attribution, Denys is a giant in Mystic Christian theology. His most famous works are *The Mystical Theology* and *The Divine Names*. These brief works exhaust the reasoning mind's tendency to codify or name God. As a result this opens the mind to mystical awareness beyond names and forms. These short works hold special importance for The Alexandrian Mystics and for the writers of *The Philokalia*. It is significant to note how much The Alexandrian Mystics on through the fourteenth century honored Denys. An example is this comment by Gregory Palamas: "St. Dionysius the Areopagite (Denys), the most eminent theologian after the divine apostles. . ."[6] Yet, in my estimation the writings of Denys need to be tempered with *Miaphysite* (The Jesus Paradox) for appropriate balance. The Jesus Paradox qualifies God (in the absolute unqualified sense offered by Denys) for Christians, tempering Denys with the mystical theology of Jesus. For those versed in Buddhism, *The Mystical Theology* and *Divine Names* of Denys have striking similarities to *The Heart Sutra*. See *Asceticism, Buddhist/ Christian Dialogue, Centering Prayer, Dispassion, Hesychasm, Mystic Christianity, The Philokalia,* and *Silent Prayer*.

Dispassion

Dispassion is a state of mind free from passion or desire for sense objects. In this state of consciousness there is no attachment or aversion to any images, concepts, or other sense objects. In other words, in this state, the mind has no desire to possess anything whatsoever. A synonym for dispassion is equanimity, a term used in Buddhist tradition. Throughout *The Philokalia,* reaching the state of dispassion is considered a major breakthrough on the spiritual path. See *Asceticism, Buddhist/Christian Dialogue, Dionysius the Areopagite,* and *The Philokalia*.

Divine Union

Divine Union is the culmination of profound devotion and diligence to the decades-long path of purification, when the practitioner experiences ineffable union with God, and the abiding joy that accompanies the experience. This state of abiding joy is in contrast to the conflicting emotions (before divine union), which are characteristic of the human condition. The inexpressible divine union that takes place in the hearts

6. Palmer, et al, *The Philokalia Vol. 4,* 386.

and minds of spiritual athletes takes place symbolically during the Eucharist/holy communion. See *Centering Prayer, Cloud of Unknowing, Deification, Dispassion, Hesychasm, Original Nature, Silent Prayer, Tabor Light,* and *Unloading.*

Dyophysite

Dyophysite (sometimes called *Diphysite*) is a Greek word that means "two natures." The Council of Chalcedon conceived of the person of Christ "in two natures." This is the unfortunate dualistic theology the West inherited. This dualistic theology was called *dyophysite* by its detractors. The Oriental Orthodox Church rejects the *dyophysite* Chalcedonian approach. In contrast, Oriental Orthodoxy embraces *Miaphysite* (The Jesus Paradox). See *Council of Chalcedon.* For contrast, see *Miaphysite (The Jesus Paradox)* and *monophysite.* See Appendix F (especially *Arius* and *Nestorius*) and Appendix G. Also see the Wikipedia article, "Dyophysite."

Emergent Church

The Emergent Church emphasizes the here and now, as opposed to future salvation. It also emphasizes social activism or "missional living." The Emergent Church is exemplified in the writings of Phyllis Tickle and Brian McLaren, among others. The movement tends to transcend labels such as conservative and liberal and breaks down any and all denominational barriers. It is anchored in the pioneering spirit of our post-modern era, which has no trouble mixing and matching apparently disparate threads of Christian tradition. See *American Friends Service Committee, Buddhist/Christian Dialogue, Catholic Worker Movement, Church of the Savior, Liberation Theology, Neo-monasticism, Quantum Physics, Vatican II,* and *World Council of Churches.*

Essenes

The Essenes were an ancient Jewish sect that predate Jesus. One distinguishing characteristic of Essene spiritual practice, reserved for its adepts, was a forty day fast. Essene writings indicate that the forty day fast was not just a fast from food, but also from speech and thought. In order to survive a forty day fast all energy was preserved, including energy expended on speech and thoughts. A number of scholars have reasoned that John the Baptist was an Essene from the community of Qumran. And that's why Jesus began his ministry with a forty day fast in the wilderness after being baptized by John in the Jordan

River, which is walking distance from Qumran. In deed Jesus' forty day fast didn't occur in a vacuum (Matthew 4:1–11, Mark 1:12–13, Luke 4:1–13). Jesus' John the Baptist/Essene connection points to the foundational significance of monastic experience in Christian tradition. See *Asceticism, Monastic Authority,* and *Qumran.*

Fox, George

George Fox (d. 1691) was the founder of the Quakers (The Society of Friends). He believed that communion with Christ in silent prayer is what gave one's voice authenticity and authority, not the hierarchy of clergy. He, like The Alexandrian Mystics, believed that authority was based on personal experience with the Divine in silent prayer, not on title, position, or rank. Early on Fox influenced William Penn (d. 1718) and Oliver Cromwell (d. 1658). And he remains influential through the centuries. See *American Friends Service Committee, Jesus' Third Way, Monastic Authority, Neo-monasticism, Peace Churches,* and *Quakerism.*

Fundamentalism

Fundamentalism (or absolutism) is the unwavering adherence to a set of irreducible beliefs. Adherence to these beliefs determines who is saved or damned, faithful or infidel. Fundamentalists don't accept this label and its negative connotations, yet for the most part the label still holds. The absolute adherence to a set of beliefs provides relief from the myriad uncertainties of our times and the challenges they present, yet absolutism contributes to subtle and gross forms of violence throughout the world today. For contrast, see *Jesus' Third Way, Mainline Christianity, New Age, Peace Churches, Progressive Christianity, Miaphysite (The Jesus Paradox), Vatican II Council,* and *World Council of Churches.*

Gospel of Thomas

The Gospel of Thomas is a Coptic Text, which many scholars concur is the oldest and most authentic of the Gnostic Gospels. It is considered by most scholars to be an important source for understanding the historical Jesus. It has many mystical sayings, which are not found in the canonical Gospels. The Gospel of Thomas was discovered near Nag Hammadi, Egypt in 1945. *Thomas* has been dated as early as 40 and as late as 140 CE. See *Contemplative Christianity, Historical Jesus, Jesus Seminar, Mystic Christianity,* and *Progressive Christianity.*

Hesychasm

Athletes of the soul from the fourth century on who followed Saint Anthony into the desert to pray were called *hesychasts*. Little is known about early *hesychasm* in the Egyptian desert because it was taught through oral tradition and was generally not written down for posterity. It's safe to say that *hesychasm* was rooted in silent prayer, which was very similar to Centering Prayer as taught by Thomas Keating and others today.

The most precise early instruction on *hesychasm* may be John Climacus in *The Ladder of Divine Ascent*: "Take up your seat on a high place and watch, if only you know how, and then you will see in what manner, when, whence, how many and what kind of thieves come to enter and steal your clusters of grapes. When the watchman grows weary, he stands up and prays; and then he sits down again and courageously takes up his former task."[7] Climacus gives a similar account in *The Philokalia*.[8] What we surmise from this quotation and others similar to it is that *hesychasm* was a vigilant eyes-open form of centering prayer, which clears the mind of all distractions and rests in primal silence. Among the more advanced circles of Centering Prayer practitioners today, there is a diversity of approaches. There are so called *breathers* (who follow the breath during silent prayer), *worders* (who use a sacred word during silent prayer), and *gazers* (who practice an undifferentiated gaze on the floor in front of them during silent prayer). Of the three, *gazers* are most akin to *hesychast* tradition. A characteristic of *hesychasm* is that purification, which takes place while practicing this silent prayer, is often accompanied by "cleansing tears" or "blessed tears." *Philokalia* writers, especially Nikitas Stithatos, often refer to these tears as part of silent prayer's purification process.[9]

The term *hesychasm* encompasses other practices, which include crouching postures, rhythmic recitation of the Jesus Prayer, and breathing techniques. These techniques were offered to beginners to break up the monotony of their prayer practices and to decrease the likelihood that they would give up on silent prayer. Yet as Gregory Palamas reiterates in *The Philokalia*, these were preliminary exercises to the more advanced and pure *hesychasm*, as described above.[10]

7. Climacus, *The Ladder*, Step 21, 27.
8. Palmer, et al, *The Philokalia Vol. 4*, 200.
9. Palmer, et al, *The Philokalia Vol. 4*, 126. Also see 79–174.
10. Palmer, et al, *The Philokalia Vol. 4*, 290.

A primary aspect of *hesychasm* is what the *Philokalia* refers to as "radical humility" before God. As more and more expansive states of consciousness are introduced, the ego gets puffed up with pride. There are many humbling methods to counter this pride. One of the most widespread is constant recitation of the holy name, Jesus, through the various derivations of The Jesus Prayer. This recitation protects the mind from egoism and keeps the mind appropriately stayed on Jesus, the founder and perfecter of Christian faith (Hebrews 12:2).

The ultimate purpose of *hesychasm* is union with God. Also see *Asceticism, Centering Prayer, Cloud of Unknowing, Deification, Dionysius the Areopagite, Dispassion, Divine Union, Jesus Prayer, Mystic Christianity, The Philokalia, Prayer of the Heart, Silent Prayer, Tabor Light,* and *Unloading.*

Historical Jesus

The Historical Jesus is the reconstruction of the life of Jesus based on critical analysis and historical methods. It is strictly concerned with the Jesus of history, not the Jesus of faith. For this reconstruction primary sources (Gospel texts) are used, along with other historical sources. Other sources include fragments of early non-canonical Gospels, the writings of Jewish historian, Flavius Josephus, and Roman documents, such as writings of imperial biographer Suetonius and the letters of Pliny to Emperor Trajan. The Historical Jesus is relevant to Christology, yet its underlying assumption smacks of the same hubris as the scientific/secular age, namely that Jesus is a historical human being, period. Divinity with a capital D, miracles, and the like are rejected out of hand by most historical Jesus scholars. See *Christology, Jesus Seminar, Progressive Christianity,* and *Miaphysite (The Jesus Paradox).*

Human Condition

According to the mystics the root of human dysfunction is our inability to find happiness. Our attempts to find happiness in fleeting sensory pleasures, in affection and esteem, in power and control, in status and position, or in financial security are misguided, leading to constant frustration, which results in a deep underlying anxiety and dissatisfaction. This is what mystics and other teachers, such as Thomas Keating, refer to as The Human Condition. Thoreau's observation that "The mass of men lead lives of quiet desperation" summarizes the human condition.[11] According to The Alexandrian Mystics and the writers of *The Philokalia*, the way to find an ever-flowing stream of happiness (not conflicting emotions) is to periodically renounce sensory stimulation and seek God in the interior depths of our consciousness, which is usually most effectively reached through disciplined silences. For contrast see *Asceticism, Buddhist/ Christian Dialogue, Centering Prayer, Deification, Desert Fathers and Mothers, Dispassion, Divine Union, Essenes, Hesychasm, Jesus Prayer, Monastic Authority, Mystic Christianity, Original Nature, Prayer of the Heart, Unloading,* and *Silent Prayer.*

Hypostasis

Hypostasis (Greek) refers to the substantial unity (*hypostatic* union) of both the incarnation ("at once God and human") and the Trinity (at once One and Three!). Athanasius and Cyril used the same Greek word, *hypostasis*, to describe both the unity of the incarnation and the unity of the Trinity. In the Nicene Creed (written primarily by Athanasius), Jesus' relationship with God the Creator is characterized as "*hypostatic* union." A key characteristic of *hypostatic* union is indivisibility.[12] Indivisibility changes our paradigm/our frame of reference. According to The Alexandrian Mystics, in actuality there is no divide and there can never be a divide when it comes to the incarnation (this divide only exists in our fragmented minds). The incarnation is indivisible. The guiding lights for the early Church's understanding of *hypostasis* were the Cappadocian Fathers (329–395, so named because they came from Cappadocia in what is now Turkey). See *Miaphysite (The Jesus Paradox), Nicene Creed,* and *Trinity.* Also see Appendix B.

Jesus Paradox (Miaphysite)

The Jesus Paradox (*Miaphysite*) is the core assertion of Alexandrian Mystics (Alexandrian Fathers) going back to Cyril of Alexandria. The Jesus Paradox (my contemporary equivalent to *Miaphysite*) is the non-dual awareness of Christ, who as Cyril of Alexandria stated, is "at once God and human." If Jesus is at once God and human, as believers we cannot refer to Jesus as God without qualifying that: "God in human form." We also cannot refer to Jesus as human only, without qualifying that: "the human incarnation of God." For more specifics, see *Hypostasis, Miaphysite,* and *Trinity.* For contrast, see *Dyophysite*

11. Thoreau, *Walden,* chapter 1-A.
12. Sellers, *The Council of Chalcedon,* 213–214.

and *Monophysite*. For a more general survey, see *Alexandrian Mystics* and *Mystic Christianity*. Also see Appendices B, D, E, F, and G, and the Wikipedia article, "Miaphysitism."

Jesus Prayer

The Jesus Prayer is: "Lord Jesus Christ, son of God, have mercy on me."[13] This prayer, based on Luke 18:13, is probably the earliest prayer of Christian tradition. Various lengths of the prayer (such as "Jesus Christ have mercy," or "Lord, have mercy") were repeated continuously, especially on retreat, by The Alexandrian Mystics. The writers of *The Philokalia* instruct monks to stick with one form of the prayer, as opposed to changing the wording, so that the prayer takes root in the mind. The Jesus Prayer was popularized among the monasteries of the Egyptian desert by a monk named Pachomius (d. 348). Along with The Jesus Prayer, Pachomius also popularized the use of prayer ropes, with variously numbered knots, to facilitate the recitation of the Prayer. The Jesus Prayer and prayer ropes remain prominent in the Eastern Church today. Prayer ropes have similarities with Roman Catholic rosaries and Buddhist malas. See Chumley, *Mysteries of the Jesus Prayer*. Also see *Buddhist/Christian Dialogue, Hesychasm, The Philokalia,* and *Prayer of the Heart*.

Jesus Seminar

The Jesus Seminar is a group of about one hundred and fifty scholars and lay representatives founded in 1985 by Robert Funk. The seminar uses votes with colored beads to decide their collective view of the historicity of the deeds and sayings of Jesus found in the Gospels. They have produced new translations of the New Testament, which includes the Gospel of Thomas. The Jesus Seminar is relevant to Christology, yet its underlying assumption smacks of the same hubris as the scientific/secular age, namely that Jesus is a historical human being, period. Divinity with a capital D, miracles, and the like are regularly and summarily rejected by fellows of the Jesus Seminar. See *Christology, Gospel of Thomas,* and *Historical Jesus*.

Jesus' Third Way

Author Walter Wink writes cogently about how many of Jesus' Gospel teachings advocate what he calls Jesus' Third Way, also known as

---

13. Palmer, et al, *The Philokalia Vol. 4*, 206.

the *Peace Testimony*. Jesus' Third Way is not fight or flight. It is a way that is both assertive and non-violent. Select Gospel passages, when interpreted correctly illuminate The Third Way of Jesus. Exemplary passages include Matthew 5:39b, Mark 15:21, and Matthew 5:40.[14] The general passage associated with Jesus' Third Way is The Sermon on the Mount (Matthew chaps. 5–7).

When I think of Jesus' Third Way, Renee Girard's profound treatment of the ultimate meaning of the Cross comes immediately to mind. For Girard, the Cross is the definitive subversion of society's underlying systemic scapegoating and violence. See *American Friends Service Committee, Catholic Worker Movement, George Fox, Peace Churches,* and *Quakerism.* See Wink, *Engaging the Powers.* Also see Girard, *The Scapegoat.*

Liberation Theology

Liberation Theology interprets Jesus' teaching in terms of liberation from economic, political, and social injustice. It is Christianity through the eyes of the poor, with Marxist overtones. Liberation Theology is well represented in Gustavo Gutierrez's book, *A Theology of Liberation.* See *American Friends Service Committee, Catholic Worker Movement,* and *Progressive Christianity.*

Logos

The Word (*Logos* in Greek) is the eternal aspect of Jesus that existed before the historic incarnation and after the incarnation (outside of time). *Logos* is referenced by many Greek monastic writers of *The Philokalia,* and others. The *Logos* is captured in the first chapter of John's Gospel, verses 1–5. The mystery of the incarnation (The Jesus Paradox/*Miaphysite*) is found in the interplay between the pregnant energizing silence of God and God's Word or *Logos.* This interplay is the basis of incarnational theology and exists outside of time. Jesus' human body, born of Mary, existed for a brief period in the fullness of historic time, yet exists for all time as the primordial and paradoxical *Logos.* See *Christology, Contemplative Christianity, Mystic Christianity,* and *The Philokalia.*

Main, John

See *Prayer of the Heart.*

14. Wink, *The Powers That Be,* 98–111.

Mainline Christianity

By *Mainline Christianity* I mean all Christian denominations represented at the World Council of Churches (WCC), including the Roman Catholic Church. The WCC includes approximately three hundred forty two denominations from over one hundred countries. The WCC tends to weed out more fundamentalist and isolationist Christian factions. To me, the WCC represents ecumenism and centrist Christianity at its best. See *Liberation Theology, Progressive Christianity, Trinity, and United Church of Christ.*

Mary Magdalene

Many feminist scholars point out that Mary Magdalene was a disciple of Jesus and may have been one of the most prominent disciples, incurring the envy of other disciples. Mary is also an important symbol for balance between male and female in Christian tradition. It's unfortunate that the early Church was threatened by Mary, and through what appears to have been a smear campaign, makes her out to be a demented prostitute, rather than a prominent (perhaps the most prominent) disciple of Jesus.

One of the most fascinating details of the Gospel accounts of the resurrection is that Mary Magdalene was the first witness to the resurrection. This gives Mary a prominent place in Christian tradition as "the apostle to the apostles." According to literary critics, this detail also contributes to the authenticity of Gospel accounts of the resurrection. For, if the story was fabricated, a man (men were considered the most reliable authorities in the patriarchal culture of the time) would have been the first witness. See *Progressive Christianity.* See Bourgeault, *The Meaning of Mary Magdalene: Discovering the Woman at the Heart of Christianity.*

Miaphysite (Jesus Paradox)

Miaphysite (The Jesus Paradox), which is sometimes called *Henophysite*, is the core assertion of Alexandrian Mystics (Alexandrian Fathers), rooted in the teachings of Athanasius and Cyril of Alexandria.[15] I refer to *Miaphysite* (Greek) as opposed to *monophysite* (Latin). I do this because *Miaphysite* is the term Oriental Orthodox tradition accepts as

---

15. Sellers, *The Council of Chalcedon*, 213. Some, like Richard Rohr, may refer to the dynamic of Miaphysite as imaginal causality. Scholastic philosophers may call it exemplary causality. Science today might call it morphogenic fields.

authentic (largely because it is the actual word that Cyril used) and because of the negative connotations associated with the word *monophysite*. *Miaphysite* is the non-dual awareness of Christ, who as Cyril of Alexandria put it, is "at once God and human." If Jesus is at once God and human, that means that as believers we cannot refer to Jesus as God without qualifying that: "God in human form." We also cannot refer to Jesus as human only, without qualifying that: "the human incarnation of God." My technical definition for *Miaphysite* is "one united dynamic nature." I distinguish between simple union (*monophysite* in Latin) and dynamic union (*Miaphysite* in Greek). The legacy of *Miaphysite* theology is preserved today in the Oriental Orthodox Church (not to be confused with Eastern Orthodox). *Miaphysite* is the crown jewel of the Alexandrian Mystics. It is the center piece that holds the various strands of Mystic Christianity together. For more specifics, see *Hypostasis, Jesus Paradox,* and *Trinity.* For contrast, see *Dyophysite* and *Monophysite.* For a more general survey, see *Alexandrian Mystics* and *Mystic Christianity.* Also see Appendices B, D, E, F, and G, and the Wikipedia article, "Miaphysitism."

Monastic Authority

Regular retreats and habitual silent prayer are the key to Monastic Authority (spiritual authority). The Alexandrian Mystics believed that spiritual authority is not derived from one's level of education, one's position in the clerical hierarchy, one's heredity, or any other designation. Spiritual authority is primarily rooted in direct experience of communion with God in prayer. This is why to this day in the Oriental Orthodox and East Orthodox traditions, there is a special reverence for monks and nuns and for monastic experience. And as the writers of *The Philokalia* often attest, it is not the robe or the monastery or celibacy that makes the monk or nun, but weeks, months, years, and decades of habitual silent prayer.[16] For me the quintessential Monastic Authorities of Christian tradition are The Alexandrian Mystics. See *Alexandrian Bishops, Alexandrian Mystics, Anthony of Egypt, Asceticism, Athanasius of Alexandria, Buddhist/Christian Dialogue, Contemplative Christianity, Cyril of Alexandria, George Fox, Mystic Christianity,* and *Neo-monasticism.*

16. Palmer, et al, *The Philokalia Vol. 2,* 106.

Monophysite

Monophysite is a heresy of the early church and was correctly condemned by early church leaders. *Monophysite* posits that the incarnation is "one simple nature," or "one compounded nature." This is in contrast to "one united dynamic nature" of *Miaphysite*. In other words, *monophysite* does not distinguish between the two aspects of Jesus (Divinity and humanity). Instead of a dynamic union there is an amalgam, where Jesus' humanity is dwarfed and overwhelmed by Jesus' Divinity, like a drop of water is overwhelmed and subsumed by the ocean. I distinguish clearly and painstakingly between simple union (*monophysite* in Latin) and dynamic union (*Miaphysite* in Greek). One challenge of adequately addressing *monophysite* is that there were many forms of it and many angles on it. For contrast, see *Dyophysite* and *Miaphysite* (*The Jesus Paradox*). See Appendices F and G. Also see the Wikipedia article, "Monophysitism."

Mystic Christianity

I prefer the terms *Mystic Christianity* or *Christian Mysticism* to the term *Contemplative Christianity*. Yet, I shy away from these terms unless they are made more precise. For me, the words that give Mystic Christianity disciplined specificity are "The Jesus Paradox/*Miaphysite*" and "The Alexandrian Mystics." These terms ground Mystic Christianity, free it from nebulous hearsay, and give it tangibility, lineage, and integrity.

Mystic Christianity is not an esoteric science that occurred among some isolated mystics outside of mainstream Christianity. It is Christianity's historic essence and core. It is Christianity rightly understood. It is to properly understand and silently behold the greatest mysteries of the faith: The Trinity and The Incarnation.

I think Mystic Christianity is convoluted in people's minds because of wave upon wave of controversy that surrounds its root concepts. For me, a basic vocabulary of Mystic Christianity would include *Miaphysite* (The Jesus Paradox), The Trinity (according to the Cappadocian Fathers), *Hesychasm* (Silent Prayer[17]), *The Mystical Theology* and *Divine Names* of Denys, and *The Philokalia*.[18] What all these subjects have in common is that they've been surrounded by controversy. The

---

17. *Hesychasm* covers a much broader spectrum of practices than Silent Prayer, yet the two are more akin than most Westerners think. See *Hesychasm* in glossary.

18. When it comes to Mystic Christianity, none of these concepts and nothing else whatsoever will substitute for the real daily practice of silent prayer.

reasons for the controversies are that mystics and mystical concepts are easily misunderstood and misrepresented. They are also threatening to people who are unfamiliar with mystical experiences, especially church authorities. Because there is so much controversy around Mystic Christianity's root concepts, most Contemplative Christians have steered clear of them. This is one of the tragedies of Christianity. And as a result, in many people's minds, there is no unified and deeply rooted lineage of Christian Mystics, nor a core of mystical concepts that hold the legacy together. As a result, many Christians who are mystically inclined turn to new age experiments or to other religious traditions that have well developed mystical legacies.

Yes, Catholic and Protestant Christianity has taught the mystics piece meal—this isolated mystic here, that one over there—*The Cloud of Unknowing* that happened to pop up there. Yet, the deeply rooted legacy dating back to the Earliest Christians is generally lost on Western tradition as a whole. To make matters worse, people genuinely inclined toward mysticism in contemporary western society are most often dismissed at best or accused of being deranged at worst, by those who have made reason and dualistic thinking their ultimate authority. [19] In this post-modern era, with its distance from the ancient controversies and its pioneering spirit, I hope many will return to Mystic Christianity's deeply rooted historic foundation. Mysticism is the deepest expression of any faith and any mysticism worth its salt must rest on a firm historic lineage and legacy. See *Alexandrian Mystics, Asceticism, Contemplative Christianity, Deification, Desert Fathers and Mothers, Dionysius the Areopagite, Divine Union, Hesychasm, Logos, Miaphysite (The Jesus Paradox), Monastic Authority, Natural Mystics, The Philokalia, Progressive Christianity, Silent Prayer, Tabor Light,* and *Trinity.*

Natural Mystics

The Natural Mysticism of Christian Tradition is epitomized in the writings of Saint Francis, Saint Patrick, and Celtic Christianity, who show profound reverence for the natural world. For these writers the way of devotion to the Creator is to fall in love with creation. This same feeling is present in many Protestant Hymns such as "How Great Thou Art"

19. Accusations of derangement seem to be an occupational hazard of Christian Mystics dating back to at least the sixth century. Maximus the Confessor writes, "For he who has been united with the truth has the assurance that all is well with him, even though most people rebuke him for being out of his mind. For without their being aware he has moved from delusion to the truth of real faith; and he knows for sure that he is not deranged, as they say. . ." (Palmer, et al., *The Philokalia Vol.* 2, 282).

and "All Things Bright and Beautiful." In his book, *Mysticism Sacred and Profane*, R.C. Zaehner draws a hard and fast distinction between religious and natural mystical experiences. I don't think it's possible to make such a sharp distinction. For Mystics like Francis, religious and natural mystical experiences flowed together. See *Mystic Christianity* and *Original Nature*.

Neo-monasticism (Neo-monastics)

Neo-monasticism is also referred to as new monasticism or lay monasticism. This term refers to people who have a regular practice of silent prayer, but who don't reside in a monastery or cloister. Neo-monastics include self identified monk-priests, monk-ministers, monk-bishops, monk-accountants, monk-lawyers, etcetera. These people have demanding occupations of various kinds, yet remain devoted to a consistent silent prayer practice. To make progress in silent prayer the recommendation of Centering Prayer communities is to practice at least twenty minutes twice a day and to do at least one silent prayer retreat per year.

Denominations that encourage and develop neo-monasticism are The Quakers (FGC), The Church of the Savior, The Episcopalians, Oriental Orthodox, Eastern Orthodox, and Roman Catholics. My hope is that more leaders of Protestant denominations will support neo-monasticism within their congregations and judicatories. See *Alexandrian Bishops, Asceticism, Church of the Savior, George Fox, Monastic Authority, Oriental Orthodoxy, and Quakerism.*

Nestorius, Nestorianism, Nestorian Controversy

See Appendix F.

New Age

The New Age was developed in the last half of the twentieth century and is influenced by psychology, parapsychology, and self-help. It experienced a kind of genesis and flowering in the 1960s, when various Indian gurus visited the West. New Age prefers an eclectic approach to the world religions and is not rooted in any one faith tradition in time. It is theologically imprecise and anti-authoritarian. It exerts a strong influence on Progressive Christianity. For contrast, see *Fundamentalism.*

Nicene Creed

The Nicene Creed (325)) is Christianity's broadest, most universal, and most uniting creed. It is also the most widely used creed or profession of faith in Christian liturgy today. It is called Nicene because it was adopted by three hundred and eighteen bishops in the city of Nicaea by the first ecumenical council.[20] See Appendix C. Also see *Athanasius* and *Hypostasis*.

Oriental Orthodoxy

The Oriental Orthodox Church only accepts three ecumenical church councils: The first council of Nicaea (325), the First Council of Constantinople (381), and the First Council of Ephesus (431). They adamantly reject the Council of Chalcedon (451), which conceived of the person of Christ "in two natures" (*dyophysite*). Instead of the dualistic Chalcedonian approach, The Oriental Orthodox Church embraces *Miaphysite* (The Jesus Paradox). See *Miaphysite (The Jesus Paradox)*. For contrast, see *dyophysite* and *monophysite*. For the demographics of the Oriental Orthodox Church today see Appendix E. Also see the Wikipedia article, "Oriental Orthodoxy."

Original Nature (Original Purity, Original State)

The terms *original nature, original purity,* and *original state* pertain to the original nature of the intellect after the purification of consistent silent prayer. These terms are found throughout *The Philokalia*.[21] In the *Philokalia* original nature is also referred to as "the pre-fallen state."[22] Our original purified nature is completely free of *original sin* or *the human condition* as it is variously called in Christianity and Psychology. It is a liberated primordial state of being that is intuitively inter-connected with both Creator and creation, to both Divinity and humanity. See *Anthony of Egypt, Deification, Dispassion, Divine Union, Natural Mystics, The Philokalia,* and *Unloading.* For contrast, see *Human Condition.*

Peace Churches

The historic Peace Churches are the Church of the Brethren, the Mennonite, and the Quakers (FGC). These traditions believe in the *peace testimony* of Jesus, epitomized in The Sermon on the Mount (Matthew chaps. 5–7). The historic application of the *peace testimony* has included resistance to serving in armed forces. See *American Friends Service*

20. The Creed only has two hundred and twenty bishops' signatures, yet it was often referred to as "The Council of The Three Hundred and Eighteen" in ancient documents.

21. Palmer, et al., *The Philokalia Vol. 3,* 314, 318; *Vol. 4,* 88.

22. Palmer, et al., *The Philokalia Vol. 4,* 212.

> Committee, Catholic Worker Movement, George Fox, Jesus' Third Way, Progressive Christianity, and Quakerism.

Peace Testimony

See Jesus' Third Way.

Philokalia

The Philokalia is a collection of texts written between the 4th and 15th centuries by spiritual masters of the Orthodox *hesychast* tradition. It is a pillar of Eastern Mystic Christianity. The texts of *The Philokalia* were originally written for the guidance of monks. The collection was compiled in the 18th Century by Saint Nikodemos of the Holy Mountain (Mount Athos in Greece) and Saint Makarios of Corinth. *The Philokalia* has recently been translated into English by Faber and Faber Publishing. *The Philokalia* illuminates subjects such as *Anthony of Egypt, Asceticism, Deification, Desert Fathers and Mothers, Dionysius the Areopagite, Dispassion, Divine Union, Hesychasm, The Jesus Prayer, Logos, Monastic Authority, Mystic Christianity, Original Nature, Silent Prayer,* and *Tabor Light* (all in the glossary).

Prayer of the Heart (John Main)

The Prayer of the Heart is similar to Centering Prayer, except that the sacred word, *Maranatha*, is repeated frequently, if not continuously during silent prayer. In this prayer form, *Maranatha* ("Come Lord Jesus" in Aramaic), serves as a kind of mantra, which is not only repeated during prayer, but also repeated when possible during the day. This practice was developed and contemporized by John Main (d. 1982) and Laurence Freeman. For more see Main, *Word Into Silence* and prayeroftheheart.com.

An ancient counterpart to this prayer form is The Jesus Prayer, which Orthodox monks repeat continuously to this day, especially on retreat. See *Centering Prayer, Cloud of Unknowing, Hesychasm,* and *Jesus Prayer.*

Process Theology

Process Theology stems from the process philosophy of Alfred North Whitehead (d. 1947), which was further developed by Charles Hartshorne (d. 2000), Marjorie Suchocki, and others.

A basic understanding of Process Theology is that we are in process with God and that over time the relationship between God and humanity is changing both God and humanity. This means that we can influence God and vice versa (Genesis 18:26–33). We are in process with God. God is not omnipotent. God shares power with us—without our hands and feet, God has no hands and feet to act in the world. We need God and God needs us. A perfect example of this is the incarnation. Through the incarnation God is in process with us. The eternal has become and is becoming temporal. See *Progressive Christianity*.

Progressive Christianity

Three hallmarks of Progressive Christianity are: 1) its inclusion of all peoples as children of God, regardless of race, class, gender, sexual orientation 2) its respect for other religions and its willingness to enter into interfaith dialogue as mutually enriching 3) an emphasis on social justice and eco-justice. Some top Progressive Christian Magazines/Periodicals are The Christian Century, Sojourners, and Weavings. Some exemplary organizations are Church of the Savior and the Sojourners Community in Washington, D.C and The Center for Action and Contemplation in Albuquerque, New Mexico.

I affirm The Eight Points found on progressivechristianity.org, while also seeking to temper points one and two by rooting them in The Jesus Paradox of the Alexandrian Mystics. See *American Friends Service Committee, Catholic Worker Movement, Contemplative Christianity, Liberation Theology, Mainline Christianity, Mary Magdalene, Mystic Christianity, Process Theology, Quakerism, United Church of Christ*, and *Vatican II*. For contrast, see *Fundamentalism*.

Quakerism

There are three streams of Quakerism today, Evangelical Friends International (EFI), Friends United Meeting (FUM), and Friends General Conference (FGC). EFI and FUM are evangelical and have paid clergy. FGC is characterized by silent meetings for worship and doesn't have paid clergy. FGC recognizes elders, who lead the community. FGC, along with the Mennonite and Brethren, are the three historic Peace Churches, who emphasize Jesus as the model for non-violence. The historic Quakers (FGC) understand the importance of keeping an exquisite balance between contemplation and social activism. See *American Friends Service Committee, Contemplative Christianity, George Fox, Jesus' Third Way, Mystic Christianity*, and *Peace Churches*.

Quantum Physics

Quantum Physics asserts that if we measure a photon of light as a wave it will behave as a wave. If we observe a photon of light as a particle it will behave as a particle. Yet, a photon can't be a wave and a particle at the same time. So, when we observe a photon of light in a certain way, we change the intrinsic nature of that photon. In other words, at the quantum level, there is no objective reality. How we observe phenomenon changes the nature of that phenomenon. Put differently, we are not observers of reality—we participate in it! See *Hypostasis, Miaphysite (The Jesus Paradox), Mystic Christianity*, and *Progressive Christianity*. For contrast, see *Fundamentalism*.

Qumran

Qumran is an archeological site in the West Bank of Israel. Most scholars believe it was an ancient site of an Essene monastic community. John the Baptist was most likely an Essene from Qumran. Reasons for postulating this are that he was known to be a desert hermit (Matthew 3: 1, 4) and Qumran was a hermetic desert community. Also John the Baptist baptized people (including Jesus) in the Jordan River (Matthew 3:13), which is in walking distance from Qumran. See *Asceticism* and *Essenes*.

Silent Prayer

Silent Prayer in the Christian context is always understood as *prayer*. Prayer is conversation and, at its deepest, communion with God. Most Christians understand prayer as a one-way conversation or monologue. Silent prayer balances this mistaken understanding of prayer by focusing on what's most important: what is being communicated from the other end of the line. This deep listening requires letting go of any and all sensory distractions. In Western contemplative tradition silent prayer is referred to as *the prayer of simplicity, the prayer of faith, the prayer of simple regard,* and *silent worship*. In *The Philokalia* silent prayer is often referred to as *watchfulness, blessed stillness,* or *noetic stillness*. See *Asceticism, Centering Prayer, Cloud of Unknowing, Deification, Dionysius the Areopagite, Dispassion, Divine Union, Hesychasm, Mystic Christianity, Prayer of the Heart, The Philokalia,* and *Unloading*.

Tabor Light

The Eastern Orthodox theology of the Tabor Light, also referred to as *Light of Tabor, Uncreated Light* and *Divine Light*, is the light Jesus emanated on Mount Tabor during his transfiguration (Matthew 7:2, Mark 9:3, Luke 9:29). This same Light is associated with Saint Paul's conversion, when he was blinded by Light (Acts 9:3–9, 22:6–11). This Light is referenced throughout *The Philokalia*.[23] This Light, revealed on Tabor, was understood to be the fulfillment of the promise that some of the disciples would not taste death until they beheld the kingdom of God (Mark 9:1). This Light is the manifestation of God's kingdom, which was not only revealed to disciples two millennia ago, but which is still revealed to Christian Mystics in the depths of prayer. See *Deification, Divine Union, Hesychasm, The Philokalia,* and *Mystic Christianity.*

Trinity

The theology of the Trinity was most fully developed by the Cappadocian Fathers: Basil the Great (d. 379), Gregory of Nyssa (d. 395), and Gregory of Nazianzus (d. 389). The theology of the Trinity pressed the "hypostatic union" of the Creator, Christ, and Holy Spirit (both One and Three at the same time). While distinct in their relations with one another, they are One. Athanasius, Cyril, and the Alexandrian Mystics pressed this same "hypostatic union" of Jesus' Divinity and humanity. While Jesus' Divinity and humanity are distinct, they are one. The Trinity and the incarnation are the ultimate mysteries of Christian faith. The biblical bases of the Trinity are the numerous scriptures which say the Creator is God, that Jesus is God, and that the Holy Spirit is God. In addition there are a plethora of scriptures that say God is One.[24] See *Hypostasis, Miaphysite (The Jesus Paradox),* and *Nicene Creed.* Also see Appendix B.

United Church of Christ (UCC)

The United Church of Christ (UCC), with its Congregational (Puritan) roots, is the oldest Christian denomination in North America. The UCC is a mainline Protestant Christian denomination, which throughout its history has emphasized Jesus' radical inclusion in the Gospels and social justice. The first woman, the first black man, and the first homosexual ever ordained in the United States, were all ordained within the UCC and its historic forbears. The UCC was also the first Christian denomination

23. See Gregory Palamas and Nikitas Stithatos (Palmer, et al., *The Philokalia Vol.* 4, 414–15, 167.)

24. Examples of scriptures that say Jesus is God: John 10:30, 5:18, Colossians 2:8–9; that say the Creator is God: John 8:41, Ephesians 4:16; that say the Holy Spirit is God: Acts 5:3–4, 28:25–26, 1 Corinthians 3:16; that say God is One: Matthew 12:32, 12:29, Deuteronomy 6: 4–5.

along with the Quakers, to formally oppose slavery in the United States. See *Mainline Christianity* and *Progressive Christianity*.

Unloading

Unloading of the unconscious, or *unloading* in brief, is a term often used in the writings of Thomas Keating and in the teachings of the Centering Prayer community. *Unloading* is the release of psycho-toxins (referred to as "passions" in *The Philokalia*) from the mind, and subsequently from the body, which accompanies silent prayer.[25] Another descriptor for passions/ psycho-toxins is the release of attachments and aversions to objects of the senses. Attachments and aversions to sensory stimulation are stored in the mind in the form of psycho-toxins and in the body in the form of muscle tension. Sometimes *Unloading* is accompanied by sensations of tingling, burning, tension, nausea, or tears. The patient endurance required to weather these painful sensations is referred to as "carrying one's cross" and "asceticism" in *The Philokalia*. On a physiological level, unloading is characterized by the gradual healing and eventual restoration of the human nervous system. The understanding of the unloading of psycho-toxins during disciplined silences is not unique to Centering Prayer and Mystic Christianity. In Theravada Buddhist tradition, fifth century author, Bhadantacariya Buddhaghosa, writes of similar phenomena throughout his classic, *The Path of Purification*.[26] It is also important to note that the healing of the human nervous system and tension stored in the body's muscle tissue can happen on different levels through various means such as regular massage, Rolfing, healing relationships, healing community, music therapy, etcetera. Yet, Thomas Keating and others maintain that the deepest and most thorough healing of the nervous system and holistic healing of body, soul, mind, and spirit is accomplished through the unloading described here, which progresses in stages, through years (usually decades) of diligent silent prayer. See *Asceticism, Buddhist/ Christian Dialogue, Centering Prayer, Cloud of Unknowing, Deification, Dispassion, Divine Union, Hesychasm*, and *Silent Prayer*.

Vatican II Council

The second Vatican Council of the Roman Catholic Church (1962–65), spawned by Pope John XXIII (d. 1963), opened flood gates to interfaith

25. Thomas Keating often refers to the term *psycho-toxins* in his talks and writings. See Keating, *Contemplative Prayer*, disc 3.

26. Buddhaghosa, *The Path of Purification*.

dialogue, more open communication with Protestants, and increased dialogue with the Eastern Church. Vatican II was a giant step toward relevancy to Twenty-first Century sensibilities like pluralism. See *Buddhist/Christian Dialogue, Emergent Church, Neo-monasticism,* and *Progressive Christianity.*

World Council of Churches

See *Mainline Christianity*

Appendix B

The Lineage of Alexandrian Mystics

CHRISTIAN TRADITION EXPERIENCED A flowering of monasteries between the third and the fifth centuries in the deserts of Egypt. The genius of this period was encapsulated in the lineage of Alexandrian Bishops
between the fourth and fifth centuries.

The Alexandrian Bishops during the period listed on the next page
are rightly considered the lineage holders of Miaphysite Theology (The
Jesus Paradox). This lineage was also embodied by most of the Desert Fathers and Mothers of the same period, living in various monastic enclaves
and associations in the deserts of Egypt. Due to the cultural context of the
time, the lineage is all male, but this doesn't diminish the relevance of their
message today.

After the Council of Chalcedon (451), the Alexandrian Mystics
experienced a diaspora, accompanied by constant theological and political struggle with Rome. During this period, representation of authentic
Miaphysite theology was spotty. But there was one champion for Miaphysite theology during the diaspora, Severus of Antioch. In my estimation
Severus was the last authentic Alexandrian Mystic lineage holder.

If you want to research authentic Miaphysite theology, don't get lost
in the byways of the diaspora (455 on up through the present day), with
its tangled web of theological and political struggles. Stick to the authentic
lineage sketched here, championed by Cyril. The lineage of Alexandrian
Bishops goes back to the Apostle Mark, who wrote the Gospel of Mark.
But, for our purposes we don't need to recount the entire lineage, just

those who carry the most pronounced threads of the *Miaphysite* legacy (especially Athanasius and Cyril).[27]

The lineage of Alexandrian Bishops, who championed *Miaphysite* (The Jesus Paradox):

- Alexander I (312–328 CE)

- Athanasius I (Primary author of Nicene Creed) (328–373)

- Peter II (373–380)

- Timothy I (380–385)

- Theophilus (385–412)

- Cyril I (412–444)

- Dioscorus I (444–454)

———————————————————Diaspora———————————————————

- Severus of Antioch (not an Alexandrian Bishop) (465–542)

27. Before the recent clarity the Oriental Orthodox Church has offered us through books such as Gebru, *Miaphysite Christology*, there was a lot of confusion about the difference between the terms *Miaphysite* (Greek) and *monophysite* (Latin). Like the Oriental Orthodox Church, I steer clear of the term *monophysite* because of the distortions and confusion surrounding it. *Miaphysite* (Greek) clarifies the distortions and accurately reflects the spirit and legacy of Athanasius, Cyril, The Alexandrian Mystics, and Oriental Orthodox theology today.

Appendix C

The Nicene Creed (325 CE)

IT'S HARD TO OVERSTATE the significance of the Nicene Creed. It's the one creed the universal church unanimously agreed on before any splits.

Even though the Nicene Creed doesn't clarify the relationship between Jesus' Divinity and humanity, the Creed's primary author, Athanasius, clarified Trinitarian Theology: "God is one and three at the same time." Holding to the same theological thread of unity within diversity, Athanasius believed Jesus is "at once God and human." This phrase championed by Cyril of Alexandria I coined "The Jesus Paradox."

Alexandrian Trinitarian theology and Alexandrian incarnation theology have the same core. In the case of Trinitarian theology the three manifestations of the Trinity are "of one being" with one another. In the case of incarnation theology Jesus' humanity is "of one being" with his Divinity.[28] In other words, the Trinity is one and three at the same time. And Jesus is God and human at the same time. These are the core nondual assertions of Christianity.

It is difficult for many with a Twenty-first Century mindset to understand the function of an article of faith like the Nicene Creed. In response to this difficulty I found Kathleen Norris' words helpful. . .

> "What am I to do. . . when I have difficulty affirming parts of the Creed—like the Virgin Birth?" "You just say it," came the response. "Particularly when you have difficulty believing it. You just keep saying it. It will come to you eventually." The student raised his voice: "How can I with integrity affirm a creed in which I do not believe?" And the priest replied, "It's not your

---

28. The technical name for "of one being" is *hypostasis* (Greek). See glossary.

creed, it's our creed," meaning the creed of the entire Christian church. I can picture the theologian shrugging, as only the Orthodox can shrug, carrying so lightly the thousand-plus years of their liturgical tradition: "Eventually it may come to you," he told the student. "For some, it takes longer than for others. . ."[29]

Here is the famous creed. I have taken the liberty of making the Creed inclusive, substituting Father with Creator, man with human, etcetera:

> We believe in one God, the Creator, the Almighty
> maker of heaven and earth,
> of all things visible and invisible.
>
> We believe in one Sovereign, Jesus Christ,
> the only Child of God,
> begotten from the Creator before all worlds—[30]
> God from God, Light from Light, true God from true God;
> begotten, not made;
> of one Being with the Creator;
> through whom all things were made;
> who because of us human beings and for our salvation,
> came down from heaven,
> being made flesh by the Holy Spirit and the Virgin Mary,
> and became a human being;
> who was crucified for us under Pontius Pilate,
> and suffered and was buried,
> and rose again the third day in accordance with the scriptures,
> and ascended into heaven,
> and sits at the right hand of the Creator;
> who will come again with glory to judge the living and the dead;
> whose dominion will have no end.
>
> We believe in the Holy Spirit, the Sovereign, the giver of life,
> who proceeds from the Creator, and from the Christ;
> who with the Creator and the Christ is worshiped and glorified;
> And we believe in one holy catholic and apostolic church;
> we acknowledge one baptism for the forgiveness of sins;
> we look for the resurrection of the dead,
> And the life of the world to come. Amen.

29. Norris, *Amazing Grace.*
30. See *Logos* in glossary.

Appendix D

Biblical Roots of The Jesus Paradox (Miaphysite)

Numerous scriptures point to Jesus' Divinity and humanity. Yet, few scriptures illuminate the relationship between Jesus' Divinity and humanity. So, I'll focus on those.

For in Christ all the fullness of the Deity lives in bodily form (Colossians 2:9, NIV)

This scripture says it all: Jesus was Divine with a capital D and human with a lower case h. Jesus is the monotheistic Deity with a capital D, not a deity in a pantheon. In other words, Jesus is the ultimate reality, yet never separate from his humanity.

Then they all said, "So you are the son of God (ho huios tou theou) then." He replied, "You are right, I am," Jesus told them (Luke 22:70, PHILLIPS)

"Son of God" is found throughout the New Testament. And believers are sometimes referred to as "sons of God" (2 Corinthians 6:18 and Galatians 4:4–6). Yet, Jesus is considered God's unique Son, not loosely, but in the strict formal sense of the word.

In the Gospels, and popularly in John 3:16, Jesus is referred to as "the only Son of God." Jesus is usually described as *ho huios tou theou*: not just a "son of God," but "The Son of God." "The" emphasizes his unique exclusive relationship to God. "The son" is the equal and sole heir of the Father (God). This is the context for understanding "Son of God." Jesus inherited everything that belongs to God (full Divinity).

For progressive Christians within our twenty-first century context, the interpretation of the father and son relationship is problematic and patriarchal. But the analogy isn't about male dominance. Jesus was extraordinarily egalitarian for his time. And as womanist writer Jacquelyn Grant affirms in *White Women's Christ and Black Women's Jesus*, Jesus' most distinguishing characteristic isn't his gender, but his humanity.

In Greek, the term *huios theou* was applied to "sons of God" in the plural ordinary sense of the phrase, meaning there are many sons of God. This ordinary sense of the word *son* is applied to Jesus only three times in the New Testament (Mark 1:1, 15:39, and Romans 1:4). Usually Jesus is designated "the (one and only) son" of God as described above.

Jesus is both the son of Mary (fully human) and the son of God (fully Divine). Some translations of Luke 22:70 are not as clear as the Phillips I've referenced above. When Jesus was asked "Are you then the son of God," some translations have Jesus replying "You say that I am." In contrast the Phillips Version asserts "You are right, I am." Nevertheless, the affirmation that Jesus is the unique exclusive human incarnation/son of God *(ho huios tou theou)* is affirmed throughout the New Testament.[31]

The word became flesh (John 1:14a)

The strong almost crude word "flesh" presses Jesus' full humanity.[32] "Word" used here is *Logos* in Greek, which means the eternal Word. "Word" is the eternal Word in Genesis 1 that created the heavens and the earth. In other words, we can substitute "The Word" in John 1:14 for "God:" God became flesh. This declaration essentializes *Miaphysite*. John 1:14 is the first biblical reference to the Word using the Greek verb "to become." Prior to John 1:14 the Greek verb "to be" is used. The verb "to become" proclaims the eternal has become temporal, the immortal "I Am" has become mortal, the absolute Deity now shares our relative humanity. The Creator has become the creature. This is the heart of Christmas.

---

31. This phrase is found in 1 John ten times, in John eight times, and in Romans and Hebrews four times each.

32. Bultmann, *The Gospel of John.*

God and I are one (John 10:30)

Jesus' statement in John 10:30 is the essence of *Miaphysite*. There's "one united dynamic nature" in Jesus. Unity is emphasized, not duality. Jesus isn't inspired by God as with other prophets. Jesus is God in human form. This exceeds traditional Jewish expectations for the Messiah. Jesus shares in the very power of God, especially in terms of life, death, and judgment. Jesus moves his audience beyond the idea of messiah to "The Son of God" (*ho huios tou theou*). Attempts are made on Jesus' life because of the claim he is "The Son of God" (John 5:18, 8:58–59, 10:30–31, 36–39). John 10:30's claim "God and I are one" is also the basis of Jesus' "I am" statements (John 6:35; 8:24, 58; 17:21–22), such as "I am the resurrection and the life, I am the bread of life, etcetera"

Jesus said to them, "Very truly, I tell you, before Abraham and Sarah were, I am" (John 8:58)

This statement echoes God's great self declaration in Exodus 3:14: "I am that I am." In this statement Jesus doesn't say "I was" but "I am," expressing his eternal being and his oneness with God. In Orthodox tradition the eternal being of Christ, which always was and always will be, which existed before and after the Incarnation, is referred to as the eternal Word (*Logos* in Greek). In John 8:58 Jesus claims pre-existence with God beyond the bounds of time. Jesus identifies himself with the divine name "I Am." So, this is an expression of Jesus' unity with God and a proclamation that Jesus is greater than Abraham (or any other prophet). Jesus is one with God and pre-existed eternally with God before the world was made (also see John 1:2–3).

God is in me and I am in God (John 10:38b)

Miaphysite (The Jesus Paradox) means "one united dynamic nature." John 10:30 also proclaims one united dynamic nature. Again there's more than a relationship here. There's a dynamic unity of Divinity and humanity. The Gospel of John uses the language of indwelling to characterize Jesus' Divinity. This isn't on the level of insight or revelation. This is a dynamic intertwined being. There is an indissoluble union of the two in Jesus (other scriptures that mirror John 10:38b: John 14:10a, 11a; John 17:21a).

Philip said to Jesus, "Lord, show us God, and we will be satisfied." Jesus replied, "Have I been with you all this time, Philip, and you still do not know me? Whoever has seen me has seen God. How can you say, 'Show us God?' Do you not believe that I am in God and God is in me?" (John 14: 8–10a)

Philip's approach is like many Christians today who've gutted Jesus' transformative power. Philip says, "Show us God." In other words, "Jesus you are the wisdom teacher who points to God like great prophets of old. Please show us God." Jesus corrects Philip and says, "How can you say 'show us God.'" "Don't you know I'm in God and God's in me?" In other words, Jesus is not inspired by God. Jesus is in God and God is in him: dynamic union.

When the disciples see Jesus they see God—God in human form. Verse ten explains that Jesus' teaching was not of human origin. There was an inseparable unity between Jesus' human words and God's words. Christians believe Jesus' humanity and Divinity are united. Disciples like Philip came to understand this through Jesus' words and works, especially his resurrection.

Appendix E

Miaphysite's Geographic Roots Today[33]

THE *MIAPHYSITE* CHURCHES OF the Oriental Orthodox Church (not to be confused with The Eastern Orthodox Church!) include:

The Coptic Orthodox Church
- Territory: Egypt, Nubia, Sudan, Western Pentapolis, Libya, and all of Africa (includes the British Orthodox Church)
- Adherents: twenty million (seven to ten million in Egypt)

The Armenian Apostolic Church
- Territory: Armenia, Nagorno-Karabakh Republic
- Adherents: nine million

The Eritrean Orthodox Church
- Territory: Eritrea
- Adherents: one and a half million

The Ethiopian Orthodox Tewahedo Church (*Tewahedo* means "one united dynamic nature" in Ge'ez, the theological language of Ethiopia)
- Territory: Ethiopia
- Adherents: forty-five million

---

33. Wikipedia, "Oriental Orthodoxy." Numbers provided are approximate.

The Indian Orthodox Church

- Territory: India and throughout the world
- Adherents: three million

The Syrian Orthodox Church

- Territory: Syria, Lebanon, Israel, Turkey, Iraq, and Iran, and throughout the world.
- Adherents: five and a half million (eighty thousand are in Sweden and the U.S.A., fifty thousand are in Germany)

Some Independent Catholic Churches, not in full communion with the above churches, also embrace *Miaphysite* (The Jesus Paradox). These include The Antiochian Catholic Church in America.

Not all the theologians of the Oriental Orthodox Church will accept the finer points of the *Miaphysite* theology presented in this book. I did have an Oriental Orthodox monk, Abba Yohannes, edit the manuscript. Abba Yohannes of the Nine Saints Ethiopian Orthodox Monastery in America went over the finer points of the *Miaphysite* theology presented here (especially in chapter 6) and verified its consistency with his understanding of *Miaphysite* in Ethiopian Orthodox tradition.

In the twentieth century *Miaphysite* has been accepted by the wider Church. Both Rome and Constantinople accepted the alternative *Miaphysite* theology as "adequate"[34]. *Miaphysite* theology is far more than "adequate." It amounts to no less than the cure for Christianity's ills. W.H.C. Frend writes, "There was nothing comparable to the school of thought, which had matured slowly through two centuries of Alexandrian church history to reach its climax with the genius of Cyril"[35]

---

34. Hastings, et al., *The Oxford Companion to Christian Thought.*
35. Frend, *The Rise of the Monophysite Movement*, 88.

Appendix F

Miaphysite versus Monophysite, and other Early Church Heresies

Monophysitism

In the following paragraphs I will very briefly distinguish *Miaphysite* from a range of heretical *monophysite* doctrines.

For the contemporary reader, these pre-scientific speculations about the nature of the incarnation may seem irrelevant to our times. Yet, these distinctions were essential for the preservation of Mystic Christianity and its jewel of non-dual awareness/paradox as found in *Miaphysite*. And in my estimation, this mystical awareness is our most noble human endowment.

Even though some of the titles of the books I refer to contain the word *monophysite* (Latin), I completely steer clear of the word, because of its association with heresy in the early church. I use the word *Miaphysite* (Greek) because it's accepted by the Oriental Orthodox Church and is free of the negative connotations of *monophysite*. My basic distinction is between *Miaphysite* (dynamic union) and *monophysite* (simple union). As Oriental Orthodox theologians reiterate, *mia* stands for composite unity and *mono* stands for an elemental unity.

Scholars who make no distinction between *Miaphysites* and *monophysites* are imprudent, because every school of thought or theology has its sophisticated scrupulous students and its gross simplistic students. To lump them all together is unwise. Unlike misguided authors

280

who lump them all together, I clearly delineate between *Miaphysites* (Greek/dynamic unity) and *monophysites* (Latin/elemental unity).

The heretical *monophysites* believed Jesus' humanity was a phantom and was unsubstantial compared to his Divinity. According to the *monophysites* there was one nature, the Divine nature, in Christ, which eclipsed the human nature.

The *monophysites* didn't understanding the economy of the incarnation. *Monophysites* thought Christ's divinity dwarfed his humanity.[36] When in truth the human became exalted and the Divine humbled. *Monophysites*, like the unbridled mystics of the East, believed Jesus' humanity was like a drop of water losing itself in the ocean of God.

For *Miaphysites* Jesus' particular humanity is never lost in the ocean of God, so to speak. For *Miaphysites*, there is always dynamic unity between the two aspects. There was no mixture or confusion as with a drop of water in the ocean, there was a dynamic—a composite union—a composition where Jesus' humanity wasn't lost in his Divinity. Neither was Jesus' Divinity lost in his humanity. The *monophysites'* simplistic sense of union (like a drop of water in the ocean) was rightly deemed heretical.[37]

Monophysites believed God was united to a less than full humanity (just the body, but not the human soul). The important distinction, which many misguided authors fail to make, is between word-man and word-flesh understandings of incarnation. Word-man (*Miaphysite*) Christologies are orthodox, affirming Jesus was both God and human. Word-flesh (*monophysite*) Christologies emphasize the divinity of Jesus to the exclusion of his full humanity. According to the *monophysites* Jesus was not like us in every respect and his flesh was simply a vehicle for the Divine.

Miaphysite rejects Apollinaris of Laodicea's (d. 390) odious *monophysite* doctrine of one simple nature after the union, where the two aspects of Christ get wiped out in the incarnation. Authentic *Miaphysite* asserts Jesus was "at once God and human" or "one united dynamic nature" or "one dynamic nature."

---

36. The most flagrant example of a divergent *monophysite* is Eutyches, who was excommunicated, then later reinstated after confessing his mistake.

37. In mystical union our humanity is not lost in Divinity. Even at the moment of the mystic's height of union with God, a dynamic relationship always remains. Christianity is about dynamic intertwined relationship. It's not about losing one's self altogether like a drop of water in the ocean.

Miaphysite describes one untied dynamic nature derived from both aspects of the incarnation, *not* one nature remaining after the destruction of one or the other aspect. *Miaphysites* believed God was united to both a human soul and a human body in Jesus (full humanity).

Arianism (Arius)

The insistence on the Divine, but ontologically secondary status of the son (Jesus) is known as the Arian heresy (fourth century). Arius (d. 336) thought the son was secondary to God. The Nicene Creed rebuked Arius' doctrine ("the Son is secondary to the Father (God)") by affirming Jesus is "of one substance with the Father (God)." Arius taught "once He (Jesus) was not," meaning Jesus' nature was not eternal—that Jesus was essentially a temporal human. The early church rightly considered this heretical. For Jesus is both eternal (the Divine *Word* or *Logos* of God, which always existed and always will exist) and temporal (coming to us in the historical Jesus in the fullness of time, who died on a cross). This is a mystery. In other words, *Miaphysite* asserts that Christ's status is in no way secondary to God.

To clarify, *Miaphysite* contends there can be no faith in God without God's distinct manifestations. God isn't greater than the Son. God isn't greater than the manifestations of God. They're two sides of the same coin. One could not exist without the other. All attempts to stress the supremacy of God the Creator and to subordinate God the Christ were rejected as "Arian" by Alexandrian tradition.

Miaphysite rejects Arius' odious doctrine of "two sons," which maintains "two natures after the union." There is one dynamic nature with two aspects, not two natures.

Gnosticism

Docetism (a form of Gnosticism) believes Jesus' body and sufferings were apparent but not real. In docetism exclusive emphasis is given to Jesus' Divinity. An example of docetism is Apollinaris, who thought Christ's body was negligible. Docetism rationally deduces that if Divinity and humanity come together, the humanity is dwarfed by the Divinity like a torch thrown into the sun. That's why Cyril said the incarnation was a divine mystery. Cyril didn't understand how Divinity and humanity came together, other than to say somehow God accepted limitation when God became human. The process by which this happened is ineffable. So, Jesus' humanity wasn't dwarfed by Divinity, but rather there was an exquisite balance and symmetry between unequals.

So, *Miaphysite* is not docetism. According to *Miaphysite* and scripture, Jesus' body and suffering are real (Luke 24:36–43).[38]

Julian of Halicarnassus (d. after 527) asserted Christ's body was incorruptible—not only from the time of the resurrection, but even from its formation in the womb. So, according to Julian, Jesus isn't human as we are human and didn't suffer on the cross.

Many Gnostics believed Jesus wasn't really human. He was God period. Gnostics to varying degrees believed Jesus' flesh was a façade. Jesus didn't suffer like we suffer because Jesus was essentially God. His humanness was a veneer—a vehicle for divine intervention. His humanity wasn't like ours. He was only human in terms of appearance and a few other selected traits. For many Gnostics, Jesus' humanity was a mask. Behind the mask was God in the unqualified sense. And, Jesus' Divinity altogether overwhelmed his humanity.

Monothelitism

Miaphysite should be distinguished from the heresy called *monothelitism*. *Monothelitism* refers to one will in the incarnation. Whereas, *Miaphysite* is the singular dynamic of two wills. Here again one will is an extreme and two wills is the other extreme. A singular dynamic of two wills (*Miaphysite*) is the balanced approach. The third Council of Constantinople (681) proclaimed *monothelitism* a heresy and confirmed two wills in Christ, Divine and human. This was the tragic logical outcome of Chalcedon's dualistic "in two natures" theology. For *Miaphysite*, there are not two wills and there is not one will. Rather there is one inseparable dynamic of two wills, preserving Christ's unity.

Nestorianism (Nestorius)

Nestorius (d. 451) believed Jesus wasn't fully God. Nestorius simply couldn't understand God crucified. Nestorians and others couldn't conceive of "God dying." For them, Jesus' humanity was mortal. However, the eternal God certainly wasn't subject to mortality. So, Nestorians and others argued the Divine and the human never came together in a substantial way.

According to Nestorius, Mary isn't the Mother of God; she's only the bearer of flesh in whom God dwelled. So there are two sons. There's the son of Mary (the flesh) and the son of God (the Spirit). In this

---

38. The opposite of docetism is ebonitism. Ebonitism placed exclusive emphasis on Jesus' humanity to the exclusion of his Divinity. *Miaphysite* rejects ebonitism.

thinking, the child was formed in the womb before the union and God simply dwelled within a human.

Nestorianism is the ancient version of much of so called theology today, which denies the full Divinity of Jesus, claiming Jesus was a prophet like others before him. This so called theology discounts the essence of the Christian testament, which is that God became human in every way, including suffering and death on a cross. This substantial union is the essence of the incarnation. Cyril reiterates this union: "God died." God isn't aloof. God entered into the thick of it and became human, even to the point of suffering and death on a cross. This is the nature of Divine love, to completely give itself away.

Dynamic Unity, Not Duality

Miaphysite is dynamic union. The vast differences between Divinity and humanity remain, but can never be separated or divided. In other words we can't refer to the Divinity of Christ in isolation. Neither can we refer to the humanity of Christ in isolation. This means Jesus can never be referred to as God period (God in the ultimate unqualified sense).[39] Jesus' humanity never existed apart from his Divinity. After God became incarnate in a particular human being, we can no longer claim God is absent from the human condition.

In spite of the extraordinary differences between Divinity and humanity, *Miaphysite* always maintains the unity of the incarnation. Just as Jesus states in the Gospels, "God and I are one" (John 10:30), so too Jesus' Divinity and humanity are united. Early Eastern churches[40] drew many other implications from the word *Miaphysite,* but the bare-bones insight is this: inseparable dynamic union. This primal interpretation of *Miaphysite* was never considered "heretical." Many[41] just thought it was a slippery slope leading to heresy.[42] The opponents of *Miaphysite* didn't realize they were also sliding down a slippery slope toward error.[43] "One nature" is a slippery slope. But so is "two natures." The *Miaphysite* mystics were the ultimate tightrope walkers, able to navigate the extremes, with Cyril as their champion. Cyril understood theology

---

39. Ultimately, God remains the primordial mystery beyond all names and forms, yet revealed to Christians in Jesus, God's unique human incarnation.

40. By "early" I mean "Pre-Chalcedonian."

41. The Chalcedonians in particular.

42. As was the case with *Monophysites.*

43. Nestorius' "two sons."

is a razor's edge requiring numerous subtle distinctions to avoid folly. And in the end, unity and dynamism win the day, not duality (two natures, two wills, etcetera). Strictly speaking Jesus is not "one nature." Nor is Jesus "in two natures" as the dualistic West has erroneously accepted. Jesus is "one united dynamic nature."

It's easy to overemphasize Jesus' humanity. It's also easy to overemphasize Jesus' Divinity. So it's vitally important that the one never loses sight of the other. The incarnation's exquisite balance never excludes one aspect or the other and never succumbs to duality. *Miaphysite* always keeps the two in tension. When we lose the paradoxical tension between Jesus' Divinity and humanity we lose our center. It's like the fret board of a guitar. If we lose tension on one end of the strings or the other, the strings no longer make music.

Particular Unity, Not General Unity

When the Alexandrian Bishops spoke of "one nature," by *nature* they meant *hypostasis*, not *ousia* (Greek). *Hypostasis* pertains to particular terms such as the individual names of people, i.e. *Rick Lincoln. Ousia* pertains to general terms such as *humans, mammals, cats.* To say Jesus is "one *ousia*" is very different from saying Jesus is "one *hypostasis*." *Hypostasis* implies a much more real, substantial, and solid union—much clearer than *ousia. Ousia* is ambiguous. *Hypostasis* is distinct. Through the centuries many have argued God united with *humanity*—a general ambiguous unity. The *Miaphysites* said God united with the Nazarene born in Bethlehem whose dad and mom were Joseph and Mary. This is very different.

For Cyril the word *physis* or *nature* in all the phrases means a concrete reality—a personal named thing as opposed to a more generalized humanity. So this unity is not a figure of speech—it's real. For the *Miaphysites*, expressions like "in two natures," "two wills," "two operations," can't conserve Christ's unity in any real sense. *Miaphysites* see Christ's unity as actual, not as abstract. From two (Divinity and humanity), Christ was formed indivisibly and his nature (*hypostasis*) is one. *Miaphysites* concede that Christ's one nature was formed in composition. Yet, that nature remains one.

God's nature took on human nature and personality, not just in the abstract hypothetical sense of the Old Testament, but in a real sense of soul, flesh, and blood. So, as believers we say in Jesus God has a unique and distinct personality.[44]

44. A great irony of the Chalcedonian debate is both sides claimed Cyril as their master. Yet Chalcedonians (*dyophysites*) co-opted Cyril, making Christ out to be like Siamese twins with two separate life systems instead of one dynamic such as the body and rational soul of a human being, which Cyril espoused. Non-Chalcedonians (*Miaphysites*) preserved the integrity of the incarnation as taught by Cyril. *Miaphysites* preserved Christianity's mystic core: The Jesus Paradox.

Appendix G

Miaphysite's Historic Roots: Redressing the Council of Chalcedon

What is forgotten cannot be healed
and that which cannot be healed easily becomes the cause
of greater evil.

–HENRI NOUWEN

I DO NOT WANT TO confuse the reader with tedious details about the Council of Chalcedon (451). Yet I can't ignore the Council. So in the pages that follow I have sketched my very brief take on the Council.

My perspective on the Council provides the context for my understanding of *Miaphysite* as presented in this book. Much of the material for this chapter is taken (sometimes verbatim) from Father V. C. Samuel's book, *The Council of Chalcedon Re-examined.*[45] I am deeply indebted to Father Samuel. Very early on, his work planted the seed for *Healing The Divide.* Throughout this section I will refer to *Miaphysite* (Greek) as opposed to *monophysite* (Latin). I do this because *Miaphysite* is the term Oriental Orthodox tradition accepts as authentic (largely because it is the actual word that Cyril used) and because of the negative connotations associated with the word *monophysite.*

---

45. Samuel, *The Council of Chalcedon Re-examined.*

The Council of Chalcedon was the confrontation over Christian theology in its most primal form (the argument over "Who is Jesus?"). At Chalcedon, we don't see the delicately handled and intricately woven debates that should have taken place and would have shed light on Christian theology for ages to come. Instead, we see an underlying power struggle between the Roman See and the Alexandrian See for supremacy. To put it crudely, Chalcedon became a pissing match between Rome and Alexandria that was more about protecting egos than about sound theology.

The conflict at Chalcedon centered on the misunderstanding of Greek concepts. Roman Catholic Pope Leo, who was most influential at Chalcedon, had no knowledge of Greek. As a result, he misinterpreted the *Miaphysite* theology of Alexandrian Bishop, Dioscorus, which was passed down to Dioscorus from Cyril and Athanasius.[46] Because Leo had no knowledge of primary Greek concepts, such as *hypostasis*, he confused the Greek term *Miaphysite* (The Jesus Paradox). He and Rome's misunderstandings of *Miaphysite* (Greek) were labeled *monophysite* (Latin) and condemned at Chalcedon.

Unfortunately, for the most part, the Roman See has not been able to look at the deeper theological issues involved at Chalcedon. As history attests, those in power often lack humility and introspection. Rome simply went on proclaiming the Council of Chalcedon and renouncing all who opposed it as heretics. Rome rarely considered the primary role it played in the first split of the Church.

The *Miaphysites'* protest against the dualistic theological notions of Chalcedon was a matter of conscience and faith, which was in line with centuries of Alexandrian Mystic teaching, especially that of Cyril. And the faithful would sooner die than accept the dualistic "two natures" of Christ.

The *Miaphysite* monks who vehemently opposed imperial authority at Chalcedon to their own hurt were the heart and soul of popular Christianity in the East. After Chalcedon, the *Miaphysite* monks were willing to put their Christian beliefs first, even if it meant banishment, maiming, or death.

It is important to note here that at the time of the Council of Chalcedon, the aura that surrounded the divinely appointed emperor was all-pervasive. At that time all disorder, especially political disorder, was regarded as the work of the devil. In this regard, *Miaphysites* gave primary allegiance to Christian citizenship and saw nationality as secondary. In

46. Sellers, *The Council of Chalcedon*, 227.

other words, like the early Quakers, these *Miaphysite* monks followed their conscience first and the State second.

"Of one nature" theology was so attractive to the Syrian and practically all the Egyptian monks in the fifth and sixth centuries because *Miaphysite* for them was Christian Mysticism. Authentic *Miaphysite* was synonymous with Christian Mysticism. Authentic *Miaphysite* pointed to the unqualified, undifferentiated mysterious source of all, which came to us in human form. It honored the paradox of God incarnate over dualistic thought.

Those unaccustomed to the deep silences of the monastery were not familiar with mystical experiences of God beyond all names and forms. Those who were not familiar with mystical experience often asserted that Jesus was God, period. Then in the next sentence they would add that Jesus was human. But for the authentic *Miaphysite* this could not be. Jesus was at once God and human in the same sentence, leading to a more nuanced faith akin to mystical experience. For the authentic *Miaphysite*, Jesus' humanity and ultimate Divinity were not separate at any time.

One hallmark of the authentic *Miaphysite* movement is the doctrinal position of the Syrian church given to Emperor Heraclius (d. 641). This written doctrine affirmed that "Jesus Christ is one, one nature, namely one person, and that he is not divided into two natures, or two persons, or two Christs, after the ineffable union."[47]

Healing The Divide is about restoring the dynamic unity between Jesus' Divinity and humanity as understood by The Alexandrian Mystics. This dynamic relationship is what's missing from Western theology today, rendering it flat and hopelessly dualistic. The profound holistic understanding of Christ's dynamic being is the mystical legacy of the *Miaphysites*.

For those who want to dig deeper into this material, I recommend reading *The Council of Chalcedon Re-examined* by V.C. Samuel and *The Council of Chalcedon: A Historical and Doctrinal Survey* by R.V. Sellers. By reading these, the general reader will quickly grasp Chalcedon's inherent problems. Separating out Jesus' Divine and human elements line by line throughout the Gospels strikes most people as schizophrenic. This schizophrenia is with us today in Christianity's fundamentalist and new age extremes.

Severus of Antioch made the following statement:

47. Sellers, *The Council of Chalcedon*

> To walk bodily on earth and to move from place to place is indeed human. But to enable those who are lame and cannot use their feet to walk is God-befitting. However, it is the same God the Word incarnate who works in both. It is this principle embedded in the tradition set up by the fathers which is being violated by the (language) "two natures after the union."[48]

The Council of Chalcedon's doctrinal formula, "Made known in two natures," smells of the Nestorian heresy of "two sons."[49] Chalcedon's doctrine of "two natures" polarized Christendom in the fifth century. And its legacy polarizes Western Christianity today. If Christ were two natures he would not be God the Son incarnate, but only God the Son dwelling in a human.

It is telling that the Chalcedonian side never tried to replace the Nicene Creed by the council's formula. This shows that there is obviously apprehension about the Chalcedonian formula. And with good reason—it has caused much division in The Church. Jesus said "A good tree cannot bear bad fruit; nor can a bad tree bear good fruit. . .you will know them by their fruits" (Matthew 7:18, 20). The fruit of the Council of Nicaea was unity. The fruit of Chalcedon was division.

What I have been writing about is a true mystical union, not a nominal union of "two natures, two wills, and two natural operations." How can there be union when everything is split into two.

The theological disparity between Roman and Eastern Christianity, exacerbated by The Council of Chalcedon, reached its apex in 1204, when the armies of the Fourth Crusade (Roman Catholic) abandoned their journey to the Holy Land and turned their attack to Constantinople (the Center of East Orthodox Christianity), inflicting massive depredations. The Fourth Crusade exponentially deepened longstanding bitterness between Byzantine and Western Christianity. The sack of Constantinople is a travesty of church history that Greek Christendom has never forgiven or forgotten.

As Henri Nouwen writes in *The Living Reminder*, "What is forgotten cannot be healed and that which cannot be healed easily becomes the cause of greater evil."[50] I don't think the soul of the church has healed

---

48. Sellers, *The Council of Chalcedon*, 248-f with notes.

49. In exile, Nestorius sometimes wrote of Christ as existing in "one *prosopon*" (person) in "two *ousia*" (natures), so anticipating the dualistic Chalcedonian formula, which was refuted by the *Miaphysites*. "In two natures" was and is anathema to *Miaphysites*. See Appendix F.

50. Nouwen, *The Living Reminder*, 17.

from the unilateral church splitting spirit of Chalcedon. So, it is edifying to address this historic split in light of our times. For, unless there is healing redress, history repeats itself. My prayer is that authentic *Miaphysite* properly understood will prevent greater evil.

In this post 9/11 age, it behooves Christians of all varieties to re-examine the finer point of their Christology in order to safeguard it against divisiveness and polarization.

The Chalcedonians took a beautiful concept (*Miaphysite*) and reduced it to its lowest possible connotation, imposing an awful caricature on the most sophisticated theological minds of the time (The Alexandrian Mystics). The same is done today by minds that have no room for the mystical/ holistic spirit of Christ. Yet, no politically motivated human authority will have the last word on Jesus.

It may surprise some people that the jury is still out on some of the most significant aspects of Christian faith. Yet this acknowledges that Christian tradition is still alive and kicking in the twenty-first Century. God is still speaking. I pray that Christianity has the courage to redress the past. Then Christianity will not be relegated to the limitations and liabilities of history, but will own up to dynamic tradition that is alive and requires redress in every generation.

How we think theologically is relevant and imperative for the formation of spiritual well-being, culture, social cohesion, and international relations.

Discord was woven into The Church as never before at Chalcedon.

In order to hope in the future, we must first put right the past. So, along with Cyril of Alexandria, V.C. Samuels, the Oriental Orthodox Church, and others, I reject the Chalcedonian formula: "in two natures."[51] Christ was not and can never be in two natures. Christ is "one united dynamic nature."

In response to the errors of Chalcedon and its divisive repercussions, this book affirms the jewel of the Oriental Orthodox Church, which holds the cure for Christianity's dualistic ills. This Jewel is *Miaphysite* or The Jesus Paradox. The Jesus Paradox represents the heart and soul of the deepest and most long standing legacy of Christian mystical theology. *Miaphysite* is nothing less than Christian Mysticism's definitive theological core.

51. Like author V.C. Samuel, I retain The Council of Chalcedon simply as an instrument through which Nestorius and Eutyches were discredited. The Council of Chalcedon did well there. It failed miserably when it came to comprehending Christianity's mystic core.

Bibliography[1][2]

*Allen, Pauline, and Hayward, C.T.R. *Severus of Antioch (The Early Church Fathers)*. New York: Routledge, 2005.

Alcock, Anthony. *The Life of Samuel of Kalamun by Issac the Presbyter*. Warminster, England: Aris & Phillips, Ltd., 1983.

Ambrose, Bishop of Milan. *Nicene and post-Nicene Fathers of the Christian Church, A select library of: A new series translated into English with prolegomena and explanatory notes*. Toronto: University of Toronto Libraries, 2011.

Anatolios, Khaled. *Athanasius: The Coherence of his Thought (Routledge Early Church Monographs)*. London: Routledge, 2004.

*Anatolios, Khaled. *Athanasius (The Early Church Fathers)*. New York: Routledge, 2004.

Aquinas, Thomas. *The Summa Theologica of St. Thomas Aquinas* (Five Volumes). Translated by The Fathers of the Dominican English Province. Allen: Christian Classics, 1981.

1. For the select bibliography most primary to this work see the authors last names preceded with asterisks.

2. Bibliography Notes: If your aim is to become steeped in the essence of Christianity's Mystic Roots, I would recommend several works cited in the Bibliography above the others. First is Keating's *Contemplative Prayer*, a Sounds True audio recording (hands down the best summary of Centering Prayer practice I've come across). Keating may not be a hesychast in the strict sense, as The Alexandrian Mystics were, but he exquisitely apprehends the Spirit of silent prayer in our present context. Second is the English translation of *The Philokalia*, with particular emphasis on the following Philokalia writers: Evagrius, Hesychios, and Didachos in Volume One; Maximus in Volume Two (my personal favorite); Peter and Makarios in Volume Three; Nikitas, Nikiphoros, and the two Gregorys in Volume Four. Third is *The Mystical Theology* and *Divine Names* of Dionysius. And fourth is Cyril's *Unity of Christ* and Gebru's *Miaphysite Christology*. These four strands: *Hesychasm*/Silent Prayer, *The Philokalia*, Dionysius, and *Miaphysite* (The Jesus Paradox), are Mystic Christianity's firm historic lineage and legacy. The biblical root of Hesychasm/Silent Prayer is Matthew 6:6. The biblical essence of *The Philokalia* is Psalm 46:10. The biblical root of Dionysius is The Second Commandment (Exodus 20:4). And the biblical root of Miaphysite is The Gospels (see Appendix D).

Bibliography

*Athanasius of Alexandria. *On The Incarnation*. New York: Saint Vladimir's Seminary Press, 2002.

*Athanasius of Alexandria. Robert C. Gregg, ed. *The Life of Antony and Letter to Marcellenus*. New York: Paulist Press, 1979.

Augustine. *Confessions*. Hollywood, Florida: Simon and Brown, 2012.

Barry, Wendell. *The Unsettling of America: Culture and Agriculture*. San Francisco: Sierra Club Books, 1996.

Basil of Caesarea. *Letters. With an English translation by Roy J. Deferrari* (Especially Letter 38 Concerning the Difference between *Ousia* and *Hypostasis*). Ulan Press, 2012.

Bethune-Baker, J. *Introduction to the Early History of Christian Doctrine: To the time of the Council of Chalcedon*. London: Methuen; 9th edition, 1951.

Bethune-Baker, J. *Nestorius and His Teachings: A Fresh Examination of the Evidence*. Eugene: Wipf & Stock, 1999.

Blackburn, Richard. Lombard Institute Mediation Skills Training. Kent, Washington: April 30-May 4, 2012.

Borg, Marcus. *The Heart of Christianity: Rediscovering a Life of Faith*. San Francisco: Harper, 2003.

Borg, Marcus. *Reading the Bible Again for the First Time: Taking the Bible Seriously but Not Literally*. San Francisco: Harper, 2002.

Bourgeault, Cynthia. *The Meaning of Mary Magdalene: Discovering the Woman at the Heart of Christianity*. Boston and London: Shambhala, 2010.

Bourgeault, Cynthia. *The Wisdom Jesus: Transforming Heart and Mind—A New Perspective on Christ and His Message*. Boston: Shambhala, 2008.

Boyce, James. Blog. Online: http://www.huffingtonpost.com/james-boyce/over-4000-people-will-die_b_147310.html

Bragg, Paul. *The Miracle of Fasting*. Santa Barbara: Bragg Health Sciences, 2002.

Brakke, David. *Athanasius and Asceticism*. Baltimore and London: Johns Hopkins University Press, 1995.

Buddhaghosa, Bhadantacariya. *The Path of Purification: Visuddhimagga*. Translated by Bhikkhu Nanamoli. Onalaska: Pariyatti Publishing, 2003.

Bultmann, Rudolf. *The Gospel of John: A Commentary*. Translated by G. R. Beasley-Murray, R. W. N. Hoare, and J. K Riches. Philadelphia: Westminster Press, 1971.

Cahill, Thomas, *Desire of The Everlasting Hills: The World Before and After Jesus*. New York: Anchor Books, 2001.

Cahill, Thomas. *The Gift of the Jews: How A Tribe of Desert Nomads Changed The Way Everyone Thinks and Feels*. New York: Anchor Books, 1999.

Carston, Thiede; D'Ancona, Matthew. *Eyewitness to Jesus: Amazing New Manuscript Evidence About the Origin of the Gospels*. New York: Doubleday, 1996.

Chadwick, Henry, and J.E.L. Oulton. *Alexandrian Christianity*. Louisville: John Knox Press, 1954.

*Chryssavgis, John. *In the Heart of the Desert: The Spirituality of the Desert Fathers and Mothers*. Bloomington: World Wisdom Inc., 2008.

Chumley, Norris. *Mysteries of the Jesus Prayer: Experiencing the Presence of God and a Pilgrimage to the Heart of an Ancient Spirituality*. New York: HarperOne, 2011.

Clement, Oliver. Roots of Christian Mysticism: Texts from Patristic Era with Commentary. Hyde Park: New City Press, 1996.

Climacus, John. *The Ladder of Divine Ascent (Classics of Western Spirituality)*. New York: Paulist Press, 1988.

Coffin, William Sloan. *The Heart Is a Little to The Left: Essays on Public Morality.* Dartmouth: Dartmouth College, 1999.

Cone, James. *God of The Oppressed.* Maryknoll: Orbis, 1997.

Crosby, Tim. "Does God Get Angry?" Ministry: International Journal for Clergy. July 1990.

Crossan, John Dominic. *Who Killed Jesus?: Exposing the Roots of Anti-Semitism in the Gospel Story of the Death of Jesus.* San Francisco: Harper Collins, 1996.

Cyril of Alexandria. *Commentary upon the Gospel according to St. Luke.* Charleston: Nabu Press, 2010.

Cyril of Alexandria. *Five tomes against Nestorius: Scholia on the incarnation : Christ is one : fragments against Diodore of Tarsus, Theodore of Mopsuestia, the ... of fathers of the Holy Catholic church.* London: J. Parker and Rivingtons, 1881.

Cyril of Alexandria. Trans. John I. McEnerney. *Letters 1-50 (Fathers of the Church Patristic Series).* Washington D.C.: The Catholic University of America Press, 2007.

*Cyril of Alexandria. *The Unity of Christ.* Crestwood: Saint Vladimir's Seminary Press, 2000.

*Davis, Stephen J. *The Early Coptic Papacy: The Egyptian Church and Its Leadership in Late Antiquity.* New York and Cairo: The American University in Cairo Press, 2004.

Davis, Stephen, Daniel Kendall S.J., and Gerald O'Collins S. J. *The Incarnation: An Interdisciplinary Symposium on the Incarnation of the Son of God.* Oxford: Oxford University Press, 2002.

de Caussade, Jean-Pierre. *The Sacrament of the Present Moment.* San Francisco: Harpers, 1989.

*Dionysius the Areopagite. *The Divine Names and the Mystical Theology.*[3] Translated by C.E. Rolt. Mineola: Dover, 1994.

Dostoevsky, Fyodor. *The Brothers Karamazov.* Translated by Constance Garnett. Mineola: Dover, 2005.

Editorial. "Bono's Thin Ecclesiology." Christianity Today. March 2003.

Edwards, Tilden. *Living Simply Through the Day: Spiritual Survival in a Complex Age.* New York: Paulist Press, 1998.

Fischer, Kathleen. *Women at the Well: Feminist Perspectives on Spiritual Direction.* New York: Paulist Press, 1989.

Fox, George. *The Journal of George Fox.* Barnesville: Friends United Press, 2006.

Frend, W.H.C. *The Rise of the Monophysite Movement: Chapters in the History of the Church in the fifth and sixth centuries.* Cambridge: Cambridge University Press, 1972.

Friedman, Edwin H. *Friedman's Fables.* New York: Gilford Press, 1990.

*Gebru, Mebratu Kiros. *Miaphysite Christology: An Ethiopian Perspective.* Piscataway: Gorgias Press, 2010.

Girard, Rene, and Yvonne Freccero. *The Scapegoat.* Baltimore: Johns Hopkins University Press, 1989.

3. It is significant to note how much the Alexandrian Mystics on through the four-teenth century revered Dionysius. His writings are revered throughout *The Philokalia.* An example is this comment by Gregory Palamas: "St. Dionysios the Areopagite, the most eminent theologian after the divine apostles. . ." (Palmer, et al, *The Philokalia Vol. 4,* 386.). See *Dionysios the Areopagite* in the glossary.

Bibliography

Gold, Victor Roland, et al. *The New Testament and Psalms: An Inclusive Version*. Oxford: Oxford University Press, 1995.

*Gorg, Peter. *The Desert Fathers: Saint Anthony and the Beginning of Monasticism*. San Francisco: Ignatius Press, 2011.

Goulder, Michael, ed. *Incarnation and Myth: The Debate Continues*. Grand Rapids: Eerdmans, 1979.

Grant, Jacquelyn. *White Women's Christ and Black Women's Jesus*. Atlanta: Scholars Press, 1989.

Greenleaf, Robert K. *Servant Leadership: A Journey Into The Nature of Legitimate Power and Greatness (25th Anniversary Edition)*. New York: Paulist Press, 2002.

Grewe, Reverend Fred. "Conversation." Forest Grove, Oregon. May 17, 2012.

Grillmeier, Aloys and Theresia Hainthaler. *The Church of Alexandria with Nubia and Ethiopia after 451*. Translated by O.C. Dean. *(Christ in Christian tradition, volume 2, part 4)*. Louisville: Westminster John Knox Press, 1996.

Gutierrez, Gustavo. *A Theology of Liberation: History, Politics, and Salvation*. Translated by Caridad Inda and John Eagleson. Maryknoll: Orbis, 1988.

Hadaway, C. Kirk. *Behold I Do a New Thing: Transforming Communities of Faith*. Cleveland: Pilgrim Press, 2001.

Hastings, Adrian, et al. *The Oxford Companion to Christian Thought*. Oxford: Oxford University Press, 2000.

Herzog, William R. II. *Parables as Subversive Speech*. Westminster: John Knox Press, 1994.

Hoyle, Fred. *Mathematics of Evolution*. Memphis: Acorn Enterprises LLC, 1999.

Jewell, John. "Homo-ousios, Homoi-ousios, Who Cares?" Sermon. June 18, 2000.

Jones, Rufus M. *The Faith and Practice of the Quakers*. Whitefish: Kessinger, 2008.

Kant, Immanuel. *The Critique of Pure Reason*. Cambridge: Cambridge University Press, 1999.

*Keating, Thomas. *Contemplative Prayer*. Louisville, Colorado: Sounds True Audio, 2004.

Keating, Thomas. *Intimacy with God: An Introduction to Centering Prayer*. New York: Crossroad, 2009.

Keating, Thomas. "Method of Centering Prayer." Online: http://www.contemplative mind.org/practices/subnav/prayer.htm

Keating, Thomas. *Open Heart, Open Mind*. New York: Continuum, 1994.

Kemper, Robert G. *Kind Words for Our Kind of Faith*. Cleveland: Pilgrim Press, 1986.

Kushner, Harold. *When Bad Things Happen to Good People*. New York: Anchor, 2004.

Lamott, Anne. *Grace Eventually: Thoughts on Faith*. New York: Riverhead, 2004.

Lamott, Anne. *Plan B: Further Thoughts on Faith*. New York: Riverhead, 2006.

Laughlin, Paul Allen. *Remedial Christianity*. Santa Rosa: Polebridge, 2000.

Leong, Kenneth S. *The Zen Teachings of Jesus*. New York: Crossroad, 1995.

Lewis, C.S. *The Lion, The Witch, and the Wardrobe*. San Francisco: HarperCollins, 2009

*Lossky, Vladimir. *The Mystical Theology of the Eastern Church*. Crestwood: Saint Vladimir's Seminary Press, 2002.

Luce, A.A. *Monophysitism Past and Present: A Study in Christology*. Ann Arbor: University of Michigan Library, 1920.

Luedmann, Gerd. "The Jesus Seminar Considers the Resurrection" Lecture. Germany: University of Goettingen. March 7, 1995.

Mackintosh, H. R. *The Doctrine of the Person of Jesus Christ*. New York: Hard Press Publishing, 2013.

Mailer, Norman. *The Gospel According To The Son*. New York: Random House, 1997.

Main, John. *Word Into Silence: A Manual For Christian Meditation*. New York: Canterbury Press, 2006.

Maximus The Confessor. George C. Berthold, ed. *Maximus The Confessor: Selected Writings (Classics of Western Spirituality)*. New York: Paulist Press, 1985.

May, Gerald. *The Awakened Heart: Opening Yourself To The Love You Need*. San Francisco: Harper, 1993.

McColman, Carl. *The Big Book of Christian Mysticism: The Essential Guide to Contemplative Spirituality*. Newburyport: Hampton Roads Publishing, 2010.

McDonnell, Thomas P., ed. *A Thomas Merton Reader*. Garden City: Image Books, 1974.

McGuckin, John A. *Saint Cyril of Alexandria and the Christological Controversy*. New York: Saint Vladimir's Press, 2010.

Meier, John P., *A Marginal Jew: Rethinking the Historical Jesus*, 2 vols. New York: Doubleday, 1991 and 1994.

Meinardus, Otto F.A. *Two Thousand Years of Coptic Christianity*. Cairo: University of Cairo Press, 2002.

Meninger, William. *The Loving Search for God: Contemplative Prayer and the Cloud of Unknowing*. New York: Continuum, 1998.

Merton, Thomas. *The Asian Journal*. New York: New Directions, 1975.

Merton, Thomas. *The Seven Storey Mountain*. New York: Harcourt, 1999.

*Merton, Thomas. *The Wisdom of the Desert*. Boston and London: Shambhala, 2004.

Meyendorff, John. *Christ in Eastern Christian Thought*. New York: Saint Vladimir's Seminary Press, 1975.

Motluk, Alison, "Meditation Builds Up The Brain." New Scientist. November 15, 2005.

Motovilov, Nicolas. "St. Seraphim of Sarov's Conversation with Nicolas Motovilov." Online: http://orthodoxinfo.com/praxis/wonderful.aspx

Nachmanovitch, Stephen. *Free Play: Improvisation in Life and Art*. New York: Penguin Putnam Inc., 1990.

Noe, K. Killian. *Finding Our Way Home*. Washington D.C.: Servant Leadership Press, 2001.

Noll, Mark A. *The Scandal of the Evangelical Mind*. Grand Rapids: Eerdmans, 1995.

*Nolan, Albert. *Jesus Today: A Spirituality of Radical Freedom*. New York: Orbis, 2006.

Norris, Kathleen. *Amazing Grace: A Vocabulary of Faith*. New York: Riverhead Books, 1999.

Nouwen, Henri. *The Living Reminder*. San Francisco: Harper, 1984.

O'Neil, John. *Success and Your Shadow*. Louisville, Colorado: Sounds True Audio, 1997.

Ottley, R.L. *The Doctrine of the Incarnation*. London: Methuen & Co; Sixth edition, 1919.

*Palmer, Parker J. *In the Belly of a Paradox: A Celebration of Contradictions in the Thought of Thomas Merton* (Pendle Hill Pamphlet; 224). Wallingford: Pendle Hill Publications, 1979.

Palmer, Parker J. *Let Your Life Speak: Listening for the Voice of Vocation*. San Francisco: Jossey-Bass, 2000.

*Palmer, Parker J. *The Promise of Paradox*. San Francisco: Jossey-Bass, 2008.

*Palmer, G.E.H, et al. *The Philokalia: The Complete Text Vol. 1–4, compiled by St. Nikodimos of the Holy Mountain and St. Makarios of Corinth*. London: Faber and Faber, 1983–95.

"Poll: Americans Shun Conversion Goals." The Christian Century. May 8–15, 2002.

Bibliography

*Ponticus, Evagrius. *The Praktikos & Chapters on Prayer.* Kalamazoo: Cistercian Publications, 1981.

Preston, Don K. "Catholics Will No Longer Seek to Convert Jews." Online: http://www.eschatology.org/all-articles-articles-211/43-the-israel-of-god/174-catholics-will-no-longer-seek-to-convert-jews

Public Broadcasting Service (PBS) Documentary. "Mother Teresa." November 28, 1986.

Ravindra, Ravi, *The Gospel of John in Light of Indian Mysticism.* Rochester: Inner Traditions, 2004.

*Robinson, Anthony. *What's Theology got to do with it?: Convictions, Vitality, and the Church.* Herndon: The Alban Institute, 2006.

Rohr, Richard. *From Wild Man to Wiseman: Reflections on Male Spirituality.* Cincinnati: St. Anthony Messenger Press, 2005.

*Rohr, Richard. *The Immortal Diamond: Searching For Our True Self.* New York: Jossey-Bass, 2013.

*Rohr, Richard. *The Naked Now: Learning to See as the Mystics See.* New York: Crossroad Publishing Company, 2009.

Rohr, Richard. *Things Hidden: Scripture As Spirituality.* Cincinnati: Saint Anthony Messenger Press, 2008.

Russell, Norman. *Cyril of Alexandria (The Early Church Fathers).* London: Routledge, 2000.

*Samuel, V.C. *The Council of Chalcedon Re-Examined.* London: British Orthodox Press, 2001.

Sanford, David. "If God Disappeared" Lecture. Turner, Oregon. August 4, 2010.

Schmemann, Alexander. *For the Life of the World: Sacraments and Orthodoxy.* New York: Saint Vladimir's Press, 1997.

*Sellers, R.V. *The Council of Chalcedon: A Historical & Doctrinal Survey.* London: S.P.C.K. Press, 1961.

*Sellers, R.V. *Two Ancient Christologies: A Study in the Christological Thought of the Schools of Alexandria and Antioch in the Early History of Christian Doctrine.* London: S.P.C.K., 1954.

Severus of Antioch and Athanasius of Nisibis. *The Sixth Book of the Select Letters of Severus, Patriarch of Antioch, in the Syriac Version of Athanasius of Nisibis, Edited and Translated by E. W. Brooks: Pt. 1-2. Text.* Charleston: Nabu Press, 2010.

Shenouda III, Pope (H.H.). *The Nature of Christ.* Jersey City: St. Mark Coptic Church (http://www.saintmark.com), 1999.

Smith, Houston. *Forgotten Truth: The Common Vision of The World's Religions.* San Francisco: Harper, 1992.

Smith, Houston. Lecture on Future of Religion. Berkeley: Pacific School of Religion. October 12, 1997.

Smith, Houston. *The Soul of Christianity: Restoring the Great Tradition.* San Francisco: Harper, 2005.

Solle, Dorothee. *The Silent Cry: Mysticism and Resistance.* Columbus: Fortress Press, 2001.

Spong, John Shelby. *Rescuing the Bible from Fundamentalism: A Bishop Rethinks the Meaning of Scripture.* San Francisco: Harper, 1992.

Sullivan, Clayton. *Rescuing Jesus from The Christians.* Peabody: Trinity Press International, 2002.

Sweet, Leonard; Viola, Frank. *Jesus Manifesto.* Nashville: Thomas Nelson, 2010.

Teasdale, Brother Wayne. *The Mystic Heart: Discovering A Universal Spirituality in the World's Religions*. Novato: New World Library, 2001.

Thoreau, Henry David. *Walden*. Philadelphia: Empire Books, 2012.

*Tickle, Phyllis. *The Great Emergence: How Christianity Is Changing and Why*. Ada: Baker Books, 2008.

Tillich, Paul. *A History of Christian Thought*. New York: Harper & Row, 1968.

Tillich, Paul. *Systematic Theology, Vol. 1 & 2*. Chicago: University of Chicago Press, 1975.

Torrance, Iain R. *Christology after Chalcedon: Severus of Antioch and Sergius the Monophysite*. Eugene: Wipf and Stock Publishers, 1998.

Truss, Lynne. *Eats, Shoots, and Leaves: The Zero Tolerance Approach to Punctuation*. New York: Gotham, 2004.

Tutu, Desmond. "God at 2000 Lecture." Corvallis: Oregon State University. February 11, 2000.

Tzu, Lao. *Tao Te Ching*. Translated by Gia-Fu Feng and Jane English. Hollywood, Florida: Simon and Brown, 2012.

"UNICEF Report." New York Times. December 10, 2004, A1.

Urban, Linwood. *A Short History of Christian Thought*. Oxford: Oxford University Press, 1995.

Voskamp, Ann. *One Thousand Gifts*. Grand Rapids: Zondervan, 2011.

Wallis, Jim. *God's Politics: Why the Right Gets It Wrong and the Left Doesn't Get It*. San Francisco: Harper, 2006.

Watts, Alan W. *Beyond Theology*. New York: Vintage, 1973.

Weinandy, Thomas. *The Theology of St. Cyril of Alexandria: A Critical Appreciation*. (Especially "The Image of God in Man: Alexandrian Orientations" by W.J. Burghardt p. 147-160.). London: Bloomsbury T&T Clark; First edition, 2003.

White Jr., Ronald C, et al. *White American Christianity: A Case Approach*. Grand Rapids: William B. Eerdmans Publishing, 1986.

Whitehead, Alfred North. *Nature and Life*. Chicago: University of Chicago Press, 1934.

Wigram, W.A. *The Separation of the Monophysites*. Brooklyn: Ams Pr Inc, 1978.

Wikipedia. "Dyophysite." Online: http://en.wikipedia.org/wiki/Dyophysite

Wikipedia. "Miaphysitism." Online: http://en.wikipedia.org/wiki/Miaphysitism

Wikipedia. "Monophysitism." Online: http://en.wikipedia.org/wiki/Monophysite

Wikipedia. "Oriental Orthodoxy." Online: http://en.wikipedia.org/wiki/Oriental_Orthodoxy#Oriental_Orthodox_Communion

Wilbur, Ken. *No Boundary: Eastern and Western Approaches to Spiritual Growth*. Boston: Shambhala, 2001.

Wilde, Oscar. *The Complete Works of Oscar Wilde: Stories, Plays, Poems, and Essays*. New York: Perennial, 1989.

Wink, Walter. *Engaging the Powers: Discernment and Resistance in a World of Domination*. Columbus: Augsburg Fortress, 1992.

Wink, Walter. *The Powers That Be: Theology for a New Millennium*. New York: Three Rivers Press, 1999.

Young, Francis M. and Andrew Teal. *From Nicaea to Chalcedon: A Guide to the Literature and Its Background*. Grand Rapids: Baker Academic, 2010.

Zaehner, R.C. *Mysticism Sacred and Profane*. Oxford: Oxford University Press, 1975.